PORTRAIT OF AN AMERICAN:
Charles G. Dawes

PORTRAIT OF AN AMERICAN:

Charles G. Dawes

by

BASCOM N. TIMMONS

ILLUSTRATED WITH PHOTOGRAPHS

NEW YORK

Henry Holt and Company

Photographs in the picture section are credited as follows: 1. Chicago *Tribune* Photo;
2. Chicago *Tribune* Photo; 6. Signal Corps, A.E.F.; 7. Kaufmann & Fabry Co.; 8.
Kaufmann & Fabry Co.; 9. Kaufmann & Fabry Co.; 10. Keystone View Co., Inc.; 11.
Kaufmann & Fabry Co.; 12. Kaufmann & Fabry Co.; 13. Harris & Ewing; 14. Harris
& Ewing; 15. Harris & Ewing; 16. Kaufmann & Fabry Co.; 17. Kaufmann & Fabry
Co.; 18. Harris & Ewing.

Library of Congress Catalog Card Number: 53-5274

PRINTED IN THE UNITED STATES OF AMERICA

To the Memory of

HENRY M. DAWES

CONTENTS

PORTRAIT OF AN AMERICAN:
Charles G. Dawes

Chapter One

✿

MARIETTA

𝕴f Brigadier General Rufus R. Dawes had found time to read his copy of the Cincinnati *Commercial* on August 27, 1865, the day his first son was born, he would have found that it was one of those whirling, news-making days that were to be symbolic of the life of that son, Charles Gates Dawes. The Atlantic cable had broken that day after being two-thirds laid; President Andrew Johnson had met with his Cabinet to consider invoking the Monroe Doctrine to drive the Emperor Maximilian out of Mexico; and now five months after the last guns of the Civil War had sounded, an authoritative source in Washington let it be known that Jefferson Davis, recent President of the Confederate States, who lay in irons at Fortress Monroe, would soon be placed on trial.

Even in the well-written column of the *Commercial's* Washington correspondent was a discussion that could not have failed to be of interest to one with a small gift of prescience, for it called the White House "a miserable old shell in which no gentleman of comfortable circumstances would, for an instant, think of living. It should," the correspondent thought, "either be abandoned or made fit for the habitation of a President."

The Dawes family into which the infant was born that day in Marietta, Ohio, was not an obscure one. The first Dawes in America, William, had come from England in 1635 as a member of the Massachusetts Bay Colony. There were some clergymen and teachers among William's descendants, but most of them became traders and merchants, one being senior partner in the mercantile firm of

3

Dawes and Coolidge; both partners were forebears of men whose names, in reverse order, were one day to form a winning Presidential and Vice-Presidential ticket.

According to irascible John Adams, there were even politicians among the early Dawes kin. One of them, Tom, may have been the progenitor of the smoke-filled rooms which were still operating on a national scale in the United States as late as 1952. In his diary, Adams complained that local Boston politicians were meeting secretly in Tom Dawes' garret.

"There they smoke tobacco until you cannot see from one end of the garret to the other," wrote the future President. "There they drink flip, I suppose; and there they choose a moderator who puts questions before the voters regularly; and selectmen, assessors, wardens, fire wardens, and representatives are regularly chosen before they are chosen in town." The group of which Adams spoke were the men later known as the "Sons of Liberty."

The first Dawes to make page-one news was thirty-year-old William, the great-great-grandfather of the man who, one hundred and fifty years later, was to be Vice-President of the United States. William rode with Paul Revere on the night of April 18, 1775. Revere took the route from Charlestown to Lexington; Dawes ducked the redcoats through meadows and marshes from Boston to Concord.

Another great-great-grandfather of Charles Gates Dawes was Manasseh Cutler, a graduate of Yale before the Revolutionary War, and a friend of Benjamin Franklin. Sagacious old Manasseh, a preacher, lawmaker, pamphlet writer, and botanist, was one of the drafters of the Ordinance of 1787, chart for the government of the Northwest Territory, and the document which planted the first substantial colony in Ohio. The Northwest Ordinance has been called the most notable law ever drafted by representatives of the American people. It provided for the settlement of the Northwest Territory and for the admission of states to be formed from it. It established a public school system and provided that no law should ever impair the obligation of contract. Its most important provision was the abolition of involuntary servitude—the first effective blow struck against slavery in this country. Cutler was also a member of the House of Representatives from Massachusetts in the Seventh and Eighth Congresses.

Marietta, in all of its customs and man-made aspects, was as near a Massachusetts village as its inhabitants could fashion it. Forests came up to the very edge of the town. It even outdid New England in one arboreous respect, boasting the Rathbone elm, the largest of record in the United States; and there were great beeches and oaks. Wild crab bloomed everywhere. Sheepnose apple trees blossomed in its orchards, and woodbine covered its houses. Its churches were replicas, and its houses copies, of those in New England.

The first Dawes to take up residence in Marietta was William Mears, son of the 1775 rider. Henry was of the second generation. For two complete centuries and a quarter of another, the Dawes family had been in the main stream of events in America; but it remained for Rufus R., of the third Dawes generation in Ohio, who came out of the Civil War a brevet brigadier general at twenty-six, to achieve fame beyond any of the name to that date, including William.

When Lincoln issued his first call for volunteers in April, 1861, Rufus R. Dawes was engaged in business at Mauston, Juneau County, Wisconsin. Accompanying the President's proclamation was an announcement that the Badger State's quota would be limited to an infantry regiment of 780 men. Two weeks later twenty-two-year-old Rufus R. Dawes had recruited 100 men, and two months later his company had been mustered into service. They bore the mellifluous title, "Lemonweir Minute Men," for the lovely river which curled from the softly swelling hills through the beautiful valley where most of the men lived. For the most part wearing the red shirts of raftsmen, some in country homespun, and a few in broadcloth and silk hats, the Dawes recruits arrived at Camp Randall in Madison so meagerly drilled that they kicked one another's heels as they walked along.

At Madison, Dawes met Edward S. Bragg, Captain of Company E, Sixth Wisconsin, who immediately impressed him as "the brightest man in the regiment." Bragg, at thirty-four, was the most influential Democrat in Wisconsin, one of the state's most noted lawyers, and a Stephen A. Douglas delegate to both the Charleston and Baltimore Democratic National Conventions the previous year; but, like Dawes, with little military knowledge.

An intimate friendship was to spring up between the men so different and yet each with a personality which put him naturally in command. Bragg, diminutive, all port and mien, swank and swagger; and Dawes, of quiet stability, were often to alternate in command of the Sixth Regiment of the Iron Brigade. Each was to be the idol of his soldiers; both were to attain the rank of brigadier general; and both were to serve in Congress.

By August 7, 1861, Company K and the rest of the Sixth Regiment were at Camp Kalorama on Meridian Heights in Washington, D.C. They went into action in June, 1862, for McDowell's ten-day wild-goose chase after Stonewall Jackson in the Shenandoah Valley; and, on July 31, when Pope had succeeded McDowell in command of the Army of Virginia, the Wisconsin men, 2,800 strong and led by General John Gibbon, moved into the bloody forty-five days covering Rappahannock, Gainesville, and the Second Bull Run, and the battles of South Mountain and Antietam in the Maryland Campaign. In those operations, Gibbon's 2,800 men suffered a loss of 1,592 and came out of the carnival of blood with the historic title, the "Iron Brigade," to be as famous for its valor in the North as the "Stonewall Brigade" in the Southland.

At Antietam, recently elevated Lieutenant Colonel Edward S. Bragg was wounded, and Dawes, now major, took command of the Sixth Wisconsin in the midst of the fierce struggle. At the battle's end, it had lost 400 men killed and wounded. A few days later, when President Lincoln came to review the Union forces, Dawes wrote:

"The flower of our regiment was slaughtered in that terrible corn field. . . . We had about 2,050 men in line for the review. . . . Mr. Lincoln was manifestly touched by the worn appearance of our men, and he himself looked serious and careworn. He bowed low in response to the salute of our tattered flags. As I sat upon my horse in front of the regiment, I caught a glimpse of Mr. Lincoln's face which has remained photographed upon my memory. Compared with the small figure of General McClellan who, with his jaunty air and somewhat gaudy appearance, cantered along beside him, Mr. Lincoln seemed to tower as a giant."

In the switching of command between quick-moving Bragg and sure-footed, bold Dawes, the Sixth Wisconsin was led by Bragg at Fredericksburg, Fitzhugh's Crossing, and Chancellorsville. From Chancellorsville, when Stonewall Jackson swept down on the Federals in the last charge of that great Confederate General, there came the first of the false reports that Dawes had been killed in battle. As that report circulated, he and Bragg were getting the first sleep they had had in many nights.

"Bragg and I lay down on the same oil cloth. I remember distinctly that Bragg wore his spurs and that he kicked in his sleep."

On the pleasant morning of June 30, 1863, when the Sixth Wisconsin in the First Battalion of the First Brigade, First Division, First Army Corps of the reorganized Army led the way for Meade's legions across the Maryland line into Pennsylvania on the way to Gettysburg, Bragg, the "Little Colonel," was again disabled, and Dawes rode at the head of his men.

"The regiment will go out strong in health and cheerful in spirit and determined always to sustain its glorious history," he had written to Mary Gates. "It has been my ardent ambition to lead it through one campaign, and now the indications are that my opportunity has come. If I do anything glorious, I shall expect you to be proud of me. . . . I have a good mount; she knows the orders of battalion drill as well as the men do. . . . If there is a battle, watch the papers to see if General John F. Reynolds and General James S. Wadsworth figure in it. By them, you can trace me."

On July 1, there came to Marietta the first flash of the telegraph from Gettysburg. It told that General Reynolds and Wadsworth's division had opened the battle and had been cut up severely in the fight.

Now Lieutenant Colonel Dawes, commanding the Sixth Wisconsin, had been detached from the Iron Brigade by order of General Abner Doubleday and rushed to the support of Wadsworth's division, which was being forced back and outflanked.

The fire of the Sixth Wisconsin checked the advancing line of the Southerners, who took refuge in a railroad cut. Dawes' mare had been shot from under him. Dawes was thrown sprawling in front of his men. The mare hobbled to the rear on three legs. On foot, Dawes charged the cut and, in the 175 paces of the advance, he lost one out of every two men in his command before he obtained the surrender of the Second Mississippi, the only regiment to surrender as an organization during the battle.

"The commander of the regiment, Lieutenant Colonel R. R. Dawes, proved himself one of the ablest officers in the field," General Doubleday said in his report. "The moment was a critical one, involving the defeat, perhaps the utter rout, of our Union forces."

To Mary Gates, Dawes wrote:

"God has preserved me unharmed through another desperate, bloody battle. Regiment lost 168 men. . . . Only four field officers in the brigade have escaped, and I am one of them."

On July 4, Dawes passed his twenty-fifth birthday supervising the burial of fallen Union and Southern soldiers. He found his mare and arranged for her keep and shipment from Gettysburg to Wisconsin, a full 1,000 miles.

Six months after Gettysburg, on January 6, 1864, the Sixth Wisconsin went back to Milwaukee for a month's furlough and to recruit. Dawes, now a colonel, stopped in Marietta and, on January 18, he married Mary Beman Gates.

Mary Gates, like the Daweses and most other Marietta families, was of New England stock. Her father, Beman Gates, had come to Ohio from Connecticut. At twenty-one, he was an editor; at twenty-four, he was of established position and income; later he became a railroad builder, and in 1863 had organized the First National Bank of Marietta.

Mary Gates had been brought up in the home at Fourth and Putnam Streets, known as "the house with the big windows." The Gates house betokened comfortable financial circumstances, and Mary Gates' windows looked out on flowering terraces, a box-bordered formal garden, the common annuals and perennials, towering trees, a spring, and the college campus.

Dawes and his bride went to Milwaukee and his furloughed regiment, traveling part of their journey in a freight caboose. Then he returned to war for the hardest campaigning of all: the Wilderness,

Spotsylvania, the Bloody Angle, Laurel Hill, Jericho Ford, North Anna, Bethesda Church, Cold Harbor, and Petersburg.

On April 14, 1865, four months and thirteen days before the birth of their son, Charles Gates, Brevet Brigadier General Dawes and his young wife arrived in Washington on their war-interrupted honeymoon. They planned to attend Ford's Theater that night, to see the play "Our American Cousin." Why they turned back their tickets and thus were not witnesses of the assassination of Abraham Lincoln was told in a letter written by Mary Dawes to her mother, Mrs. Beman Gates:

"We barely escaped seeing the whole affair. Just after we got into Washington Friday, we heard that Grant and President Lincoln were to be at Ford's Theater that evening, and we made our arrangements to be there; but we walked over the Capitol grounds and around the streets so long before supper that I was so completely tired out that I told Rufe that, if there was any possibility of seeing President Lincoln anywhere else, I just could not go to the theater. So we contented ourselves to give up seeing him for the evening, fully expecting to see him Sunday at Dr. Phineas D. Gurley's New York Avenue Presbyterian Church, which he scarcely ever failed to attend."

The Marietta Iron Works, manufacturers of railroad iron, prospered; and, as his fortune grew, Rufus Dawes looked for other investments. Oil-and-gas exploration was under way in southeastern Ohio, and he made money in that, too. Successful in all operations he undertook, within a few years he was rated wealthy.

By 1872 his attention was devoted almost wholly to the Marietta Iron Works. A kinsman, William P. Cutler, was a prime mover in the building of the Hocking Valley and other short lines in Ohio, Indiana, and Illinois, which would later become parts of the Illinois Central, Baltimore and Ohio, and of the Pennsylvania Railroad systems. Cutler and his associates had been the largest customer for Dawes' rails. Now, in 1872, Dawes was to land the biggest customer of them all. Jay Cooke wanted all the production the Marietta plant could give him for his extensions of the Northern Pacific and other western railroads.

The panic of 1873 brought sudden and complete financial disaster to Rufus Dawes. Jay Cooke and other railroad builders to whom he had been furnishing great quantities of iron rails were unable to pay for consignments already delivered, and gave no more orders. The rolling mill closed, never to open again. General Dawes soon engaged in the wholesale lumber business and, although he never recovered the fortune lost in 1873, he eventually became moderately prosperous.

In 1880, Rufus Dawes received the Republican nomination for Congress in his district. His opponent was Adoniram Judson (Silver Bill) Warner, like Dawes an ex-Union general. Their units had fought within 200 yards of one another at Gettysburg. They were warm friends; and the campaign, while fiercely partisan, was personally friendly, but not intended to be as friendly as young Charles Gates Dawes made it.

On the eve of election, the Warnerites organized a torch-light parade. It marched up Fourth Street past the Dawes home and, to the consternation of others of the Dawes family sitting on their front porch, Charley Dawes was in the front rank of the band, playing a flute. He explained, when he returned home that night, that it was a purely professional appearance for which he had been paid. But to the others of the family it was heresy, compounded by the fact that the remuneration he had received had not even been in sound money; the pay had been a silver dollar!

Dawes won the election. Fifteen-year-old Charles, grown a little more orthodox in his Republicanism, always vividly remembered March 4, 1881; for on that day, not only did his father become a member of the House of Representatives in the Forty-seventh Congress, but Senator John Sherman of Ohio provided the youth with a ticket to the members' gallery of the Senate. Young Charles saw Rutherford B. Hayes go out as President and James A. Garfield come in; watched Vice-President Arthur in one of the few times he was to preside over the Senate; listened to James G. Blaine of Maine speak on the last day before he resigned from the Senate to become Garfield's Secretary of State; and thrilled to the majestic oratory of Senator Roscoe Conkling of New York, who found an occasion to speak, as he always did when the Senate galleries were crowded.

When young Dawes went to John Sherman's tiny office in the

Capitol to thank him for his courtesies, he found the Senator and his brother, General William Tecumseh Sherman, together, and remembered that the lawmaker addressed his soldier brother as "Cump."

Congressman Rufus Dawes found the Republican side of the House of Representatives well filled with ex-Union soldiers, from privates to major generals. On the Democratic side, there was a mixture of ex-Union and ex-Confederate veterans. His old friend, ex-Brigadier General Edward S. Bragg, the "Little Colonel" of the Sixth Wisconsin, sat as a Democrat from that state.

Dawes was but one term in Congress; but his service was notable for two things: one, a piece of legislation; the other, a vote. He introduced and pushed to passage legislation establishing diplomatic relations between the United States and Persia.

Congressman Dawes was one of the small group of thirty-five House members who voted against passage of the Chinese Exclusion Act. Senator Henry Laurens Dawes, of Massachusetts, was one of the six Senators so aligned. Whatever the merits of the bill, failure to support it was a fatal political error. Organized labor in his Ohio district arose en masse against him. In Marietta, the Chair Makers Union, the district's largest labor union, marched in a body to the polls to vote against Dawes and for (Silver Bill) Warner, from whom he had wrested the seat in 1880. Warner won the close election by 600 votes.

Rufus R. Dawes never again held public office after leaving Congress. He had strong support for the Republican gubernatorial nomination in 1889, but his health had begun to fail, and the nomination went to Joseph B. Foraker.

In August of that year, the wiry man who, in 1863, had gone through a half-dozen pitched battles and many skirmishes and, for a period of eight months, had never once slept in a house, became critically ill of exhaustion. He partially regained his health but never again was able to walk. He continued, however, to conduct his lumber business. New inventions helped.

"The development of the long-distance telephone has been of immeasurable help to me with my restricted activities," he wrote. "As early as January, 1886, from Marietta, I talked business with perfect ease with men in Parkersburg, West Virginia, over our telephone. Now I am able to reach more distant places."

The Dawes family was closely knit, not only in the ex-Union officer's immediate family, but there were close ties among the Gateses, Cutlers, Bartletts, Millses, Elsworths, Bosworths, Shedds, and other kinsmen.

All the Daweses seem to have had an uncommon affection for one another. In letters and journal entries, Charles Gates Dawes was to tell with pride of the achievements of his brothers Beman, Rufus, and Henry, and his sisters Mary and Bessie.

But each Dawes had a mind of his own. Although his father was a member of the Loyal Legion, Charles Gates wrote a letter to the Cincinnati *Commercial Gazette* attacking the Legion's principle of primogeniture and its requirement that its members wear full-dress suits at the annual banquets. And when Charles Dawes wrote a letter to the Marietta *Register* warmly endorsing legislation pending in Washington to establish the Interstate Commerce Commission to regulate railroads, his brother Rufus Cutler Dawes wrote an answering letter, blistering the argument point by point.

Young Charles did things young men of those days did. He engaged in athletics, won a bicycling prize, was a good debater and a regular attendant at the First Presbyterian Church.

He seemed little interested in politics after his father left Congress; but when, during the Cleveland-Blaine campaign in 1884, both Blaine and Thomas Brackett Reed of Maine spoke in Marietta on the same day, he thought it was a great event. There were torchlights and a great throng; and Grandmother Gates, who was also there, said it was the biggest political event in Marietta since the "Tippecanoe and Tyler, Too" campaign of 1840.

From Marietta College, Dawes was graduated fourth in his class. He took great pride in his alma mater. Not so good a student was his brother Beman, whose antics brought a series of suspensions.

When they returned for commencement exercises a few years later, Charles said reverently, "This old school has turned out some great men."

"Yes," replied Beman, "it turned me out three times."

At Cincinnati Law School, Dawes studied in the law office of the dean of the school, former Major General Jacob Dolson Cox. Cox, a handsome man, six feet three inches in height and of military bearing, had been a Civil War division commander, first Governor of Ohio at the end of the war, member of Congress, and Secretary of Interior in the Cabinet of President Grant.

Dawes' diligent study attracted the attention of General Cox, and the veteran barrister gave his protégé careful tutoring. Cox also came to have great faith in the business judgment of Dawes, and to be his financial backer.

Dawes' high examination grades were marked up by a young Cincinnati lawyer, William Howard Taft, later to be President and, afterward, Chief Justice of the United States.

The paths of Taft and Dawes, who were one day to have desks 100 feet apart in the Capitol at Washington, one as Vice-President and the other as Chief Justice, never crossed until years later, when both were in public life.

A Marietta College student was Byron Bancroft Johnson, later to be one of the organizers, and lifetime president, of the American League of Professional Baseball Clubs. Johnson was no scholastic wizard, but Dawes put him down as the student most likely to succeed financially.

Johnson decided the Marietta baseball park needed a fence, and set out to raise the funds. On his list of prospects was Beman Gates, grandfather of Charles Gates Dawes. Beman Gates, though perhaps a distant kinsman of "Bet-a-Million" John W. Gates, was no spiritual kinsman of that picturesque plunger in free-handed money matters.

"I could not believe it when Johnson told me he had induced my grandfather to contribute twenty-five dollars," Dawes said. "When he convinced me, I told him that a man capable of getting that amount from Beman Gates was destined to succeed financially."

Johnson went on to Cincinnati Law School with Dawes, and was a fellow student in General Cox's law office.

Another classmate of Dawes at Cincinnati Law School was George Buckland, of Freemont, Ohio, a son of Major General R. P. Buckland. General Buckland was a business associate of ex-President Hayes. Dawes wrote an account of a summer visit to Fremont, as a guest of General Buckland. He spent a day and night at the home of the ex-President, as a guest of his son, Webb, and heard reminiscences of General Grant, who had just died at Mount McGregor.

Participating in the discussion of why Grant sought a third term as President were Ohio's four most eminent citizens: Senator John Sherman, Hayes, and Generals Buckland and Cox. Dawes had not yet started his diaries, but he made a record of the conversations of the four most distinguished men he had ever seen together in a private gathering up to that time.

The sort of man he was to be was very clearly indicated by now.

"Henry," said Bill Riley, brakeman on the Marietta, Columbus and Northern Railway, "your brother Charley Dawes is the commonest man I ever saw."

"What do you mean by common?" Henry asked a little dubiously.

"Well," said Bill Riley, "you know how common I am. I've got no education, and I don't live in the best part of town. Charley, he's got education and he knows all the big people. So he got on my train, and I told him I was going to get married. 'That's fine, Bill,' he says, 'when is the wedding?' I told him. 'Bill,' he says, 'I'm coming, and I'll be your best man.' He did come, sure enough, and everyone liked him. He was the commonest man in the crowd."

General Jacob D. Cox was struck by "his intense energy and his vigorous independence of thought."

Atlee Pomerene, a Cincinnati Law School mate, afterward to be a Democratic United States Senator from Ohio, called Dawes "a man of friendships, . . . a very definite person."

Grandmother Dawes, in her diary, referred to his "warm thoughtfulness and great consideration of others."

During his college and law-school years, Dawes worked the summers as surveyor for the Marietta, Columbus, and Northern Railway. Both at school and in his work, he gathered an infinite number of friends, and kept them through the years.

The Dawes family had been a journal-keeping one, even back to old Manasseh Cutler, whose papers had come into the possession of the family in the boyhood of Charles Gates Dawes. Old Manasseh's frankness had shocked Grandmother Dawes, a prim lady of the 1880's, who "didn't like the notion of the old clergyman going to horse races and dances and balls, and drinking wine at dinners, and she doesn't want our boys ever to know, so she will guard these papers pretty closely as long as she lives."

When Charles Gates Dawes, at the suggestion of his grandfather Beman Gates, began keeping the diary, he was a graduate of Marietta College and held a degree he had obtained from Cincinnati Law School before he reached twenty-one. Marietta, oldest town in the Northwest Territory, had only 5,000 population and, although he had once written in unconditional glorification of his birthplace, "Nature made no errors in the creation of this Muskingum country," it afforded no glowing opportunities for young lawyers.

While Dawes nursed his law degree and waited for the arrival of his twenty-first birthday and a suitable location for his legal talents, he entered into partnership with his father in the production of railroad ties and car timbers. His first diary entry was dated January 3, 1887:

"I went to Dexter City on train but missed seeing my man, so walked to South Olive to look after some badly hewed railroad ties," he wrote. "While there, a freight train was wrecked and a passenger train blocked. Found Father and General Lew Wallace, the author of *Ben Hur*, on the passenger train, and we three went to supper at Captain J. Woods while the wreck was being cleared. At Caywood, we were delayed by another train wreck, but the General delivered his lecture, notwithstanding. I went with Bessie Putnam.

"Had a pleasant time with General Wallace. Received a very different impression of him than I received at the age of twelve years (I think). I took dinner with Mary Elston at his home in Crawfordsville. He made too much fun of Mary and me at that time."

The name of General Wallace was only the first of those of famous Americans with which his diary was to be studded. In a long career, he kept this diary, the totaled entries of which not only made him his own best historian but, kept contemporaneously as it was, gave on-the-spot illumination of some of the world's greatest events. Its second entry contained the name of a Cincinnati Law School mate, and the man with whom he had the longest of all his friendships, Atlee Pomerene.

"Arrived at Canton. Atlee Pomerene was at the depot to meet me. Went to the hotel where he is boarding and, after supper, to a little gathering he had arranged for me. Atlee had Harry Frease to dinner with us. As Atlee is candidate for city solicitor, he made me meet all his political friends."

Early entries showed his interest in music and the stage. To most of the infrequent plays which came to the Marietta city hall, he went with Ward A. Holden, later an eminent New York City physician. "Ward and I always get the cheapest seats," he wrote. On March 19, 1887, he put down for the first time the name which was to occur most often in his diary: Caro Blymyer.

Caro Blymyer two years later became his wife and walked by his side the remaining years of his life.

Subsequent entries were to record his impressions of almost every musical and stage star of the last decade of the nineteenth and first decade of the twentieth centuries. He was interested in music, also something of a flutist and pianist in his own right. On some occasions at Marietta musicals he played the flute, and his mother was his accompanist on the piano.

Charles Dawes' thoughts of a location turned west, as did the thoughts of most young men similarly situated in those days. Kansas City and Omaha had highest priority on the list of possibilities. He finally decided on Lincoln, Nebraska.

On a night late in April, he walked to the registry desk of the Commercial Hotel in Lincoln. On the desk, there rested a familiar object of Western Americana of that day, a stub-pointed pen jabbed into a huge, splotched Irish potato. He took the pen and wrote a scratchy signature on the register. He was too tired for a scotoscopic view of the town which was to play such an important part in his life, and went immediately to bed.

Chapter Two

❁

NEBRASKA YEARS

$\mathcal{T}$he Lincoln which greeted Charles G. Dawes when he left the Commercial Hotel to view it on the morning of April 27, 1887, was no scenic treat to the young man whose life had been passed among the wooded hills, the green valleys, and the clear, clean streams which flow into the winding Muskingum River and on into the turbulent Ohio.

Twenty years earlier, the first legislature of Nebraska had sent a commission to choose a site for a state capital, the paramount stipulation being that, when located, it should be called Lincoln, in honor of the man who had not only saved the Union but had signed that charter for the settlement of an infinite expanse of the arable West, the Homestead Act, which President Buchanan had vetoed. On treeless salt plains, in a hamlet formerly called Lancaster, 100 miles from the nearest railroad, was built first a state capitol, then a state university, a penitentiary, and a hospital for the insane. A railroad came five years later.

The combination of the Homestead Act, the magnetic pull of the romantic West on the Easterner, the promise of "land for the landless," and the constant reiteration, by Horace Greeley, of his slogan, "Go west, young man; go forth into the country," had at first failed to bring the expected influx of settlers. But, where all other inducements failed, the panic of 1873 succeeded; tens of thousands had gone west in search of a living. In the early eighties, Lincoln had mushroomed from a little over 10,000 population to a figure which the 1890 Census showed to be beyond 55,000.

But on that spring morning in 1887, Lincoln still had the new, tentative look of a Western town which might, overnight, double its population or, just as quickly, lose half of it. It was, for the most part, treeless, for long periods rainless, a town of dirt streets, its houses scattered over a wide expanse of prairie. Nor had he, Dawes was soon aware, come like a bee to a clover patch. Opportunities for a young lawyer just six months past his twenty-first birthday were little brighter in Lincoln than in Marietta.

"I was quickly convinced," Dawes recalled years later, "that Horace Greeley's advice, 'Go west, young man,' was not good short-range pecuniary counsel. I had come out West under the impression that it would be comparatively easy to get rich. But migration acts as a cream separator; and, when I got here, there were gathered some of the brightest young men of the East, all of whom had come here under the same circumstances and with the same aspirations as I. I could have done better had I gone to an Eastern or a larger Midwestern city. There would not have been the same relative competition. Here, there were seven men for every dollar; I could have gone where there were seven dollars for every man."

His early impression that real-estate trafficking offered a path to riches also was soon dissipated. His arrival and the collapse of the mid-eighties city real-estate splurge were practically simultaneous.

"I struck Lincoln right at the top of a boom; then it started sliding," he said.

The early struggles of a young lawyer in these surroundings emerge vividly from the terse notes in his diary:

"*May 21:*   Engaged desk room in Academy of Music at $6 per month.

"*May 24:*   Ordered business cards and started out the profession of law.

"*May 25:*   Spent day trying to drum up business. Called on Attorney General Lease, an old Washington County, Ohio, man at the Capitol. In the evening, went to see the 'Beggar Student.'

"*May 31:*   Accomplished nothing much this day. At office and around collecting (or attempting to collect) bad bills.

"*June 1:*   Got a large amount of collection work today and unexpectedly. Spent morning and afternoon at it. Made about $5, little enough for the detestable business.

"*June 8:* Made arrangements with Weeks, chief engineer of the B. & M. Railway, to collect a $50 note I had against one of his level men. Thus an embryonic lawsuit was spoiled which, otherwise, would have been my first. . . .

"*June 21:* Was sworn in as a practicing Nebraska attorney, by Judge Chapman, on motion of A. W. Field. . . ."

Dawes had no relish for the kind of law practice which would probably come his way. In August, two months after he was admitted to the bar in Nebraska, he became counsel for the Lincoln Board of Trade in a fight against discriminatory freight rates. He could have found nothing quite so likely to establish himself as a public figure, or so financially unrewarding. He received no retainer, and never asked for or accepted a fee in his long freight-rate litigation. "It is a good, steady job without pay," he wrote.

Perhaps anyone who made a trip from Marietta, Ohio, to Lincoln, Nebraska, in an open-windowed, cindery railroad coach in the eighties, computing the miles traveled, the hours consumed, and the transfers and waits at terminals, would have ended the trip with a conception of distances involved, and the urgent necessity of reasonable transportation rates. Dawes believed these transportation charges were the No. 1 economic problem of the western country.

Dawes pursued the rate combat with all the zeal of a crusader. When other men in Lincoln became complacent, he shook them up, painting a picture of prosperous Nebraska commercial towns processing the products of prosperous Nebraska farms. His earnings from other law cases were not enough to support him and his cause; and, for a period in the most crucial part of the fight, his father sent him $50 per month to assist him in making ends meet.

Dawes' rate fight is one of the best documented of all the activities of his life. When in 1951, sixty years later, John E. Pixton made a study of "Charles G. Dawes and the Nebraska Freight-Rate Fight" for the Nebraska State Historical Society, he found, in addition to collections which the Historical Society had made, papers in public libraries, railroad archives, newspaper files, state capitols, and in private hands.

Freight-rate controversies were nothing new in the West when Dawes arrived in Lincoln. Iowa, Nebraska, and Texas were the three states where freight rates aroused the highest passions. The battles in Texas, led by James Stephen Hogg, and in Nebraska, spearheaded by Dawes, were under way simultaneously. But where Hogg made his effort first as attorney general and then governor, Dawes carried on as a private citizen, with funds for expenses raised by the Trade Board's solicitations.

Dawes was pitted against the rich resources and the formidable legal talent at the disposal of the Burlington, the Union Pacific, and the Missouri Pacific. Arrayed against him were such lawyer giants as craggy-faced Joseph William Blythe, John M. Thurston, and T. M. Marquette. The briefs and legal arguments he prepared to use against the railroads Dawes himself pecked out on a venerable caligraph, forerunner of the typewriter.

The contention of Dawes was that the disproportion existing between the high local rates in Nebraska and the lower "through" rates from outside points to the state shut out the producers of interior Nebraska from dealing with their natural home market, the cities of southern and western Nebraska. Under the long-haul theory of rate-making, he argued, railroads discriminated against those industries of southern Nebraska which produced for the state market, and encouraged only industries producing for a distant market on which the carriers got a long haul. This system of rate-making, he contended, prevented development and diversification of the industries of interior Nebraska upon natural lines.

John Utt and the other members of the Lincoln Board of Trade which sponsored them placed no great reliance in the Dawes-originated replevin suits as a means of reaching their ultimate objectives; but Utt, in the cattle-country idiom of the day, thought such cases in sufficient numbers would "raise hell among the yearlings," and might have the effect of softening the attitude of the truculent railroads. Dawes' somewhat ingenious argument was that failure of a carrier to deliver goods to a consignee upon payment of a "reasonable" charge constituted unlawful seizure of the consignee's goods.

Thus it was that the cause which was to win Dawes nationwide fame started with a simple replevin suit against the Burlington, three months after his arrival in Lincoln.

Dawes had fought only the opening skirmishes of the freight-rate war when he began the acquaintance with William Jennings Bryan which ripened into life-long friendship and political opposition. Dawes had arrived in Lincoln on April 26. Bryan came six months later, on October 22. Dawes, twenty-two, with smooth-shaven cheeks and looking even younger than his years, and Bryan, twenty-seven, and wearing a big, black beard, met at a banquet of the Irish National League of America, in Lincoln. Dawes was soon convinced that Bryan was an orator of stature. Placed far down on a list of speakers headed by T. P. O'Connor and H. Grattan Esmonde, Irish members of Parliament, Bryan spoke so eloquently that the diners, who had not correctly understood his name when he was introduced, punctuated his speech with cheers: "Hurrah for O'Brien!"

Dawes and Bryan soon had offices in the same building, the Burr Block. Bryan was on the fifth floor, Dawes on the third. Bryan had formed a partnership with Adolph R. Talbot, an established lawyer. Bryan's part of the firm's income was so small that, while waiting for Mrs. Bryan to come out, he slept in the office to save expenses. The two young lawyers were to be ranged against one another at the famous Round Table, a Lincoln discussion club, in courts, and on political hustings.

At the end of the year 1887, the personable young Ohioan had established himself in Lincoln. Older lawyers had learned that he was a young man of intense seriousness, driving energy, and re-sourcefulness.

The hard Nebraska years were decisive in molding the kind of man Charles Gates Dawes was to be. His widening circles of friends included such pioneer Nebraska figures as S. H. Burnham, I. M. Raymond, D. E. Thompson, F. W. Little, E. E. Brown, and Stephen S. Geisthardt. Financial success would not tap his shoulder for some years; but, at the first year's end, he wrote to his father in Marietta that he would be able to manage without any financial assistance, even though he gave a great deal of time without re-muneration to the prosecution of the railroad cases.

The first tangible success in the railroad cases came to Dawes exactly a year after his arrival in Lincoln. He had made his first appearance in the Nebraska Supreme Court in a suit attacking the lease of the Atchison and Nebraska Railroad by the Burlington. Dawes, who had prepared his case with great care and rehearsed it orally in his room, claimed that the lease of the line running from Atchison, Kansas, to Lincoln was really a marriage in violation of the laws of the state prohibiting the consolidation of the franchises of competing lines.

Dawes' adversary before the Supreme Court was T. M. Marquette, the Burlington's brilliant general solicitor. The Court, in its decision, upheld Dawes' contention and declared the lease void. Dawes got the news in a telephone call from Attorney General Lease, and wrote in his journal: "This is a great victory, and indicates a successful termination of that suit. . . . One year ago today, I arrived in Lincoln."

Dawes' first friends in Lincoln had been among older men. Bryan was the first of his age group. From then on, the names of others of similar age began to appear in his diary, among them Second Lieutenant John J. Pershing, with whom Dawes formed a friendship which was one of the closest of his life, and certainly the closest Pershing ever had; Bruce Coffroth, an attorney, and later his law partner; Dan Wing; and Gus Hanna. Wing, who became a New England financial leader, was perhaps the first of the young men Dawes launched on their careers.

Dawes' judgment in financial matters had gained him the confidence of General Cox, his Cincinnati law-school teacher, and many others. Soon he was asked to make investments for them.

"I picked up, in these investments, some valuable experience," he related later on. "I bought one building for General Cox, paying $32,000 for it, which was a great sum of money in my imagination, and the most I had ever handled, up to that time.

"The man from whom I purchased the building was a hardcrusted, touchy-tempered old lawyer. After I took possession of the property and examined into the situation, I felt that, from a moral standpoint, some of its tenants left a great deal to be desired. The second floor housed the biggest gambling joint in town. A part of the building, which was residential, had female tenants whose source of income was being widely discussed in the town. I gave notice to both the gamblers and the jolly women to vacate. Some of the shadiest characters were the personal friends of the former owner, and bewailed to him the homeless state in which I had cast them. A few days later, the old lawyer met me on the street. He was much displeased.

"'Young man,' he snorted, 'if you have started out singlehanded to moralize the world, you'll find out you have a hell of a job on your hands.'

"His advice on that particular case may not have been entirely unbiased and pertinent but, as an over-all postulate, it is one which can be valuable to both individuals and nations."

The Lincoln *State Journal* of January 1, 1889, described Dawes in a list of matrimonial eligibles: "Anti-monopoly agitator; 125 pounds, neatest moustache in Lincoln. Has disposition to go back and see someone in Ohio, but is worth trying again."

Eighteen months after his arrival in Lincoln, Dawes, still short of money, returned to Cincinnati and married Miss Caro Blymyer. Early pictures show her as a delicate, dark-haired girl, with a fine oval face, dominated by her large, dark, thoughtful eyes. Her father, W. H. Blymyer, of Pennsylvania Dutch stock, was a manufacturer of such miscellaneous things as steam engines, sorghum machinery, and ice machines. He had erected one of the first tall buildings in Cincinnati, and was president of the Cincinnati Exposition. Caro Blymyer was a direct descendant of Miles Standish and of Paul Fearing, the first delegate to the Continental Congress from the Northwest Territory. She was also a descendant of Major General Israel Putnam, of the Revolutionary War, and of Michael Hillegas, the first Treasurer of the United States.

"When I was getting ready to go home and get married, I couldn't afford a dress suit, so I went to the Chancellor of the University, who had one and let me have it second-handed," Dawes wrote. "About the same time, Lieutenant John J. Pershing needed one. The tails of his had worn bare. He told me he went to a tailor and had him cut a tail out of an old pair of pants. Then he bought a new pair of trousers for $6.

"Mrs. Dawes and I came back to Lincoln and started housekeeping in a little six-room cottage at 1400 D Street. The phrase of the wedding service, 'With all my worldly goods I thee endow,' was a hollow mockery in my case for, after the ceremony at Cincinnati, the railway fare to Lincoln consumed the bulk of my 'worldly goods.' But it was a glorious time, when we figured we could live on $80 per month. It took close to $100. Mrs. Dawes was a good manager, or we could not have got through on that; but I found, at the end of the first year, I had earned enough to spend $100 per month on our living, and had $400 left over for furniture; and then, after a time, came little Rufus Fearing and then little Carolyn, and life was wholly complete."

The first Bryan-Dawes silver debate occurred at the home of S. H. Burnham, Lincoln banker and businessman.

"I don't know anything about the silver question, and I want to learn," said the man who was to carry the 16-to-1 free-silver flag as the 1896 Democratic Presidential candidate.

One of the witnesses to the debate was Judge S. B. Pound, father of Roscoe Pound, later renowned dean of Harvard Law School.

Bryan and Dawes, whose houses were a block apart, continued their vehement argument as they walked home together. Dawes was an enthusiast for his point of view, Bryan an evangelist.

"Mrs. Bryan and Mrs. Dawes walked ahead of us," Dawes wrote. "They got home and had to come back and get us out of our argument. We had stopped on a street corner, and were going at it again, hot and heavy."

The Lincoln Round Table, of which Dawes was to be the last living charter member, was similar to hundreds of such discussion clubs scattered throughout the nation. The membership was heterogeneous: lawyers, physicians, ministers, bankers, businessmen, mechanics, and, in university towns like Lincoln, faculty members. They discussed issues of the day, and often expressed grass-roots sentiments which party politicians heeded in writing state and national platforms. There were discussions of such subjects as "Annexation of Hawaii to the United States," the "Hatch Bill in Regulating Dealings in Commodity Futures," "Nebraska Freight Rates," and "How the United States Government Should Raise Its Revenue."

"There would be a general discussion and the expression of able men of extreme views on every subject, successfully designed to create irritations and 'comebacks'," Dawes wrote. There sometimes were distinguished visitors. Among such, Dawes listed Robert G. Ingersoll and Bill Nye, the humorist.

Dawes remembered that one of the subjects Bryan suggested for debate at the Round Table was: "Resolved, That Private Fortunes Should Be Limited to $100,000 for Each Individual."

Many years afterward, when Dawes visited the Bryan home in Florida, the Commoner showed him over the Bryan property.

"Now suppose your $100,000 limitation had been adopted," bantered Dawes.

"Circumstances alter cases," Bryan replied with a sly grin.

Bryan, before the end of the eighties, had decided on public life as a profession. Dawes was just as determined not to get into politics, at least from the standpoint of holding office himself. Bryan sought every opportunity to get speaking dates and appear in public. His name stayed on the office door as Talbot's partner, for he was certainly an excellent public-relations man for the firm.

Bryan chose the tariff as the most vote-worthy issue when he was elected to Congress in 1890 for the first of his two terms, in the Fifty-second and Fifty-third Congresses.

Pershing never attended sessions of the Lincoln Round Table, but participated with Bryan and Dawes in "debates at the Square Table" in Don Cameron's Restaurant, a place around which many Dawes and Pershing legends revolve. There were even more numerous legends about Cameron himself.

There has been a romantic report that Cameron was a one-time Spanish grandee on his uppers, who introduced the most peppery version of Spanish cooking to the West. In fact, he had been a cook for the lumberjacks of Minnesota and Wisconsin, then hit the old fur-traders' trail through the Platte Valley and over the South Pass, to cook for mining outfits in Colorado and Wyoming. He fed them superlatively well, and won their robust approval. When these activities began to lag, he had taken himself, his skill, and his skillet to boom town Lincoln, halfway between the lumber and mining camps.

The fame of Don Cameron's place has been heard by many more present-day Lincolnites than have ever heard of the Round Table. For nearly a half century, Pershing and Dawes were to make reference to it in conversations and correspondence; and, after

Pershing had commanded the AEF and Dawes had been Vice-President, they joined to finance the comfort of Cameron in his last days.

An appearance by Dawes as a witness before the Committee on Railroads of the Nebraska State Senate on February 25, 1891, as a "people's advocate against the railroad lobby," enhanced his reputation. His enviable renown as a rate expert was in no way lessened when, on the following August 13, he appeared before the State Board of Transportation and held the floor for more than two hours, and was given the close attention not only of the Board but of the most important railroad men in Nebraska. Dawes amazed his audience by quoting from memory 150 alleged discriminatory rates. When Auditor of State Benton heckled, Dawes got into one of those acrimonious colloquies which he had frequently precipitated:

"I will say to you, Mr. Auditor Benton, that it is a good deal better for you to make this investigation right here at home than it is riding in special cars at the expense of the railroads."

Benton replied:

"I guess you would ride, too, if you had the chance."

"Not if I were drawing a salary as a state auditor and a member of the Board of Transportation, and was paid by the people to stay home and protect their interest and do my duty," Dawes shot back.

In the exchange, Dawes had had opportunity to focus attention on the point which he had been seeking to bring to the public's notice: that state officials who took passes from railroads could not be expected to do their full duty to the public, and that leaders in private life also shared the blame. How many railroad passes were issued in any one year, in the era when they were handed out so freely, was never ascertained. In Texas, Governor Hogg claimed 232,000 passes were in use at one time, and were in the hands of most state, county, and city officials.

Even William Jennings Bryan was a pass taker.

"But since I have been a candidate for public office, I have paid every nickel of my railroad fare," Bryan said.

"There is today, in this state, a great public grievance, exorbitant local rates on railroad freight," Dawes wrote. "And yet, the leading men of the state and of this city pose as apologists for this robbery, because they fear the robbers. They stand by and see the proper internal development of the state retarded by these high local rates, and keep their mouths shut, lest their annual passes take wings and fly."

About the Dawes appearance which saw his clash with Benton, an Omaha newspaper commented:

"C. G. Dawes, the young Lincoln attorney who appeared before the State Board of Transportation Friday and disturbed the serenity of that somewhat slow-moving and complacent body by a few startling facts, has already gained state-wide renown."

On April 22, 1891, the New York *Post* gave editorial attention to Dawes and his freight-rate fight. The 1,500-word leading editorial in the *Post* was the first mention he had ever received in an Eastern newspaper.

He was still short of his twenty-sixth birthday.

The year 1893 saw Dawes a dynamic part of the life of Lincoln. He had two children and had moved into a larger house. His law practice had grown. The breadth of his interests was constantly expanding.

S. H. Burnham had organized the American Exchange National Bank, and asked Dawes to be one of the directors. Along with Burnham and G. M. Lambertson, Dawes then brought about a consolidation with the State National Bank, to make the new American Exchange Bank the second largest in the city.

In part with his savings and in part with loans from General Cox and others, he founded the Dawes Block Company, owning and managing a number of office buildings in Lincoln's business center. He was one of the incorporators, vice-president, and held one of the three controlling interests in the Lincoln Packing Company.

On February 4, he was able to announce the acquisition of what he regarded as the best business location in Lincoln, the building on the northwest corner of Thirteenth and O Streets. "My children will live to see the corner always a family possession," he wrote. He retained the property all his life.

One striking note ran through all Dawes' entries on business deals. He rarely entered into a business venture without inviting one or two of his friends to share the profit with him.

His friend John J. Pershing was discouraged at his prospects. He had the impressive title of Professor of Military Science and Tactics, and Commandant of Cadets, at the University of Nebraska. But he was thirty-five years old and still a second lieutenant and, at the going rate in the Cavalry, would not reach the grade of major until retirement age. He had acquired a law degree while teaching the Nebraska cadets.

Pershing told Dawes that the only thing he really knew was the business of Indian fighting, which he had learned in skirmishes against the Sioux. Indian fighting was in the doldrums, and he had no bidders for his law talent. But when he mentioned the subject of a partnership to Dawes, his friend warned him:

"Better lawyers than either you or I can ever hope to be are starving in Nebraska. I'd try the Army for a while yet. Your pay may be small, but it comes very regularly."

In a journal note of January 1, 1893, Dawes wrote: "We are living in a rapid time." His diary attested that these were whirling days for him. For recreation, he boxed, played tennis, skated, swam, danced, and even took up the game new to the West, golf. He was good at billiards, belonged to a whist club, but was a poor card player. He played the piano and flute at social affairs, and was a regular church attendant.

The theater was his principal diversion. He loved it with a passion shared with no contemporary some-day-to-be-famous American, with the possible exception of Woodrow Wilson. He was always taking his pretty young wife to see people like Edwin Booth, Henry Irving, Ellen Terry, Julia Marlowe, Nordica, Clara Morris, W. J. Florence, Sol Smith Russell, Lillian Russell, and Marie Tempest.

When the radiant, voluptuous English singer Lottie Collins came to town in flesh-colored tights and with a gravel voice, much foot stamping, and many muscle-shaking spasms sang the St. Louis-born ragtime, "Ta-Ra-Ra-Boom-Dee-A," hit song of 1891, Dawes recorded laconically:

"Saw 'Miss Helyett,' a very poor comic opera. Miss Lottie Collins, the famous dancer, appeared in the second act and displayed remarkable agility, among other things."

It was an era of great American neighborliness, hand-shaking, and visiting. Nowhere was the spirit of friendliness and helpfulness so generally practiced as on the new, raw Great Plains. Dawes' journal entries reflect all this with accounts of the calls he made, the people with whom he talked, the business which occupied his mind, and the events of local, state, and national interest which drew his attention.

Dawes was interesting himself in all manner of civic affairs. He had by now relatively as wide an acquaintance as he had in Marietta and was later to have in Chicago, and in all three cities during his residence he had as wide an acquaintance as any man there. The Burnhams, Raymonds, and others with whom he had business dealings, in associations which ripened into enduring friendships, were the oldest citizens, but they had been there only a decade or a decade and a half longer than he; for when Dawes, at the age of twenty-two years, went to Lincoln, he was two years older than the twenty-year-old town.

In the bitter-cold months of January, February, and March, 1893, much of it subzero temperatures, Dawes wrote, in a relaxed manner, of what seemed to be a very furious rate of life: of law, business deals, meetings of the Round Table Club, of his views on monopoly, politics, and politicians. The three-month period is typical of the life of activity he led. He wrote capsule reviews on musical events he attended or theatrical performances he saw, and made notes on impressions of books he read. Two of these books were the essays of Arthur Schopenhauer, the German philosopher, and *La Débâcle*, by Emile Zola.

When Rutherford B. Hayes, the first of the fifteen presidents of the United States whom he was to know, died on January 17, 1893, Dawes commented in his diary that he had seen Hayes many times and been entertained in his home.

"President Hayes was a great man, much underrated by the public."

When the death of Blaine, a little more than a week after that of Hayes, symbolized the end of an era, Dawes wrote of the plumed knight:

"*January 27:* Worked a little and loafed a little.

"James G. Blaine is dead. He was a striking figure in current history. I saw him frequently at Washington and, again, when he spoke at Marietta during his canvass against Cleveland for the Presidency. He lived in a turmoil of excitement, harassed by ambition and by false friends. He was surrounded by the rich, their business associate and intimate adviser, yet was the idol of the poor. He was the most wonderful example of a successful alloy of demagogism and statesmanship. His impulses came from the brain and not the heart, in all public matters; yet he was not a cold calculator, by any means, his greatest mistakes being in hasty decisions."

He deplored the tendency "toward consolidation and concentration of wealth and power in the hands of a few."

In midwinter of 1893 scandal broke which set all Nebraska talking. Of it, he wrote:

"Exposure shows gross neglect and carelessness in the letting of large contracts, on the part of the Board of Public Lands and Buildings in this state, and impeachment is suggested. Many investigating committees have been appointed, and good results seem likely to be obtained. It seems probable that the Dorgan-Mosher penitentiary-asylum combine is broken forever."

In a talk before the Round Table, Dawes related the Nebraska scandal "to the concurrent upturnings which political scoundrels are receiving all over the world." He listed "similar awakenings of the people to unsuspected corruption, such as the cozy kinship between crime and the police in New York City, as shown by the Parkhurst crusade; the exposure of the great Panama Canal frauds, and convictions of prominent men in France; the prosecution of the whisky trust; the exposure of bank scandals in Rome, Italy; and other instances.

"Too often in the past, the good results have been negated when the people lapsed into apathy and listlessness. Let us hope that we are on the threshold of an era when people will take more time to examine into their public affairs. Until men have the same vigilance in their government as they have in their private business, we will always see the infringements on the rights of people meet with imperfect vindication."

Dawes gave many evidences that he was no hide-bound partisan. He wanted his party "to win only when it deserved to win," he wrote. He thought its rebuke in the election of Grover Cleveland as President in 1892 would have a "chastening and salutary effect" on it nationally, and the great gains of the Populist Party in the

West "ought to have the effect of bringing the Republican Party back closer to the people's will in this section." He detested party machines, and the record of his Nebraska years is replete with his appeals to the people over the heads of languid or venal office holders.

"I have scratched my ticket a little, for good reasons," he wrote. Dawes' ticket scratching did not extend far enough to favor William Jennings Bryan in either of his Congressional races, being confined to "some of the state candidates under the domination of the railroads."

"I would support you if your economics matched your oratory," he told Bryan.

A diary item dated February 6 read: "The Populists and Democrats in the legislature combining, W. V. Allen was elected United States Senator from Nebraska, by a majority of five. He is a better man than the candidate of the Republican Party, John M. Thurston, the attorney of the Union Pacific. The people have gained a victory, and all friends of good government ought to rejoice. Although a Republican, I am for honest treatment of the desires of the people to have railroad domination in politics ended."

There were squalls on the economic horizon when the Round Table met at the Dawes home in midwinter to discuss the silver question. Round Table Member William Jennings Bryan was not present at this meeting; he was busy with his Congressional duties, but stories had drifted back to Lincoln, and Bryan was the chief topic of conversation.

One of Bryan's colleagues in the House of Representatives was brilliant young Joseph Weldon Bailey, of Texas, three years Bryan's junior. Bryan asked his advice on good books to read on the money question. Bailey turned over to him such books as General A. J. (Silver Bill) Warner's *Appreciation of Money, Source of Value in Money,* and numerous pamphlets of the Bimetallic Union, of which Warner was founder and president. The young Texan also took the Nebraskan to a secondhand book store, and Bryan left with an armful of books on gold and silver. Soon Bryan, according to reports in Washington and Lincoln, was giving every spare minute to a study of the money question. Bryan, Round Table members heard, was preparing himself to ride the "white" money horse against the "yellow" steed in a race for higher office.

By the next meeting, Bryan was home, and Dawes recorded: "Attended a meeting of the Round Table at the home of Congressman William Jennings Bryan, where we discussed a good supper, as well as the silver question."

There was no doubt in the minds of those attending that meeting that Bryan's study of the writings of General Warner and his close association with Congressman Richard P. (Silver Dick) Bland of Missouri had vastly increased his information on money. He was, in fact, even then preparing for the speech he was to make in Congress four months later, advocating the free and unlimited coinage of silver as the cure for the nation's ills.

For all the Congressman's boning on the subject, Dawes thought Bryan's logic was weak. He combated his arguments, and apparently carried a majority of the Round Table with him. Dawes did not regard himself as a reactionary; he regarded himself as a "progressive conservative," but he told his fellow Round Tablers that, on his record, probably he was considered radical. He thought sound money was progressive. Dawes did not fail to recognize that any sort of cause backed by Bryan's oratory would have an increasing number of converts; he believed the Government had already gone too far in silver legislation, such as the Sherman law, "which compels the Government to buy silver bullion which is worthless for purposes of redemption."

Dawes began to be an eager student of banking matters from the time he was elected to the directorate of the Lincoln bank. That study, plus preparation he made for his debates with Bryan, sent him delving deep into monetary problems and led to his first book, published by Rand McNally in 1894, under the eighteen-word title, *The Banking System of the United States and Its Relation to the Money and Business of the Country.* In the months intervening between his first scribbled notes for the book and its publication, he was to have opportunity to test his theories in a crucible which the nation little expected. When the book did appear, it advocated guarantee of bank deposits, which came thirty-nine years later, in a more critical banking situation than that which was to come in the summer of 1893.

Dawes made his first visit to Texas in the spring of 1893. He was so favorably impressed with the future of that section that he looked for an investment there. He wrote to Francis Beidler, in Chicago:

"There will surely arise, here on the Gulf Coast of Texas, one of the nation's truly great cities, certainly the metropolis of the new South."

But he saw barriers which would have to be surmounted, for he told Beidler that "Galveston has no adequate protection against Gulf floods, and Houston does not have access to deep water. Houston people talk glibly of moving the sea inland, but that is a formidable undertaking."

He had, Dawes went on in his letter to Beidler, "talked to Mr. Julius Runge, the President of the First National Bank, concerning an alliance for the purpose of controlling the Galveston Gas Company; and, if further investigations confirm my first impressions, I would want your cooperation in this deal. Neither Galveston, which has less than 30,000 people, nor Houston, which has two or three thousand less, are yet much more than half as large as Lincoln."

Dawes, through some legal matters he had handled in Nebraska, had become interested in the manufacture of artificial gas, and believed it offered a profitable future. This Galveston move, although nothing came of it, was his first toward entering the business.

When Dawes returned to Lincoln, it was no longer breathing the heavy air of a boom. High-level business activity, which the whole state had enjoyed, was ending. The darkest part of the picture neither Dawes nor anyone else foresaw.

In the spring of 1893 the West talked principally of the World's Fair, which was being rushed for summer opening in Chicago. Its wonders had been ballyhooed until the nation's imagination had been fired and its sight-seeing appetite whetted.

To the Dawes family, it had an especial interest; and there had been much correspondence between Dawes and his father-in-law, W. H. Blymyer, of Cincinnati. Chicago had wanted something spectacular, which would cause as much talk as the Eiffel Tower, built for the Paris exposition. A young Pittsburgh engineer, George A. W. Ferris, thought he had the answer, and talked so convincingly that Blymyer, an intimate friend, had given him financial backing.

Blymyer had been president of the Cincinnati Exposition, had learned something about show business and what it took to draw crowds. Ferris went before the Columbian Exposition officials and proposed to erect, on the Midway Plaisance, a wheel 250 feet in diameter, to be known as the Ferris Wheel. He could build, he said, a concrete foundation capable of supporting the vehicle and resisting a wind velocity of 120 miles an hour.

There would be, Ferris explained to the wide-eyed officials, thirty-six cars suspended from the wheel, each car being 27 feet wide and 9 feet high, and having forty chairs of fancy twisted steel screwed to the floor. The carrying capacity of all the cars would be 1,440 passengers and, when loaded, the entire weight of the structure would be 1,500 tons. Its highest point would be 268 feet above the ground.

One revolution of the Wheel could be made in ten minutes; and a passenger's ride would be two revolutions, with six stops to each revolution, permitting the emptying and filling of six cars from twelve raised platforms.

With an exhibition providing such a thrill ride as no one in this country had ever taken, made absolutely safe by powerful air brakes, and certain to be very profitable, argued Ferris, "Where would your Eiffel Tower at Paris be?"

Chicago fair officials snapped up Ferris' project.

When Dawes took his first trip on the Ferris Wheel in June, 1893, people still shied away from it. But in July a hurricane, blowing at 110 miles per hour, swept Chicago. It was the ill wind of the proverb. At the height of the storm, Ferris, his wife, and a newspaper reporter went for a test ride. After the newspaperman announced that the Wheel "hardly trembled," visitors began to crowd it.

Ferris' project and Blymyer's judgment had been vindicated. No one ever built a second Eiffel Tower; but London built a duplicate Ferris Wheel, even bigger, for its Earl's Court exhibit the following year. People came to Chicago to ride the Wheel, even after the fair closed; and smaller Wheels became standard amusement features at every fair and carnival in the nation.

In one of his few bad business guesses, Dawes, in the spring of 1893, noted the untoward economic situation, but wrote: "The general business condition is such that a disastrous panic, such as that of 1873, seems improbable, if indeed not impossible."

For Dawes' optimism, there is this extenuating circumstance: Few men who have gone through a depression believe there can be a future one as harsh as the one they have experienced. Yet he took no chance on being caught flat-footed, and immediately began to put his affairs into shape for what he called a "long pull," if one came.

In mid-April, he wrote: "Almost a money panic prevails in the land. The long-continued export of gold has led people to fear a premium on gold, and the consequent degradation of our currency. The 100-million-dollar gold reserve has been encroached upon, but the banks are affording relief by furnishing some gold to the United States Treasury in return for greenbacks."

In May, conditions grew worse.

"*May 15:* There is a panic on Wall Street, but it does not extend over the country. Stocks took a drop, and a few failures are announced. The time has long since passed when a clique of gamblers can break this country, though there is no doubt they can do great harm, especially the grain and provision gamblers."

Disaster soon began to strike closer and closer to home. There were bank failures in Sioux City and Denver. In Chicago, the Columbia National Bank closed its doors, and long lines began to form in front of the windows of the Chicago savings banks.

The American Exchange National Bank had, by now, become "the strongest in Lincoln, and can successfully withstand a severe strain, should it come." There had been a run on another bank in Lincoln, and wisdom demanded preparation for a possible emergency. Dawes, with E. E. Brown, another director, was sent East, with the difficult assignment of finding a loan of $100,000.

Although money was scarce all over the nation, one half of the loan was subscribed by the forceful and picturesque president of the Chicago National Bank, John R. Walsh, from County Cork, Ireland, who was then at the height of his meteoric career.

The swift initial success was so unexpected that Dawes tele-

graphed to their anxious fellow directors that the mission on which
they had set out was half accomplished. The novitiate financier
made an impish entry in his diary: "Mr. Brown and I celebrated by
going to see 'Ali Baba' at the Opera House."

Dawes found New York gloomier than Chicago: "Those who
knew the most were those who seemed most alarmed." But he got
the balance of the money the Lincoln Bank needed.

The American National weathered the storm, though a stream
of withdrawals reduced its deposits by two thirds. But all over the
nation banks closed, factories shut down, railroads went into the
hands of receivers, and long lines of unemployed gathered in front
of the soup kitchens.

Dawes' diary in these months was a recital of heavy and continuous financial catastrophes. Twenty years before he had seen his
father's fortune melt under just such an upheaval. Dawes owed
$200,000, a considerable debt for a young man of twenty-eight; but
he had taken steps to ward off personal disaster. That winter, in a
small way, he was able to begin the charities he was to continue all
his life.

"Want and misery exist on all sides," he wrote. "There will be
widespread distress this winter, which it will be the duty of everyone to help alleviate. I am trying to help a few families."

To the nation, the year 1894 brought the march of Coxey's
Army and the great Pullman strike. Depression had followed panic.
In the summer of 1894 savage winds and the smoldering heat lashed
humans, animals, and vegetation on the Great Plains. The thermometer rose as high as 105 degrees, winds above forty miles an
hour.

"Thousands of acres of corn, dark, healthy, and promising, had
become a sacrifice to the insatiable appetite of embattled elements,"
said the Lincoln *Star*. "Crop failure was complete. The spirits of the
pioneers drooped; the outlook was bleak. Banks, merchants, and
business concerns went down in Lincoln. Lawyers and doctors
moved away. Buildings were vacant; there was no work; many were
hungry."

To those who stayed, Lincoln was a place of thwarted hopes.
Those who emerged passably intact from the panic were few, and
Dawes had done better than most. But he was faced with the neces-

sity of getting income from other sources to protect his Nebraska investments.

A year before, his friend Francis Beidler of the Chicago Power Supply Company had suggested a Chicago location to Dawes, a suggestion to which he gave little heed at the time. He liked the idyllic neighborliness of Lincoln.

In July Dawes acquired the entire capital stock of the LaCrosse Gas Light and Coke Company of LaCrosse, Wisconsin. Late in the year he bought the Northwestern Gas Light and Coke Company at Evanston and, in January, 1895, moved to Chicago, which was to be his home for the remaining fifty-six years of his life.

Chapter Three

❁

CHICAGO

"J feel that, in changing my home to Chicago, I am entering into a field of great possibilities," Dawes wrote in his diary in January, 1895. He was certain it was the last move he would make. Chicago would be his home for the balance of his life.

Dawes' closest business associate at the outset indicated that business, not politics, was his interest. He was John R. Walsh, a Democrat of Democrats, then Chicago's most impressive and spotlighted citizen, and the man who had come to Dawes' rescue when the Lincoln bank needed money.

Walsh confided to Dawes that he did not consider himself a president maker, but was deeply interested in seeing his friend Vice-President Adlai Stevenson succeed Grover Cleveland in the White House. Once Dawes had been in Walsh's office when Stevenson and his son, Lewis, came in. Walsh introduced Dawes to the Vice-President and, when Stevenson had departed, remarked:

"I don't know whether Adlai can make it or not. That crazy man in Springfield, who is barred himself (Governor Altgeld was of foreign birth and, therefore, ineligible for President), does not like him."

If Altgeld's opposition could be overcome, Walsh thought, Stevenson would be high on the list of eligibles, for he was generally a well-liked man, comfortable for all factions to get along with.

Walsh said Stevenson was a silverite, although he had been the ticket mate of Gold Bug Grover Cleveland. Publicly, Stevenson was noncommittal in his attitude on money. He had darted flirtatious glances at both monetary wings of the party. Walsh told Dawes of a waggish quip of which Stevenson was the butt, because of his indecision:

"Adlai is a friend of the white metal and a great admirer of the yellow."

His paramount desire, far transcending any other ambition, Walsh said, was to own a railroad. Dawes was in no position to give Walsh any comfort in the matter of getting Stevenson into the White House, but he told the banker-publisher he had a cousin, Henry Bosworth, who was receiver for a railroad of a sort (the Chicago, Peoria, and St. Louis), and would, no doubt, be glad to be rid of its rusty nails and rickety rolling stock.

"I took quarters at the Union League Club, to which I had been elected a member through the introduction of my friend, John R. Walsh, and lived there until Caro and the children arrived on January 26, when we took three rooms at the Auditorium Annex Hotel," Dawes put down in his own account of his beginnings in Chicago. "I am making some valuable new acquaintances. My financial affiliations are with the Globe National (E. H. Pearson), with the Equitable Trust people (L. A. Walton, Secretary), and with John R. Walsh, President of the Chicago National Bank."

Dawes' own account of his start in the McKinley campaign, in the management of which he eventually had a greater hand than any man except Mark Hanna, is told in a diary entry of March 10, 1895:

"During the year 1894, I met Major McKinley in Columbus, Ohio; and, also, in the fall, in Lincoln. In his interest, I did considerable work among the politicians of Nebraska, Wyoming, and North Dakota.

"In January of this year, I met M. A. Hanna, of Cleveland, and had a conference with him over McKinley's plans to secure the nomination for the Presidency. My plan of enlisting support for McKinley is being followed in the West, and Mr. Hanna has given my work full endorsement.

"Hanna is in full charge of the McKinley campaign throughout the entire country. He wrote me yesterday that McKinley would soon join him at Thomasville, Georgia, where they would meet many people. He said things look very favorable in the South. He has asked me to look after matters in Illinois, in this connection.

"McKinley seems to be the coming man."

If Dawes had wished to make a money wager on that last observation, any politician in the country would have given him liberal odds that McKinley had no such sunlit prospects. Mountainous, tart-tongued Thomas Brackett Reed, Speaker of the House of Representatives, the highest office held by any Republican at that time, was first in the field. Reed's campaign was managed by Joe Manley, who had been Blaine's manager. Benjamin Harrison, only sixty-two, and four years out of the White House, was believed to be receptive for another try. James Clarkson, the most potent of the Western king makers, would be for Senator Allison, of Iowa. Tom Platt would be for Governor Morton, who had won the gubernatorial election in New York by a record majority. Matt Quay, of Pennsylvania, would play it cagey, trying to land in the winner's circle. But Quay did not like McKinley.

McKinley was not without strength. His long service in Congress had brought him to the favorable attention of the party. In the Republican National Convention of 1892, where he had served as permanent chairman, he had polled 182 votes in a revolt against Harrison's renomination. In the good Republican off-year campaign of 1894, he had made 371 campaign speeches and appeared in 300 cities and towns in sixteen states, traveling an estimated 12,000 miles and addressing two million people.

Against McKinley stood the fact that his second term as Ohio Governor was coming to an end, and he would soon be out of office. No one except Hanna, a Cleveland coal man, seemed actively interested in consolidating such scattered support for McKinley as existed.

Hanna's admiration for McKinley dated back to the year 1876 and a pitched courtroom battle in Canton, Ohio. There had been strikes and riots at the Rhodes Coal Mine in Stark County, Ohio, which had resulted in the arrest of a number of strikers. Hanna, then general manager of Rhodes and Company, had looked on while young Lawyer McKinley took, without fee, the case of a group of strikers and secured the acquittal of most of them. Hanna had at once sought the acquaintance of his young opponent and cultivated that friendship ever since.

Hanna in 1895 had only limited acquaintance with politicians who could be expected to control convention votes. Platt, Quay, Clarkson, and Manley ignored Hanna as one hardly worth their time. Even William E. Lorimer, a lesser boss, snubbed Hanna.

Lorimer, born in Manchester, England, and just four years older than Dawes, had begun his career in Chicago at the age of twelve. He had been a newsboy and a sign painter's apprentice, had worked in the packing houses and on a street railway, and finally became a brick manufacturer and builder. He had taken over the Republican machine in a rough-and-tumble fight and forced it to give him the Republican nomination for Congress. In 1895 he held the Congressional seat, dominated the Illinois machine, and, in a play for national recognition, was backing the favorite-son Presidential candidacy of Senator Shelby M. Cullom, a man of high character and great prestige in his home state.

Dawes' March diary entry was the last on politics to appear for some time. The Republican National Convention was still fifteen months away, and business demanded attention. Dawes was negotiating for the purchase of several gas plants, and acquired those at Kenilworth and Wilmette in Illinois, and Akron in Ohio.

Perhaps the most character-illuminating of all his diary entries, in that eventful year for him, were those having to do with human suffering. For the first time in his life, he found himself face to face with the bleak, desperate poverty and human misery which are bred in a large city. He had seen hard times in Marietta and in Lincoln. There had been crop failures and unemployment; there had been people suffering, in the middle-sized town as well as the small one. But when Dawes looked at the despair which had made its home in young, teeming, vigorous Chicago, a metropolis of 1,300,000, he was shocked.

Charles Dawes never learned to look upon human misery without being moved by it or without trying to do something about it. Before six months after his arrival in Chicago had gone by, he was urging city officials and newspaper editors to get behind an effort to double Cook County's appropriation for charitable purposes. His diary tells the story:

"I saw H. H. Kohlsaat, the publisher. I am getting him to advocate, in the *Times Herald,* the increasing of the annual appropriation, for charitable purposes of Cook County, from $100,000 to $200,000. Kohlsaat promised to look carefully into the matter; and, with his aid, I can accomplish the desired results. Saw O. D. Wetherell, City Comptroller, in the same connection. This year is only half gone; yet the county agent has distributed over $80,000 of his $100,000 appropriation, and the cold months of November and December are still to come."

And, a week later:

"I talked to William Penn Nixon, publisher of the Chicago *Inter-Ocean,* about getting the appropriation for charities for Cook County raised to $200,000. He promised to take the matter up in due time. I will have to keep at it for a while yet, but I expect to accomplish it."

Dawes' campaign was crowned with success two months after it had been launched. He had carefully avoided becoming connected with it publicly, and he saw to it that all credit for the enterprise went to those who had helped him.

Throughout the years, as his efforts to help the needy continued without flagging and soon began to involve the expenditure of steadily mounting sums from his private fortune, his name became as well known in the places of poverty as in the places of the mighty. But he never ceased to be embarrassed by any expression of gratitude, however well deserved. Fate was kind to him, he felt, and it was only natural that he should give a hand to his fellows who were down and out. That was all there was to it. In the end, he formed a habit of warding off thanks with a display of crustiness which amused, but could not deceive, those who knew him.

In Mark Hanna's room in the Wellington Hotel in Chicago, in May, Dawes agreed to lead the fight for McKinley in Illinois. Dawes was surprised to find that Hanna looked without awe on such bosses as Platt and Quay. He belittled the candidacy of such Easterners as Reed and Morton. Hanna considered the East the habitat of Vice-Presidential, not Presidential, eligibles. When the Republicans made a try with an Easterner at the head of the ticket, they lost, Hanna emphasized. The West would nominate the Republican candidate, and it would be McKinley or Allison.

At Columbus, where he talked over campaign plans with McKinley, Dawes thought the Ohio Governor had a far greater familiarity with the political realities than Hanna. Except for Ohio, McKinley thought the bosses would be in control of all the states with big convention delegations, unless Illinois could be wrested from them. A spectacular victory in such a pivotal Northern state as Illinois, third largest in population and delegate strength, could be the decisive turn in the contest for the Presidency.

"McKinley also places great importance on the selection of a convention city," Dawes wrote. "He thinks Chicago the best place for him, especially so if we can win the Illinois delegation for him."

Hanna summoned Dawes to his home in Cleveland in September. There might be an important break coming, he said. Quay had indicated that he and Platt would like to talk to Hanna. Hanna went East, saw the bosses, and reported to McKinley the conditions under which he would be able to secure Eastern machine support. The terms were plain: Tom Platt wanted to be Secretary of the Treasury and be assured of all federal patronage in New York; Matt Quay wanted to be the sole job dispenser for Pennsylvania.

Hanna apparently did not think these terms exorbitant. But McKinley would have nothing to do with the "bartering bosses." He answered flatly:

"Mark, there are some things which come too high. If I were to accept the nomination on those terms, it would be worth nothing to me, and less to the people. If that is the only way I can achieve the nomination, I prefer to retire from the race."

McKinley went on to talk of the sort of campaign he wished to wage. Hanna enthusiastically agreed. Shut out of the boss-controlled states, the McKinley campaign, more than ever, needed the prestige it would get from a victory in Illinois. Illinois began selecting its delegates early in the Presidential-election year, and finished by electing delegates from the state at large in April.

Bracketed with a victory in Illinois, in advertising value, was little Vermont, which also chose its delegates early. The Green Mountain State was the most rock-ribbed of all in its Republican allegiance. It nestled between lean Tom Platt's New York and fat

Tom Reed's Maine, and Reed's managers claimed all the Eastern states for him. McKinley wanted to upset that claim. Dawes noted:

"McKinley has privately determined to exert his influence to have the National Committee select Chicago for the place of the convention."

Then came a sobering setback. The Republican National Committee met in Washington, and the anti-McKinley forces chose St. Louis instead of Chicago.

Dawes met with McKinley and Hanna in Cleveland to take stock of the situation. All agreed that a victory in Illinois was, more than ever, a vital necessity. Hanna still thought an agreement might be made with the Illinois machine. With this, Dawes disagreed in toto. He was certain the Illinois machine would have to be met head on and soundly whipped. McKinley agreed with Dawes.

By the middle of January, less than two weeks after his meeting with McKinley and Hanna, Dawes had started his organization in every one of 102 counties in the state. It was a curious organization, but far from nondescript. Its main strength consisted of political amateurs, Union veterans, businessmen, and more or less prominent Republican Party members not then in politics. Dawes himself had never voted in Illinois or attended an Illinois state political convention.

The young campaign manager was soon to have a test of his new organization and to find out the strength of the opposition. The Republican State Central Committee was to convene in Springfield on January 28 to choose a meeting place for the April state convention. So sure were the Republicans of November victory that they advertised the state committee meeting as a love feast. The meeting turned out to be more of a dress rehearsal for the coming campaign than had been anticipated; for, after the shouting and cheering for the leading candidates had finally died down, the mention of McKinley's name, made merely as a matter of national courtesy, invoked such an applause that the machine was jolted.

Dawes' organization had done its work well. He himself was so busy that he found time for only two short entries in his diary:

"*January 27:* Arrived at Springfield. Saw W. E. Mason about referring to McKinley in the meeting tomorrow. In consultation all day with Republican leaders over the state, planning district campaigns for McKinley. . . . Cullom is furious at McKinley's invasion of Illinois, which he considers his own particular and personal property.

"*January 28:* Went to love-feast meeting. . . . Cullom's name as a Presidential candidate was mentioned while he was on the stage. Even then, McKinley's magic name brought forth the most thunderous applause. All day long, the overwhelming McKinley sentiment in the state manifested itself. It is McKinley against the field, against the bosses, against everything the bosses can bring to bear."

Blond Billy Lorimer appealed to Illinois to "stand solidly for Shelby M. Cullom. He is as big as any man in the field."

The ruthlessness of the machine Dawes had set out to wreck was soon manifest. McKinley supporters, in search of meeting places, found all available halls rented for weeks in advance, by the opposition, and standing empty. All vehicles for hire were somehow engaged elsewhere. Dawes wrote in his diary:

"*February 1:* Hanna is being greatly disappointed in his canvass for funds. The great trouble with our campaign is the lack of money for legitimate purposes."

The turning of the tide came on February 12, 1896, the date when Lincoln's birthday was being observed as a national holiday for the first time. A month earlier, Hanna and Dawes had arranged that McKinley would open his campaign on this day with a speech at the Marquette Club in Chicago. They had spared no effort to secure the presence of as many influential Midwestern Republicans as they could reach.

The man who was, perhaps, the most charming of modern Presidents was never more irresistible. In Dawes' private room at the Auditorium Annex, he captivated politicians, singly and by delegations. Master of the felicitous word and the apt phrase, McKinley was superb at the great banquet, where he spoke to an audience of a thousand. Soon after this, Dawes' diary began to reflect the first successes.

On March 4, Dawes' own Congressional district, the Seventh, chose the first two instructed national-convention delegates in the nation. They were for McKinley.

In mid-March, an emissary informed Hanna that there was a possibility that Cullom might withdraw, under certain conditions.

It was a critical moment in the campaign, and, on March 29, Dawes wrote the uncompromising answer to the Cullom feelers: "The Governor told me he proposed to take this place, if it came to him, unmortgaged."

On March 31 Dawes was to make a very happy diary entry: "Received a telegram that Cullom's home Congressional district instructed for McKinley, which is a great victory for us."

By mid-April most of the Illinois district delegates had been won for McKinley. The big test of the state convention lay ahead. By what his friends called a firm hand and his opponents called autocracy, Dawes had made political enemies in no small number. He had to deal with jealousy, personal ambition, and defection in his own ranks.

One of his allies was reform Mayor Swift, of Chicago, a man with great personal ambition.

At a caucus before the state convention at Springfield, on April 24, Dawes came near packing his own meeting against himself, by inviting in some delegates who gave their allegiance to Mayor Swift rather than himself. Dawes had outlined a well-thought-out plan of procedure in the convention. Swift proposed a change, and suggested that the decision on tactics be postponed until a larger caucus could be held. Dawes, who seldom in his life lost his temper without benefit to himself or his cause, jumped to his feet and shouted to Swift:

"The proposition you make means that we go into the convention a disorganized mob. McKinley holds ninety of the one hundred counties in this state. We are not going to allow personal ambitions and personal jealousies to defeat the purposes of this caucus. We are going to demand that the order of business be changed so as to have Presidential instruction voted on before nomination of candidates for state office. The anti-McKinley minority in this convention is not going to fox us into a position where, after state candidates are nominated and delegates at large chosen, a tired convention can be tricked into adjournment without voting Presidential instructions. This is the time for decisiveness, not hesitation. There are not going to be any more caucuses. That's the way it is going to be; and, if you, Mayor Swift, don't like that procedure, you can get the hell out of here."

Swift accepted the Dawes plan.

After a record-breaking three days of caucuses and conferences, and two full days of the convention session, accompanied by all the drama usually reserved for the national convention, Dawes won instruction for McKinley by a majority of 329.

From Canton, a jubilant McKinley wrote:

"There is nothing in all this long campaign so signal and so significant as the triumph in Springfield. I cannot find words to express my admiration for your high qualities of leadership. You have won exceptional honor. You had, long ago, won my heart."

Vermont instructed for McKinley a few days later. The Illinois victory had had the expected psychological effect. Even while Tom Platt, the "easy boss," announced that "The McKinley claims do not seem to have much substantial basis," Indiana, Michigan, Wisconsin, Kansas, and Arkansas followed suit. The McKinley band wagon was rolling.

Chapter Four

❁

MC KINLEY FOR PRESIDENT

*N*ever did a young man of thirty look forward with deeper personal interest than did Dawes to the Republican and Democratic national gatherings in 1896.

He had become convinced, in April of that year, that William McKinley, whose nomination he had confidently predicted two years before when McKinley was a very chancy long shot, was certain to be the Republican convention's choice.

In his confidence that McKinley would assuredly be the Republican standard bearer, Dawes was now in numerous company. Platt, Quay, Manley, Clarkson, and the other bosses opposing McKinley had never gotten together on any effective "stop McKinley" strategy. They had plied their opposition to the Ohioan separately, and evidence of this lack of integration was readily apparent. Benjamin Harrison and most of the favorite sons had dropped out of the race.

Dawes had been making another prediction, for many months. It was that, for the first time in history, the two parties would nominate men with the same first name. His Democratic William was Bryan. This prophecy was hedged with the proviso that Bryan, in some way, manage to get to the rostrum and make a speech. The serious mention of Bryan brought him some good-natured jeers. When he made it to Hanna, he would get the reply, "It will be Dick Bland." McKinley, a personal friend of Bland, agreed with Hanna.

Dawes and Abner McKinley, brother of the Presidential candidate, left Marietta for St. Louis on June 10, six days before the convention. They found a stricken city. For two weeks now, St. Louis had been burying its dead and clearing away the debris left in the wake of a cyclone which had torn a path a mile and a half through the center of the town.

Mark Hanna had arrived a few hours before Dawes. After the St. Louis convention, he was to rank as incomparably the greatest political manager ever to come on the national scene. The Hanna legend would grow lustier and lustier; soon he would be said to have his hands on wires he never touched, and to have accomplished feats he never attempted. But on that hot, humid St. Louis night, there was about Hanna nothing of the superman. Not a notably careless dresser, he had gotten off the train wearing a cheap gray suit and an old straw hat, front side back. His feet already hurt him before the convention started, and his small, well-shaped hands had begun to swell from too much handshaking. As soon as he arrived at the Southern Hotel, he ordered quantities of ice water, stripped off his coat, and began holding shirt-sleeve interviews and conferences, with his historic Room 88 door wide open. Two floors above Hanna, Dawes, in his own room, took care of the overflow.

Tom Platt came in from New York, denying that things were so conclamant for McKinley. He still insisted McKinley would be defeated. Hanna, never suspecting such an unkind fate, was to inherit, and unwillingly wear for life, a distinguishing emblem which Platt wore only for a day. The New York boss reportedly was in possession of an immense fund to promote Levi P. Morton's Presidential aspirations. A cartoonist depicted Platt arriving in St. Louis, his valise covered with dollar marks. Later, the badge was to be transferred, by unfriendly cartoonists, to Hanna's garb. It was a made-to-order prefix for his first name, and he was to be labeled "Dollar Mark" in two Presidential campaigns.

The entries in Dawes' diary for these days are scanty, indicating that they were written at great haste. Between last-minute campaigning and the preparation of the party platform, he had little time left. But among the entries there is one, the only on-the-spot record concerning the much-disputed question of who wrote the gold plank, which went much further than McKinley had ever gone or had ever been expected to go:

"*June 15:* Attended informal conference at which was drawn up the money plank of the platform. Participated in discussion of same. The plank here agreed upon was afterward adopted by the convention. Present: Hanna; Governor Merriam (of Minnesota); Myron Herrick; H. H. Kohlsaat (uncertain of Moses P. Handy); Melville Stone, head of the Associated Press; Henry C. Payne; and perhaps one or two others. Hanna submitted a draft which had been approved by Governor McKinley. Some discussion took place as to the word 'gold' in connection with 'existing standard.' Went over to the St. Nicholas Hotel and took a hand in the Vice-Presidential campaign. Did not get much sleep."

The plank, as adopted, said, in part: "We are therefore opposed to the free coinage of silver, except by international agreement with the leading commercial nations of the earth, which agreement we pledge ourselves to promote; and, until such agreement can be obtained, the existing gold standard must be maintained. All of our silver and paper currency must be maintained at parity with gold, and we favor all measures designated to maintain inviolably the obligations of the United States, and all our money, whether coin or paper, at the present standard, the standard of the most enlightened nations of the earth."

This part of McKinley's platform was a calculated risk. It meant the certain bolt of Western silverites, among them Senator Henry M. Teller of Colorado, the "stalwart," who had been present at the birth of the Republican Party.

The Eleventh Republican National Convention does not rank among the more dramatic ones in history. Perhaps its most moving moment was when the Senator from Colorado, known as "Crying" Teller, rose to make his expected speech against McKinley's gold plank. He was wearing the old-fashioned frock of the old-fashioned statesman.

"You may nominate, in this convention, any man you choose," he said between tear drops. "If you will put him on the right kind of platform, I will vote for him. But, if you ask me, as an honest man, to surrender my principles, that I cannot do. When the Republican Party was organized, I was there. It has never had a candidate since, that my voice was not raised in his support. If my stand takes me out of political life, I will go, with the feeling that at least I maintain my consistency and my manhood, that my conscience is clear, and that my country will have no right to find fault with me."

Teller received an ovation. But, when the applause had subsided and the roll was called, the gold plank was adopted as written, by a vote of 818½ against 105½. The silver men walked out.

The rest was a foregone conclusion. Over the noisy long-distance telephone wire which had just been strung to St. Louis, the first such telephonic communication that far west, Tom Reed (from the Speaker's office in Washington) had shouted to frail, soft-spoken Murray Crane: "Put my name before the convention, even if I am the last man to oppose McKinley."

McKinley won the nomination, in a landslide, over Reed, Allison, Morton, and Quay. Reed, the runner-up, had only 84½ to McKinley's 661½. Dawes had delivered 46 of Illinois' 48 votes to McKinley. Lorimer's own delegate vote and another which the blond boss controlled went to Reed. In his far-off Canton, Ohio, home, the nominee came to the telephone to listen to the cheering, shouting, and singing of his victorious followers in the St. Louis convention hall.

The high-riding McKinley forces refused Platt and Quay even the consolation of the Vice-Presidential choice. Hanna picked squat, solemn Garrett A. Hobart, of New Jersey, for that place. Noting in his diary that he had arranged for Illinois to vote for Hobart, Dawes wrote: "I think the position taken by Illinois practically settled that question."

In the press gallery of the Republican convention, a short distance from where Mr. and Mrs. Dawes watched the proceedings, sat an editorial contributor to the Omaha *World Herald,* now turned reporter. His name was William Jennings Bryan. Two weeks later, in another convention, he would supply drama such as no political convention ever held on American soil had witnessed.

When his term in Congress had come to an end in 1895, Bryan had taken the newspaper job as a stop-gap, at a starting salary of $30 per week, and begun his efforts to secure the Democratic nomination for the Presidency. So far, he had barely won a mention among the Democratic possibilities. The leading contender was undeniably Richard P. (Silver Dick) Bland, of Missouri. But more than twenty men anxious for the lightning to strike their rods, some with new Presidential booms and others with shop-worn ones, would lug them to Chicago.

Dawes was more than ever certain it was just Bryan's kind of convention. The old party warhorses, who were mostly gold men, had lost delegate contests to men whom Henry Watterson called devils of fiatism, and these newcomers would sit in the convention. But Dawes still had little company in believing Bryan would walk off with the nomination if he could manage, in some way, to get to the convention's platform and make a speech. A newspaper item of the day had said:

"Just three people believe the boy orator of the Platte, who speaks in platte-te-tudes, has a chance for the Democratic nomination. They are: Bryan himself; his wife; and Dawes, a Republican."

Although a native of Illinois, Bryan had not even been mentioned in the Altgeld-dominated Illinois Democratic convention, held only three weeks before the national convention. He was so little known, when he arrived in Chicago, that one newspaper referred to him as "Thomas" Jennings Bryan.

Dawes went from one Chicago hotel lobby to another in search of Bryan's headquarters. He found no less than three headquarters of "Silver Dick" Bland, the cravatless Missouri favorite. At the main headquarters, dapper Colonel Joe Rickey, inventor of the gin rickey, was informing the public of the overwhelming merits both of his candidate, Bland, and of his own concoction, of which, he assured all comers, "A man can drink four times as many as any other drink."

Colonel Rickey, a master of repartee, was no mean antagonist. One of the opposing candidates had just come out with the remark: "A man who never hides his collar button with anything but a napkin might antagonize the prejudices of America's erstwhile friends when it comes to the Presidency of the United States." Rickey shot back: "Why does Bland need a cravat? His beard covers not only his collar button, but a heart which beats for all the people."

But Dawes found no Bryan headquarters. For Bryan, so far, was merely a member of a contesting delegation from Nebraska, and the rival delegation would be on the temporary roll of the convention. When the session opened, he and his fellow silverites from Nebraska were cooling their heels outside. But Bryan and his delegation were seated on Thursday, June 7. On Friday, Bryan stepped up to the rostrum.

It was the first full-dress political event in the history of the spick-and-span new Coliseum, such a meeting place as the nation had not seen before. The sun rays, falling through the glass dome, lit up every part of the hall, giving brilliance to the banners and paintings hanging from walls and ceiling.

As Dawes entered the convention hall, he passed the Nebraska delegation, some of whom he knew. Bryan was holding a large fan in his hand.

"Bryan was not sitting with his Nebraska delegation," Dawes recalled. "He was just across a railing from them. He had on an alpaca coat. Although most of the delegates were coatless, Bryan had added something. He wore a low-cut white vest, like those usually worn with full-dress suits. He looked heavy-eyed and tired, although he seemed fresh once he faced the delegates. His appearance was changed from when I first knew him. In those early days in Lincoln, he had worn a full black beard. Now he was clean-shaven.

"Bryan had outmaneuvered the conservatives, and even his allies, in the division of time and the order of its use. The conservatives put up their champions first: Senators Hill, of New York, and Vilas, of Wisconsin; and ex-Governor Russell, of Massachusetts. Hill seemed tired, and his voice did not carry. Vilas was given narrow courtesy by the delegates. Russell, who lived barely two weeks longer, was so hoarse that he could be heard only with great difficulty.

"Ben Tillman's speech had taken up fifty minutes of the allotted time, leaving Bryan only thirty minutes. It was all he needed to make himself complete master of the situation.

"He got his first demonstration of approval at the very outset, when he asked the audience not to measure his abilities against 'the distinguished gentlemen to whom you have listened,' but: 'The humblest citizen in all the land, when clad in the armor of a righteous cause, is stronger than all the hosts of error.'

"Bryan waited for the demonstration to subside, then stepped a little further forward on the stage. His youthful voice was clear, resonant, and pleasant. His tone was captivating; his diction, as always, good. The great size of the hall seemingly put no strain upon his voice. He spoke without notes. It sounded like extemporization. He made few gestures. His greatest applause came when he described his businessman:

" '*We say to you* (addressing the gold delegates) *that you have made the definition of a businessman too limited in its application. The man who is employed for wages is as much a businessman as the merchant of New York; the farmer who goes forth in the morning and toils all day, who begins in the spring and toils all summer, and who, by the application of brain and muscle to the natural resources of the country, creates wealth, is as much of a businessman as the man who goes upon the Board of Trade and bets upon the price of grain. The miners who go down 1,000 feet into the earth or climb 2,000 feet up on the cliffs, and bring from their hiding places the precious metals to be poured on the channel of trade, are as much businessmen as the few financial magnates who, in a back room, corner the money of the world. We come to speak for this broader class of businessmen.*'

"From that moment on, he had his audience at his feet, leaning forward so as not to miss a word. His closing sentence, '*You shall not press down upon the brow of labor this Crown of Thorns; you shall not crucify mankind upon a Cross of Gold,*' which gave the speech its name, did not attract great attention then. This peroration was merely anticlimax. Long before this was reached, he owned the convention, body and soul, and it had worn itself out, cheering."

Before the cheering was over, Dawes walked out of the convention hall and wrote out a telegram to Major McKinley, saying flatly that Bryan would be nominated. That evening, he wrote into his diary:

"*June 8:* Went to the Democratic convention. Sat on platform. Heard my old friend, William J. Bryan, make his speech on the platform's silver plank. His oratory was magnificent, his logic pitifully weak.

"I could not but have a feeling of pride for the brilliant young man whose life, for so many years, lay parallel to mine, and with whom the future may yet bring me into conflict, as in the past.

"The scene was memorable. I had for weeks (knowing so well the oratorical capabilities of Bryan) predicted his nomination, if he made a speech on the silver platform."

Grimly, the backers of the other candidates went about the business of placing their principals in nomination. Vest, of Missouri, nominated Bland. But, so far as the convention was concerned, he might as well have been reciting his "Tribute to a Dog," an effort which had won him his greatest fame. His voice could not be heard fifty feet from where he stood. His unheard speech was studded with Vestian nifties, such as:

> "Give us Silver Dick and silver quick
> And we will make McKinley sick
> In the ides of next November."

But the delegates knew they were not going to give the nation Silver Dick and they didn't care to hear Vest. The Cross of Gold speech had been enough oratory to last them a lifetime.

The nominating speech for Boies, of Iowa, stirred hardly a ripple. Senator Turpie tossed in the name of Hoosier Governor Matthews. A Georgia delegate, named Lewis, rather gratuitously nominated Bryan. It was an entirely unnecessary gesture. A dozen more nominators droned their way through speeches.

The nomination would come from a party split squarely down the middle. A Democratic President sitting in the White House had been insulted, time and again.

The chairman of the New Jersey delegation announced that his state, which had always hitherto been dependably Democratic in Presidential elections, would withhold its vote on the convention's ballot. Ex-Governor Flower announced that New York would not vote. Diminutive General Bragg of the old Iron Brigade, he of the famous statement, "We love Grover Cleveland for the enemies he has made," announced that Wisconsin was abstaining from voting. In all, 185 delegates skipped the roll call.

Bryan was nominated on the fifth ballot. Dawes was not present when it happened. His diary states the reason:

"*July 10:* Did not go back to the convention, as I knew the nomination of Bryan was inevitable."

Bryan was on the hustings almost as soon as the Chicago convention adjourned. He was to make the most strenuous political campaign in history, riding in a special railroad car inappropriately named "The Idler."

The "Black Eagle of the Platte," as the former "Boy Orator" had now come to be called because of his jet locks, was running on three platforms and with two Vice-Presidential running mates. He had been given the nomination of the coatless, cravatless, and, in some instances, sockless Populists at St. Louis, a sort of Wild West pow-wow, whose delegates the conservative newspapers derisively described as "representatives of the sage brush, jack rabbits, and free coinage." It had presented to him, as his ticket companion, lean, rabble-rousing Tom Watson, of Georgia, and had implored him to ditch Sewell, the Democratic Vice-Presidential candidate, and run in double harness with the Atlantan. The Free Silver convention, apparently recognizing that Bryan was already too heavily laden with Vice-Presidential entanglements, gave him a third platform to stand on, endorsed his candidacy, and let it go at that.

Bryan, sweating through the alpaca coat in which he had made his Cross of Gold speech, soon was drawing audiences which were measured only in acres.

How McKinley would meet the challenge of his silver-tongued antagonist had not been decided when Hanna, Dawes, and other members of the Executive Committee of the Republican National Committee went to Canton on July 16 and heard from McKinley his irrevocable decision to stick to front-porch campaigning. He was sure, he said, that Bryan would plead poverty, and try to capitalize on the plea.

"I will not try to compete with Bryan," Dawes quoted McKinley. "I am going to stay here and do what campaigning there is to be done. If I took a whole train, Bryan would take a sleeper; if I took a sleeper, Bryan would take a chair car; if I took a chair car, he would ride a freight train. I can't outdo him, and I am not going to try."

A front-porch campaign was not a new idea for a Presidential candidate. Harrison had used it in Indianapolis in 1888. But McKinley made an excellent platform appearance and had a winning way with crowds. In past stumping, he had displayed great endurance. In a prenomination effort in Kansas in the year 1895, he had spoken to 150,000 people in two days. Once, in the Sunflower State, he had spoken twelve times in one day; another time, he had made twenty-one speeches in sixteen hours. His decision disappointed many Republicans. But Dawes, the only member of the Executive Committee who knew Bryan, believed McKinley's plan would be the most effective.

In another diary entry concerning the July 16 meeting at Canton, Dawes wrote: "McKinley and Hanna told me they wanted me to be responsible for the proper handling of funds." He added a footnote, that Hanna had been more explicit four days later, that Dawes would handle *all* funds. He was then within forty days of his thirty-first birthday.

Dawes set up the Chicago office, then went back to Canton. On August 23, Dawes sat with McKinley in the twelve-by-eighteen library of the nominee's two-story yellow-frame house in Canton, while McKinley read him his acceptance letter, page by page. "I suggested two or three minor changes, which he adopted," Dawes wrote. "It is a very able document."

There was no doubt of the potency of McKinley's promise to banish bread lines; put an end to the depression, which had already lasted three years; "give the workman an honest dollar for honest toil"; and bring the country a new deal. Although McKinley did not actually use the words "new deal," other Republican orators did.

Part of Dawes' duties in Chicago was to audition campaign songs, which poured in for what was to be a singing, slugging contest. One of the first submitted put the New Dealer label on McKinley. The song, set to a grave tune of the grave nineties, went:

What matter if all goods are cheap, our clothing and our hash,
If we can get no work to do to bring the ready cash?
The ring of empty dinner pails is but a mournful tune.
There's got to be a new deal sure, for there's blood upon the moon.

There's blood upon the moon, oh, yes! A dark and dismal stain.
But better days are close at hand, when light shall shine again.
The winter's discontent will turn to summer's breath of June.
McKinley'll bring a new deal sure; there's blood upon the moon.

In August Bryan, en route to New York, passed through Canton. He was greeted by a crowd which filled every inch of standing or climbing space around the station.

"I am glad, in this city," he announced, "the home of my distinguished opponent, to testify to his high character and personal worth." Then, by sudden impulse, he climbed down from the train and, with Silver Dick Bland at his side, drove over to the McKinley home to greet his opponent. The nation was getting the first taste of the high drama that was to follow.

On September 14, Bryan invaded the Blue Grass State to speak at the little town of Henderson. He found that the population of a half-dozen western Kentucky counties, and some from Indiana, had come to hear him. As he swung into the East, he drew great crowds at Baltimore and Wilmington. In Philadelphia, dozens were injured in the crush. At Brooklyn, a howling, tumultuous throng greeted him. On September 25, 70,000 hailed him on the Boston Common. His argument may have been tongue-worn and illogical, but Bryan was making it as only Bryan could.

He turned west for a spectacular trip through West Virginia, then to Illinois, into Tennessee, and back into Indiana for a speech at Indianapolis on October 6. Up to now, his Boston Common crowd had been his greatest. But Indianapolis gave him a con-queror's reception. In a parade from the railroad station, the Cleveland Club of Indianapolis, in Prince Albert coats, marched ahead. These were old Grover's boys, named after the President; but they were not withholding their support from Bryan, as Cleveland was.

Behind the Cleveland Club, Bryan rode in a white carriage drawn by four white horses caparisoned in silver harness. At the circle where he made his speech, every available inch of space was taken, and the sea of people stretched away in the streets which formed the circle's spokes.

McKinley's certainty that many people would come to see him was borne out. Visitors started even before the nominee had made the announcement that he intended to keep to his own front porch. On June 18, when the telegraph wires were humming with the news of his nomination, his Canton and Massillon neighbors were already giving him a serenade. Two days later a New York delegation stopped on its way home from the St. Louis convention. On June 27, the date of his official notification, there appeared a crowd of 16,000 people.

By July 1, the visitors had trampled down McKinley's lawn and obliterated his carnation beds. By the first of August the ground around his home was bare, beat-up earth. Enthusiastic supporters had pulled the pickets from his white fence and taken them home for souvenirs.

Yet the greatest pilgrimage of American political history was merely beginning. From mid-September until the last Saturday in October, special trains brought railroad men, millworkers, miners, potters, and workingmen of all kinds, schoolteachers, commercial travelers, bishops, preachers, evangelists, merchants, bankers, Southern planters, and Northern farmers, men of every trade and profession. Visitors would start arriving at dawn, and continue coming all day. From 800 to 1,000 letters a day poured into McKinley's study. Republican processions marched and remarched past the modest McKinley home. Bands played; enthusiasts cheered; and steam calliopes contributed their "music."

Canton liked it all. The town decorated its homes. Citizens, wearing enormous red badges, their carriages shiny and their horses well groomed, met and welcomed the visitors, which many days reached as high as 10,000 and on one day 50,000.

Occasionally the old white horse which pulled McKinley's carriage would trot to the depot to bring an important visitor to the house. The country over, squads of white horses were being used to pull the white-money man. Bryan rode in carriages which had been painted white and silver-plated, with white horses wearing white silver-plated harness. Every white horse was a potential Bryan parader. Only the old McKinley white horse was exempt.

Sometimes McKinley spoke from the front porch, sometimes from the highly polished hickory stump sent to him by east-Tennessee admirers, and sometimes from the bandstand. In bad weather, or for especially large crowds, he used a tabernacle.

Finally, the "wheeled might of the nation" came to Canton.

Dawes, himself a bicyclist, and Hanna, interested in anything mechanical, had given special attention to the cyclists of America. In Chicago headquarters four times as much money had been allotted to the wheelmen's department as to the women's department; for, while women were voting only in Wyoming, Colorado, and Utah, the wheelmen were organized in every city in the land.

The McKinley and Hobart Wheelman's League was going to give the Republican candidate the show of his life. Battalions of wheelmen, two and four and six abreast, swung into alignment. Most of them were in uniform, some in suits of pure white, faced in red, others in white capes with huge magenta collars. There was the inevitable bicycle float, showing McKinley and Hobart riding tandem in the lead, Bryan and Sewell second. Tom Watson rode alone, a touch of levity in the grave nineties. Marchers followed, carrying bicycle rims with pictures of McKinley and Hobart in the circles.

The peddling wheelmen performed intricate mass-formation rides they had practiced for weeks. Finally, they halted in front of McKinley, dismounted, and raised their front wheels in salute. Their spokesman addressed the candidate:

"The wheeled hosts of the nation came to avow their allegiance to you. . . . Our bond of brotherhood is our wheel; not a mere toy or simple source of pleasure, but a great commercial auxiliary, the acme of mechanical skill in the evolution of vehicles."

McKinley replied: "In this country of inventions, I doubt if any means of locomotion was ever so favorably received. Rapid transit in this novel form depends largely upon a single condition, good roads (*loud applause and ringing of bicycle bells*), and I am for them. There are 800,000 bicycles being produced each year. The bicycle has beaten the best time ever made by a running horse."

That same night, 25,000 railroad men in working clothes surged through the Chicago Loop for McKinley and sound money, carrying railroad lanterns instead of the usual torches; and on October 8, Chicago Day, that city saw the biggest public procession of the nineteenth century, with 100,000 men with golden badges, gold hats, gold caps, and gold shoes, marching for five hours before a crowd of half a million people. Although it was an all-civilian event, the procession moved like an Army corps on dress parade. Civil War veterans were putting their military knowledge to peaceful uses.

The Chicago Day parade also saw the first use of a device which was soon in use everywhere. "It was seen everywhere during the parade," a newspaper account said. "It is an instrument called the 'megaphone,' which first came into use on bicycle tracks, and is calculated to make the most inoffensive whisper sound like a fog-horn. When it comes to noise, its success yesterday must give it recognition in all future demonstrations."

The effort to convince the electorate that McKinley, and not Bryan, was the friend of the people was going forward with wither-ing effectiveness.

Dawes had set up national campaign headquarters in Chicago, with little of the money he was generally supposed to have at his command. "The pressure for places is simply overwhelming," he had noted on July 23. "Met 100 or so people, all of whom had a plan of campaign involving their employment as an incident." The Hanna legend, fed by cartoonists who portrayed him in suits checkered with dollar signs and wading in lucre up to his knees, worked a powerful attraction upon people of every description, not all of them above suspicion. "The usual crowd of place hunters," Dawes noted, a few days later. "It involves a strain upon the sympathies to turn away some of the poor fellows."

Hanna had arrived in Chicago on August 10, a day of swelter-ing heat, but he did not bring campaign funds with him. He in-spected Dawes' headquarters, then put an extra supply of collars into his hat, and went on a round of money-raising visits. After pounding the Chicago pavement for several days without much success, he went East on the same errand. A week later, Dawes recorded:

"Received letter from Hanna. The outlook for money for cam-paign purposes is very poor. Our plans will have to be cut down."

Not until September did money begin to flow into Republican coffers.

"*September 9:*   Have now received, as committeeman, nearly $300,000 since the campaign opened."

"*September 11:*   At lunch, Mr. Hanna handed me an envelope containing fifty $1,000 bills, being a contribution of a railroad to the Republican fund. Deposited a check for a similar amount from an-other source. These will be the largest contributions of the cam-paign. Spoke to about 5,000 people at South Side meeting, and was well received."

On October 1 Hanna could report that he had collected the

largest single campaign contribution made by an individual so far when he received $35,000 from E. H. Harriman in New York, while Dawes had received a contribution of $10,000 from Marshall Field, the Chicago merchant.

Dawes made almost weekly trips to Canton to report on the progress of headquarters work to McKinley. He made this notation of his one meeting with Bryan during the campaign:

"Bryan and his wife were at the Auditorium Annex. I called upon them and had quite a talk. Bryan, somehow, imagines he has a chance to be elected President. He referred to our old silver debates and gave me a conditional invitation to visit him at the White House."

Charles Dawes' diary reflects a furious round of activities during the last month of the campaign. He was running campaign headquarters on a business basis, including meticulous accounting for every penny of campaign funds. His public speeches and private conferences followed each other in rapid succession. But on November 1 he could enter:

"*November 1:*   The campaign, one of the most notable the country has ever passed through, is drawing to a close. I write this on Sunday evening, before the eventful Tuesday. I am so confident of victory, and have always been, that I cannot even contemplate defeat as a possibility. It has been a great privilege to be connected with the campaign as one of the Executive Committee; and I have appreciated and, I think, improved my opportunities for gaining political knowledge and experience. I have kept my hands clean, and finish the campaign with a clear conscience."

And, the next day:

"*November 2:*   This is the eve before election, an event upon which my future course in life will largely turn. I believe we will have an overwhelming victory."

On that same day, Bryan traveled 290 miles in Nebraska, making daylight speeches at Lincoln and eight other stops. At Omaha, he made seven speeches at night, winding up with a great rally. At the end of his sixteenth speech of the day, and the three thousandth speech of the campaign, the 16-to-1 candidate's voice was unimpaired, his physical condition better than when he started. Next day, Nebraska was in his column.

"*November 3:* Election day. Major McKinley was elected President of the United States. There is an overwhelming majority for him, and a large majority in the electoral college. Voted at Evanston in the morning. Spent the rest of the day, and most of the evening, at national headquarters, where we received the returns. In the evening made a short address at the Auditorium, where 5,000 people were listening to the election news. Telegraphed congratulations to the Governor and to Hanna."

The majority was "overwhelming" only in the relative sense that it was much greater than the difference between the parties in any recent election. McKinley led Bryan by 567,692 in the nation. Yet the race was so close, in a number of states, that the Chairman of the Democratic National Committee did not concede the election until Thursday. That night, Bryan wired to McKinley: "Senator Jones has just informed me that the returns indicate your election, and I hasten to extend my congratulations. We have submitted the issue to the American people, and their word is law."

There was no law, in those days, requiring the publication of campaign contributions and expenditures. When Bryan and Dawes met for the first time after the election, Bryan asked:

"Charley, how much did you fellows spend to beat me?"

"We spent $3,562,325.59," said Dawes.

Bryan was amazed.

"Why, Tom Lawson told me he saw Pierpont Morgan give Hanna a check for five million dollars!"

Chapter Five

❁

A GOOD STEADY JOB *WITH* PAY

*T*he unofficial picking of a President's Cabinet for him, which is an American custom, began within a week after McKinley's election. The Cleveland *Leader,* published in Hanna's home city, which had been the first newspaper to favor McKinley's nomination and was supposed to have sources of information not open to others, forecast that Dawes would be Secretary of the Interior.

There were other plausible selections, including Benjamin Harrison for Secretary of State, and Theodore Roosevelt for Attorney General, in the *Leader's* list. Hanna's own name did not appear. What was not known at the time was that neither Hanna nor Dawes expected or desired to be rewarded with a Cabinet portfolio. Hanna had aspirations for a public career, but he wanted it in the legislative branch of government, as United States Senator from Ohio.

Dawes also entertained an ambition, to be United States Senator from Illinois. But he was barely thirty-one years old. In all the history of the republic, not a handful of men had been elected to the Senate at his age. In addition, he had been a citizen of Illinois for less than two years. His senatorial designs would have to be postponed.

Speculation that Dawes would be in the Cabinet continued as McKinley went about the business of assembling his official family. Newspapers commented that, if Dawes did get a Cabinet post, he would be the youngest man ever appointed to such a place, younger even than was Alexander Hamilton when George Washington put him in the Treasury. Men of political weight, including such McKinley intimates as Judge Peter S. Grosscup and General John McNulta, scheduled a trip to Canton to urge Dawes' appointment as Secretary of the Treasury. Dawes vetoed it.

"I am approached constantly by influential friends," he noted in his diary, "who proffer their support to me for the Illinois Cabinet position. I ask of these to refrain from addressing Governor McKinley."

In December, with Hanna, he visited the President-Elect to make plans for the inauguration which, in Hanna's words, would be "purely democratic, but grandly magnificent." Dawes' diary records:

"*December 15:* The President-Elect again discussed the question of a Cabinet position with me. He said he often thought he owed his nomination, in great part, to my effort in Illinois, and was anxious to know whether his failure to give me a Cabinet appointment would, in any way, alter our intimate and constant friendship; that he would not have these relations altered for three Cabinet positions. He spoke with deep feeling, and touched me greatly. I replied that nothing could alter or lessen my regards for him. He talked over the Cabinet personnel with me."

But, on the train en route to Chicago with McKinley, who was to be a guest in his home, Dawes wrote: "The President-Elect urged me to consider the appointment of myself as Comptroller of the Currency, if a Cabinet position for me should prove impracticable."

If Dawes was to accept an executive office in Washington, that of the Comptroller of the Currency was the one he preferred above all others. The office had been created during the Civil War, along with the national banking system. Congress, the sad experiences with the politically dominated United States Bank still fresh in its mind, had done a painstaking job to assure the political independence of the Comptroller. His term of office was five years, one year longer than the President's term.

In his quasi-judicial functions, the Comptroller was not controlled by any higher official. His annual reports were made to Congress directly, which rendered him independent of the Secretary of the Treasury, and allowed him to present to the legislature his own views on the banking and currency needs of the country. While in

later years the Comptroller's office became obscured by the creation
of the Federal Reserve Board, the Reconstruction Finance Corporation, and the Federal Deposit Insurance Corporation, there was no
doubt that, in the late nineties, it held far-reaching powers. It was an
office which demanded exceptional skill and placed an uncommonly
heavy burden of personal responsibility upon the shoulders of its
holder. These were the considerations which prompted Dawes pres-
ently to inform McKinley:

"I would gladly accept the appointment as Comptroller of the
Currency, and consider it a crowning honor."

McKinley made Dawes his emissary to ascertain if Senator Allison would accept appointment as Secretary of State. Allison desired
to remain in the Senate, so McKinley named Senator John Sherman,
of Ohio, his cabinet premier, thus providing a place for Hanna in
the Senate.

When Representative Nelson Dingley, of Maine, declined to be
Secretary of the Treasury, McKinley considered Dawes for that post.
Dawes countered by presenting to the President a candidate of his
own, white-whiskered Lyman J. Gage, a Gold Bug Chicago Democrat. McKinley promptly commissioned Dawes to ascertain Gage's
views on the tariff and, also, if he was interested in the Cabinet
place. The interview was satisfactory, and Gage was appointed.

With Mr. and Mrs. Abner McKinley, Dawes went to Washington for the inauguration. He noted:

"By a curious coincidence, my old associates, Mr. and Mrs.
W. J. Bryan, and their little daughter, were in the same parlor car
with us. I introduced them to the McKinleys and had a long talk with
them. Bryan did not express any disappointment. I had a talk
with Mrs. Bryan. She spoke very sensibly and pleasantly about 'old
times' and her husband. She somehow believes her husband will
lead to triumph, in a Presidential race, the elements which stood
for him in the last conflict."

How effectively Congress had safeguarded the Comptroller's
office against political influence became evident at once. McKinley
wanted Dawes to take office immediately. But James H. Eckles,
then Comptroller, declined to resign before the completion of his
term.

Dawes stayed on in Washington for a while, part of the time living, at the President's invitation, in the White House. He recommended W. J. Calhoun, who had been his floor leader when Dawes fought for McKinley delegates at the Illinois Republican convention, as a proper man to make the study McKinley wanted made of the Spanish-Cuban situation. He went with the President to New York for the dedication of the tomb of General Grant; accompanied McKinley to the Nashville Centennial on the first of the President's good-will tours to the South; recommended General Jacob D. Cox as Minister to Spain; and carried McKinley's offer of the, at the moment, most vital of all diplomatic posts to General Cox, which Dawes' old law teacher declined because his health was not vigorous enough to cope with the rapidly deteriorating relations between the United States and Spain.

Dawes urged that former Vice-President Adlai Stevenson be the Democratic member of the commission the President was sending abroad in an effort to effectuate his party's sound money platform. Stevenson, with the other commissioners (Senator Wolcott, of Colorado; and Charles J. Paine, of Massachusetts), departed in April. The commission got no encouragement from Great Britain, France, Russia, Japan, and India, all of whose assent was necessary for an international bimetallism agreement. Its mission eventually failed.

With Mrs. Dawes, the future Comptroller of the Currency went on their first European trip during the summer. He, of course, knew of the failure of the Bi-Metallism Commission, and realized that it would have an effect on the office he was about to assume. Unlike that of the Commission, his own trip was unofficial, intended only to gain such information as he could in preparation for his future duties.

When Dawes returned in August of 1897, he found a country emerging from the depression which had gripped it for four years. On his arrival in New York, he noted:

"Wheat sold at $1.00 per bushel today, the highest price since 1891. Prosperity seems to be dawning at last."

While waiting for the office of the Comptroller to become vacant, Dawes returned to Chicago with every intention of continuing his researches and studies on monetary matters. But he had no sooner come home than he found himself chosen the foreman of a grand jury. Although he could have evaded the distasteful assignment, he had vowed he would never dodge a civic call.

"It is a mournful duty and a rather trying experience for one who endeavors to be conscientious," he wrote.

But in three weeks the jury had disposed of 745 cases; had visited jails, infirmaries, and an insane asylum; and Dawes, as foreman, had written a report calling attention "to the grave faults of our present system of disposing of minor civil and criminal cases." When the jury was finally disbanded, Judge Ewing complimented it with the statement that "Its record has not been surpassed in the history of Cook County, and vindicates the new jury law." Judge Chetlain added: "Its record is the most outstanding of any jury in the history of this county."

In numerous meetings with Dawes, McKinley completed his currency recommendations during the autumn. The finishing touches were added at Canton. Dawes' journal threw light on the happy family life of the McKinleys. One entry:

"We talked, for a time, about his mother, who is eighty-nine years old; and of his sister, Miss Helen. His mother kissed him good-night, saying, 'William, I am going to bed now. You will find some pie under a cloth on the dining-room table, which I have put there for you.' After she and Mrs. McKinley and Miss Helen had retired, the President and I went out and tried the pie, at which we were soon joined by Mark Hanna and Senator Burrows, of Michigan."

On November 26, Dawes made this diary entry: "Mr. and Mrs. Albert J. Beveridge took dinner at the house, and spent the evening with us." The entry was notable because it was his first diary mention of Beveridge, later to be a United States Senator from Indiana, and one of Dawes' closest friends.

On December 16, 1897, James H. Eckles resigned as Comptroller of the Currency. An hour later, the President sent the nomination of Dawes to the Senate. Mark Hanna, although suffering from hives and rheumatism, began to hobble about the Senate Chamber, with Senators Cullom and Mason of Illinois trailing along behind him. In two hours he had polled the Senate Finance Committee and obtained unanimous approval of both Republicans and Democrats. Dawes was confirmed at once. He had just passed his thirty-second birthday.

Back in Lincoln days, Dawes used to refer to his running battle with the railroads as "a good steady job without pay." When he assumed the Comptroller's office, he began to draw a regular salary for the first time in his life. It amounted to $5,000 a year.

"*January 3, 1898:* I enter my responsible office fully impressed by its obligations, and resolved to administer it without timidity or favoritism, striving only to do that which is right and consistent with public and private honor.

"I believe it to be my duty to refrain from any acts which might give the impression that, as an administrator of law and a public official, I am more intimate with those the law is destined to restrain than with those it is designed to protect. Accordingly, I declined an invitation of John J. McCook to meet the bankers of New York at a banquet to be given by him."

Dawes did not have to wait long for an occasion to demonstrate that he meant what he had said about timidity. Among the first callers was Representative Charles Curtis, later to be United States Senator, Republican Majority Leader of the Senate, and Vice-President. He was swarthy, stocky, raven-haired, part Kaw Indian. In the course of his life, he had worn a blanket on an Indian reservation, been a jockey and, later, a hack driver. He had the forthright vocabulary of his background.

At the moment Curtis was outraged by the fact that Dawes, without consulting any Kansas politician or political organization, had appointed a Kansas bank examiner. The Senator, who was accompanied by two important Kansas bankers, had planned a fearsome exhibition of his indignation, calculated to win the admiration of his influential constituents.

"What do you mean," he roared, "by appointing a nonresident, nonpolitical nonentity as Kansas bank examiner? I want you to explain it to me, if you can, so I can explain it to my people!"

Dawes shouted back as loudly as Curtis:

"You won't have the slightest trouble about that. By the Eternal, you just tell anyone who is interested that you talked to a

Comptroller who feels competent to fill his job, is conducting the office exactly the way he sees fit, and, as long as he is here, is going to continue to do so."

Curtis left the office, muttering that Dawes would hear from him again. He never did.

Two weeks after coming into office, Dawes discovered that the banks of New York, Boston, and Chicago were in the habit of employing his own bank examiners, for a goodly compensation, to make extra examinations of their banks for the bankers' own uses. "This is an outrage," he announced, "and shall be stopped today. No man can serve two masters." The banks protested vigorously, but Dawes stood firm.

The severest test of his stamina and character came with the closing of the Chestnut National Bank in Philadelphia. This huge institution was closely tied up with the sprawling interests of William H. Singerly, banker, paper-mill owner, and newspaper publisher.

The ramifications of the failure affected the interests of numerous leading financiers, among them many Republican political leaders, and a liberal sprinkling of top Democrats. These leading interests had, among themselves, worked out a plan of the order in which the creditors of the institution were to be paid off. Dawes rejected the plan as unfair to the other depositors, and the storm broke.

"Great pressure is being brought to bear on me to modify my position in the Singerly matter, but I cannot and will not yield," Dawes wrote.

"The Mayor of Philadelphia called and made an argument endeavoring to have me modify my conditions of January 24.

"Senator Penrose, the State Treasurer, and the Lieutenant Governor of Pennsylvania came to my office relative to a deposit of the state in the Chestnut Street National Bank, with a proposition which was unfair to other depositors, and which I refused to consider, in consequence."

Dawes went himself to Philadelphia. When he stepped off the train on the cold morning of January 28, a tall, silk-hatted, immaculately dressed man was waiting on the platform. He extended his gloved hand and introduced himself as Edward Townsend Stotesbury.

Stotesbury had been a partner of Drexel and Company, and was now a member of the firm of J. P. Morgan and Company. He was a member (in many cases, the chairman) of the boards of directors of some of Pennsylvania's largest manufacturing and transportation companies. He headed local patriotic societies, civic organizations, and Philadelphia sportsmen's clubs. He was, moreover, a staunch Republican and heavy campaign contributor.

Stotesbury and Dawes talked only briefly. Stotesbury asked for a later appointment to discuss the situation in detail; but wished, at the time, to urge the Comptroller to beware of George H. Earle, and to see that he had no part in the management of the bank's estate.

Dawes went to the Chestnut Street National Bank, then had lunch with Earle. He observed Earle carefully all during the conference. When the luncheon broke up, Earle remarked that he believed it necessary, in the interest of the depositors, to have a receiver appointed as quickly as possible.

"I have decided to make you receiver," Dawes surprised Earle.

Dawes had picked the right man. Earle did his job so well that he not only managed to pay all depositors out in full and to return all assessments made against stockholders, but he even accomplished the astounding feat of paying to each stockholder $40 per share. This performance was made possible, in part, by the fact that Dawes, in his capacity as Comptroller of the Currency, continued for a while to publish the Democratic Philadelphia *Record*, and to run it so profitably that, eventually, it could be sold at the then extremely high figure of $2,800,000.

Dawes' administration was characterized by the vigor which had come to be expected of him. When there was a defalcation in the New York bank of powerful United States Senator Tom Platt, Dawes promptly closed its doors. There was no guilt attached to Platt, Dawes announced. But a politically minded man might have found a way not to close a Platt bank.

He sent thirty-one-year-old Dan Wing, whom he had known as a minor employee in a Lincoln bank, to clean up the Boston financial mess caused by the failure of the Globe National and Broadway National Banks. He would not listen to the Boston protest that Wing was too young a man for the task. Wing fixed things up, stayed a half century, and became one of the leading New England bankers.

Dawes found underpinning for shaky financial institutions in New York, Buffalo, Pittsburgh, and other cities. Chief Joseph, chief of the Nez Perces Indians, wearing long black hair and wrapped in a blanket, came to see him about the failure of a bank which had caused much distress to his tribesmen. When Dawes straightened it out, the great warrior called him "Big wampum man."

"I went to the White House," Dawes noted, "and got the President to go to the basement to sit ten minutes for a sculptor who had waited three months, and over, for the opportunity. The bust is for the Government building at the Paris Exposition."

Getting the President to sit for his sculptor was probably the smallest service Dawes ever performed for the White House; for the President, like so many other men, had come to rely more and more on Dawes' judgment. When McKinley accumulated savings, Dawes found investments for him, the largest in Lincoln, Nebraska.

"In the evenings, at ten o'clock, I frequently walked from my house, at 1337 K Street, to the White House, and went to the old Cabinet room, where I would wait for the President to come upstairs," he wrote. "This he did almost every night, to finish up the business of the day with his trusted friend, George B. Cortelyou, first his Assistant Secretary, then his Secretary.

"The President, on these occasions, was usually relaxed. Much of the work was formal, and consisted of examining and signing papers covering decisions made during the day, or before, and the President would often talk freely of the things involved. General Corbin, the Adjutant General, would generally be there with important matters from the War Department. I shall never forget these visits late at night."

Although Dawes always disclaimed ever having had any decisive influence on McKinley's decisions, he was never reticent about his own opinions. "If you think you have commonsense notions, you need not think them out of place in any company," he had written in 1895, when he had informed McKinley of his views on the silver question. The problems with which McKinley was now faced were more serious than the silver issue; for, to William McKin-

ley who, as a volunteer in the Civil War, had worn Union Blue for
four years, who had seen some of its bloodiest battles, and who
regarded war as the ugliest of human activities, there fell the task
of leading the United States into another armed contest.

There is no doubt about Dawes' own position toward the events
which led from the mysterious explosion of the battleship *Maine*
in the harbor of Havana on February 15, 1898, to the declaration
of war on April 27.

"The history of war which is true mingles acts of heroism with
details of the slaughterhouse," he had written at Lincoln in the
winter of 1893. "It tells of the game of chess played by generals,
and of the mechanism and reasons for the movement of great masses
of men; then, in the same breath, of disemboweled men, of splintered
bones projecting through bleeding flesh; of the butchery of men
more cruel than that of cattle; of horrible gaping wounds, headless
bodies, decaying and putrescent corpses." He had not changed his
views.

Dawes' office in the Treasury Building looked out upon the
White House, a scant 200 feet away. Two or three times a week
he had lunch there with the President. He often joined the President
and his wife for dinner as well. Dawes saw President McKinley
more often than any other man in his White House office.

Sometimes, when he was troubled, the President would ask
Dawes to go on long, slow walks with him. Sometimes they would
go for rides in a one-horse trap. "The President would drive at a
fast clip," Dawes wrote.

Assistant Secretary of State William R. Day, who carried all
the burdens of that office for the now senile John Sherman, liked
to relax by riding a roller coaster. Dawes frequently noted streetcar
trips with Day to Glen Echo, the national capital's Coney Island.

No less than thirty-six journal entries made during the two and
a half months preceding the outbreak of the war tell of conversations touching upon that subject.

"*March 9:*   I had a talk with the President, congratulating him
on the great compliment paid to him, and the great good to result
from the placing, by unanimous vote of Congress, of fifty million
dollars at his disposal for purposes of defense.

"The President stands for any course consistent with national honor which will bring peace. In his hands this immense sum will be a great instrument for good, if war comes; but the fact that it is placed in his hands is a vindication of his policy, and adds to his power to control the situation in the interests of honorable peace.

"*March 19:*   The President seemed to feel in better spirits than usual, although he is always cheerful. In the afternoon I was with Judge Day at the State Department. Theodore Roosevelt came in, urging war and emphasizing the danger of delay, having learned of the sailing of the Spanish torpedo flotilla. I went driving with Judge Day and we discussed Cuba. The situation grows more perplexing and ominous. War will be difficult to avoid. The President will do what he believes to be right. If he is right, the future, when all events are judged in the keen light of conscience and knowledge, will vindicate his course.

"The sensational papers make more difficult the situation. If war comes, it will be because the starvation and suffering in Cuba is such that the United States orders it stopped, on the ground of humanity and outraged judgment, and that order of intervention is resisted by Spain.

"*March 22:*   The President again talked of the Cuban situation. His great line of policy is being assisted by events. He had hoped, and still hopes, to stop the suffering in Cuba without war. But he expects it to be stopped. Intervention will be on broader grounds than the question of responsibility for the disaster to the *Maine.*

"*March 26:*   Saw the President at 1 P.M. A peace delegation of Quakers called and came into the Cabinet room while I was there. Was at the White House again at 4 P.M. The Naval Commission reports the *Maine* explosion was an external one first, followed by an explosion of one of the smaller magazines. This report will go to Congress, with a brief message from the President on the Cuban situation, asking an appropriation to feed the starving. This aid granted, he will proceed to feed these people, whether Spain objects or not. He will not request their recall, as this might be acceded to by Spain, placing him under obligation. Again, if they were recalled, and hostilities should open shortly after in Havana Harbor, he would be accused of treachery and bad faith.

"*March 27:*   Talked over the Cuban situation with Judge Day. He has been in constant communication with Madrid. The Spanish cabinet is intimating further concessions, and will probably consent to the feeding of the *reconcentrados,* and that the *reconcentrados* be allowed to return to their homes and farms. It is expected that Spain will further propose an armistice after this is accomplished. Day hopes they will propose that this armistice shall continue until October 1, when the President of the United States shall, as mediator, settle the dispute finally and without war.

"Neither the President nor Sagasta desires war. But the President proposes to intervene to stop the suffering. His purpose is in accord with the dictates of humanity. If this purpose of relieving suffering is interfered with, he will use force, and his conscience and the world will justify it.

"*March 28:* Was at White House. The callers are all more or less agitated over the situation in Congress. The President's message went to Congress.

"He expects abuse for his efforts for a peaceful settlement of the Cuban situation; but, when his policy and acts are all known to the public, they will know his true strength and moral courage. The weak man, in his place, would long ago have been rushed into war under the awful pressure exerted. He had, some time ago, taken the steps which the press demands should have been taken. He has notified Spain that the *reconcentrados* must be released and allowed to go to their homes. The public does not yet know this; but, when they do, a portion of the public will still demand unreasonable haste. War may be very near.

"*March 29:* There is great indignation, among the more radical members of Congress, at the President's message, which was not warlike enough to suit them.

"*March 31:* Congress is awaiting a report from the President on Monday as to the situation, by which time Spain is to answer the President's demands.

"*April 4:* Saw the President at noon. In the message, he will not recommend the recognition of Cuban independence, but will defend the right to stop the trouble, upon the broad grounds of humanity, by force if necessary.

"*April 7:* The President and I took lunch alone in the library; and afterward I went driving with him for an hour. He discussed the situation with his customary frankness. He read his reply to the joint note of the ambassadors of the six Great Powers, expressing hope for peace between this country and Spain. War seems inevitable.

"*April 20:*   Today, the President signed the joint resolution of Congress, and sent an ultimatum to Spain.

"*April 22:*   Our battleships are seizing Spanish vessels.

"*April 29:*   An engagement is expected by Sunday between our Asiatic Squadron and the Spanish ships at Manila."

True to Dawes' prediction, Commodore Dewey steamed into Manila Bay at dawn on May 1, 1898. When he had come within range of the Spanish fleet, he issued the famous order: "You may fire when you are ready, Gridley."

On May 3, Dawes wrote in his diary: "Had lunch with the President. He will make Commodore Dewey an Admiral.

"*June 4:*   News comes of the bravery of Officer Richmond Pearson Hobson and his crew, in sinking a large collier in the mouth of Santiago Harbor, under the fire of Spanish guns. The hope is that this imprisons Cervera's fleet.

"*July 4:*   During the day we heard of the destruction of Cervera's fleet at Santiago."

The war, which lasted three months, three weeks, and three days, was soon ended. At the White House, Dawes noted in his diary, he saw recently demobilized William Jennings Bryan, whose 208 days as the colonel of a Nebraska regiment had been spent in an Army camp near Jacksonville, Florida. Another colonel, Theodore Roosevelt, whose 132 days of service had been action with the Rough Riders, was also back. Bryan was preparing to try again for the White House, Roosevelt for Governor of New York.

Dawes' final entry concerning the Spanish-American War is dated August 22:

"Went with Abner McKinley and others on a Government tug down the Hudson, and met the flagship *New York*. Was introduced to Admiral Sampson. Gage, Wilson, Smith, Griggs, and Bliss, of the Cabinet, were there. Heard the Mayor of New York's address to Sampson, and his reply. Abner went back to the tug; but, upon invitation, I stayed and took the trip up the Hudson. Most of the time I was on the bridge of the ship.

"It was a most wonderful greeting which the battleships received. The river was filled with shrieking whistles; cannons were firing; and immense crowds everywhere were cheering. The ships in the parade were the *New York, Indiana, Iowa, Oregon, Massachusetts, Brooklyn,* and *Texas.* Admiral Schley boarded our ship in the afternoon.

"Two incidents aboard the *New York* made what I think will be lasting impressions on me. On the deck of every ship, bands were playing the National Anthem. On our deck I saw one young captain of the Marines, the tears running down his face, walking up and down, saying, 'This is my country! This is my country!'

"At noon, I saw old Secretary of Agriculture Wilson walking alone on the quarter deck, and I said: 'Mr. Wilson, they are serving luncheon below, and you had better go down.' Secretary Wilson is a typical American citizen from Iowa, a farmer, dignified, without affectation, and he said to me: 'I don't make it a rule to go where I'm not asked.' 'But,' I replied, 'nobody will regret the oversight more than the officers of the ship; you should go down. You have had nothing to eat since four o'clock this morning.' He said, 'My boy, I will tell you something. Thirty-five years ago, I came up this same river with my Scotch father and mother, in the steerage of a little ship; and now I come up it on this great warship, a member of the Cabinet of the President of the United States. I want to walk here and think about it. I can get along without lunch today.'"

"*December 31, 1898:* With Frank Lowden, Gus Hanna, and my brothers Rufus and Beman, I saw the old year out at the Union League Club. Thus ended an important year in my life, the year of greatest work thus far, and a year of progress, I think, all things considered. I am deeply grateful for all which has come to me, and anxious to be found worthy of it."

Chapter Six

⚙

FIN-DE-SIÈCLE WASHINGTON

"*The* real things of life are the simple things; the real attachments are the home attachments." Thus Dawes had written in his diary after a visit to his old home in Marietta.

His house at 1337 K Street, in Washington, was such a home. It was gay with the presence of Caro; little Rufus, now eight; and Carolyn, now six years old. While Senator Wolcott, of Colorado, was making the streets of the national capital unsafe with a single-seated, rubber-tired Victoria, Washington's first automobile, Dawes' stable housed a team of carriage horses of which he was proud. The Dawes house was within walking distance of the White House and the homes of his friends; for, in that *fin-de-siècle* era, almost all the homes of executive officials, Supreme Court justices, senators, and embassies were clustered in a small, tree-shaded area.

Friends had always been an indispensable element in his life. With the turnover in officialdom for which Washington is noted, new names began to appear in the diary. William Rufus Day, Dawes' closest friend, with whom he lunched two or three times a week at a famous table in Losekam's F Street restaurant, had departed, and John Hay was Secretary of State. George B. Cortelyou, McKinley's secretary, was his closest friend now, with the possible exception of Albert Beveridge. The name of George W. Perkins, soon to be a J. P. Morgan partner, appeared frequently. Theodore Roosevelt had become Governor of New York, and had much correspondence with Dawes, principally in connection with federal employment for ex-Rough Riders, to whom Roosevelt referred, in his letters, as "my

78

troopers." Another newcomer with whom Dawes was greatly impressed was Elihu Root, who was succeeding the beleaguered Russell A. Alger as Secretary of War.

His diary tells of the many informal social gatherings at the White House, which were the principal relaxation of the President.

"I joined the President and Secretary Gage in singing Methodist hymns. Senator Hanna was present, but he did not sing."

Or:

"I went with Caro and Howard O. Sproggle, of Chicago, to the White House, where Mrs. Lawrence Townsend, wife of the Minister to Belgium, played and sang. She had a marvelous accompanist. Mrs. Townsend is one of a number of fine musicians the President has had at the White House. About all the members of the Cabinet in the city, and their wives, were present.

"The President knew that Seward Webb, Cortelyou, and I played the piano. The President has a good sense of humor, so he commanded all three of us to play.

"Miss Flora Wilson, who was studying voice, was asked by the President to sing. When she refused, her father, Secretary of Agriculture Wilson, volunteered: 'Mr. President, I will sing.'

"I played the piano as his accompanist, and he sang some Scotch songs, or at least recited the words, along with some of the weirdest noises I have ever heard. Ineffectual efforts were made to draft other local talent into the concert. It was a very jolly affair, for the contrast between the finished performance of Mrs. Townsend and that of the rest of us was amusing, and was what the President was evidently seeking to emphasize."

Then there was the stage, Dawes' abiding passion. Since the President was an infrequent theatergoer, but liked to work deep into the night, Charles and Caro Dawes had developed the custom of taking Mrs. McKinley to the theater frequently. The President would remain in his study, and Dawes would often join him there after the play or concert to review the day's business or discuss the problem of the morrow.

"While I sat with the President late at night, he went through a mass of official business, and made decisions. He would often pause and tell me why he was deciding as he did," Dawes wrote. "One thing he told Cortelyou and me made a life impression upon me.

He was considering the appointment of a minister to a foreign country. There were two candidates. The President outlined their qualifications, which seemed almost identical. Both were able, experienced, honest, and competent. Each was equally entitled to preference from a political standpoint. Then he told this little story, an incident apparently so unimportant that, except for its consequences, it never would have been told; an incident so trivial that the ordinary man would have forgotten it. But McKinley was not an ordinary man.

"The President said that, years before, when he was a member of the House of Representatives, he boarded a streetcar on Pennsylvania Avenue one stormy night, and took the last seat in the car, next to the rear door. An old and bent washerwoman, dripping wet, entered, carrying a heavy basket. She walked to the other end of the car and stood in the aisle. No one offered her a seat, tired and forlorn as she looked. One of the candidates whom the President was considering—he did not name him to us—was sitting in the seat near which she was standing. He was reading a newspaper, which he shifted so as not to seem to see her, and retained his seat. Representative McKinley arose, walked down the aisle, picked up the basket of washing, and led the old lady back to his seat, which he gave her. The present candidate did not look up from his newspaper. He did not see McKinley or what he had done.

"This was the story. The candidate never knew what we then knew, that this little act of selfishness, or rather this little omission of an act of consideration for others, had deprived him of that which would have crowned his ambition of perhaps a lifetime.

"We never know what determines one's career in life. Indeed, it may be these little forgotten deeds, accumulated, are the more important factors; for it is they which must, in many cases, provide us with the opportunity to do the greater deeds, and we unconscious of it. Why comes this reward in life? Why that disappointment or failure? We cannot know with certainty. This we can know, however, and this story illustrates it: There is no act of kindliness, however small, which may not help us in life; and there is no act of unkindness, however trivial, which may not hurt us. More than that: The habitual doing of kindness always adds to our happiness, for kindness done is duty performed. Unkindness always breeds an unhappy spirit, for unkindness is duty neglected."

While growing prosperity throughout the nation soon began to reduce sharply the number of bank failures and other financial upheavals, and so lightened somewhat the burden of one phase of work in the office of the Comptroller of the Currency, work increased in another. Dawes was championing efforts to bring about a sound emergency currency to lessen the danger of financial stringencies; and, at the same time, fighting legislation for asset currency, which he considered a dangerous nostrum.

"We want some sort of currency which can come out in panics, which can be used at such times to carry us through, and not a currency which will help us into a panic when we are out of one," Dawes explained.

He won the support of President McKinley and such powerful senators as Allison, Aldrich, and Burrows, for the plan on which he worked many months. He had hoped to get it into the Gold Standard Bill, and it was inserted in the Senate. When the bill went to conference between the Senate and the House, it snagged. Speaker Henderson, anxious to get legislation which would redeem the 1896 platform promises, ordered the bill stripped of all such controversial amendments as the Dawes currency plan, and it was not in the Gold Standard Bill which McKinley signed into law on March 14, 1900.

The Spanish-American War had established the United States as a naval power to be reckoned with. Her voice began to be heard around the world.

John Hay was negotiating with the European powers for the open door in China. Congress was debating the recognition of the revolutionary government in Cuba and the Puerto Rican tariff. Thomas Brackett Reed retired from public life in protest against "imperialism."

The United States had Cuba, the Philippines, Guam, and Puerto Rico on its hands, and debated what to do with them. George Frisbie Hoar, the old man eloquent, had parted company with McKinley on the issue of expansion, leaving the administration without a spokesman in the Senate. There were frequent references to Beveridge in Dawes' diary:

"Beveridge is Presidential timber, if he can restrain his intense energies and commanding talents, and have the patience to exercise tact and discretion," he wrote.

Beveridge had, by now, won a Senate seat; and the daring strategy had been devised of filling the vacuum of the administration on foreign policy in the Senate by making him its spokesman. This explained the Dawes diary item: "I am trying to help Beveridge get on the Foreign Affairs Committee of the Senate."

Ten days after Beveridge was elected to the Senate came Aguinaldo's insurrection in the Philippines. Captain John J. Pershing, then in Washington to organize the Bureau of Insular Affairs in the War Department, and in line to become its chief, declined the promotion in order to join the fighting.

Dawes' restless energy was being expended in many ways. He had become concerned over the rapid growth of trusts in the field of business which were taking place despite the Sherman Antitrust Act of 1890, and were to culminate in the organization of the United States Steel Corporation, the nation's first billion-dollar enterprise. Four entries in 1899 pointed up his concern with the situation:

"*March 24:* The enormous capitalization of industrial concerns, and the combinations in apparent effort to control and raise prices, are deeply stirring the people, and will force the question of further legislation on the subject into the next campaign.

"*March 28:* I talked over the matter of the unprecedented growth of trusts with the President, and the position in reference to them and their evil tendencies which our party should assume. He told me he intended to call the attention of Congress to the matter in his next message, and would lead in a movement for their proper restriction."

"*Waldorf Hotel, New York. April 23:* In the evening, Mr. and Mrs. George C. Boldt entertained us at dinner. The hotel is full of business schemers. Combinations of corporations of every kind are being made, and the 'money changers' are at all the tables.

"*September 22:* At 10 P.M., went over to the White House and stayed with the President until 11:30. Discussed finance, and read my speech on 'Trusts,' which I expect to deliver in Boston."

In his speech before the Merchants Club of Boston on October 17, Dawes called "the taking of positive action against the present and prospective evils of the trusts one of the necessities of the hour. The question of the nature of that action is one of the issues now before the people, and will remain before them until properly settled."

Beveridge had come back from his trip to the Philippines just before Dawes made the Boston speech. Although Congress was in recess and Beveridge had not yet taken his Senate seat, and it was yet ten months before even the 1900 Presidential ticket would be named, Dawes recorded:

"Beveridge announced to me that he was a candidate for the Presidency in 1904 and, whether I would be for him or against him, he proposed to make me his Secretary of the Treasury."

Dawes regarded Beveridge's statement as an amusing absurdity. But he was greatly interested in another pronouncement, that the Indianian expected to put himself prominently before the country by a speech defending the administration against the Democratic charge of "imperialism."

Beveridge began the three-month writing of the speech in Dawes' house. He made the speech on January 8, 1900, one of the great days in the history of the United States Senate. All morning, landaus, victorias, stanhopes, surreys, and carriages of all descriptions, drawn by horses which were the pride of their owners and grooms, discharged their freights of smartly dressed women and silk-hatted gentlemen. Admiral George Dewey, who had come home for his welcome seventeen months after the Battle of Manila, was in the gallery, resplendent in gold lace, and accompanied by his bride, the auburn-haired former Miss McLean of Cincinnati.

Beveridge, freshman Senator from out of the West, was to make his debut in that august body in a role never before or since entrusted to one so callow in Senate service. Unknown yet, even by sight, to most of his colleagues, he was to be spokesman for his President and party on an issue which might dominate the forthcoming Presidential campaign. "Expansionism," the administration called the issue; "imperialism," cried the opposition, and even some of the most stalwart Republicans.

Every Senator was in his seat, and members of the House stood in the back of the Chamber when Beveridge walked in. He had been in his hotel room, going over with Dawes, for the last time, some of the revised portions of the speech. Dawes had been hearing parts of that speech since October; he had made suggestions; and only now it was ready.

At 12:30, Beveridge sent this resolution to the Senate presiding-officer's desk: "RESOLVED, That the Philippine Islands are territory belonging to the United States; that it is the intention of the United States to retain them as such, and to establish and maintain such governmental control throughout the archipelago, as the situation demands."

Beveridge had no notes or manuscript. Never once did he halt for a word; never did he stumble. He spoke too fast for the Senate stenographers to take his speech down completely; but each word was distinct as his rippling sentences poured forth.

He took note of Secretary of State John Hay's recent diplomatic triumph, an assent from the great powers to the principle of the open door in China, and went on:

"From Hong Kong's heights civilization is irradiating all the Orient. If this be imperialism, its final end will be the empire of the Son of God.

"The power which rules the Pacific rules the world; and, with the Philippines, that power is, and will forever be, the American Republic."

Beveridge ended his speech in exactly two hours. It filled twelve columns of newspaper type. As he finished, a storm of applause rolled through the Senate hall from floor and galleries. Senate graybeards, who had sat fascinated, violated all rules to cheer. Beveridge was famous at a leap.

Of that exciting day in the Senate, Dawes wrote:

"In the morning, at Beveridge's request, went to his room, where he read some revised extracts of his speech. With Sadie Burnham and Caro, I went to the Senate at 12:30 to hear him make his speech, upon which he had been working for months. It was a great scene and a great triumph for Albert, who delivered his address with power and matchless grace. We sat with Secretary Gage in the President's reserved seats and had a fine view of the notable event. Beveridge's speech will be long remembered as making his advent into greater affairs."

Two months later, on the party-splitting Puerto Rican tariff bill, Beveridge was outside of the administration breastworks. Dawes wrote:

"*March 13:* In the evening Beveridge came over and read me his constitutional arguments on the Puerto Rican bill, parts of which are very remarkable. As usual of late we got into a heated argument, to our mutual amusement. Mrs. Dawes did not consider it so amusing, as we upset a bottle of ink on a prized rug of hers."

For the next few days, Dawes and George W. Perkins had many stormy sessions with Beveridge, in an effort to obtain his support of compromise Puerto Rican legislation. Beveridge finally agreed:

"If it had not been for Perkins and myself, I think, without question, Beveridge would have read himself out of the party and joined Mason and others in refusing to accept the best attainable, and thus endanger the solution of the Puerto Rican Government, which is far and above the lesser question of a temporary and small tariff," Dawes wrote. The bill squeaked through Congress and headed for a court test, and Dawes noted: "The precedent is fixed for the Philippines."

It was the Philippine Insurrection which was indirectly responsible for the only scolding McKinley ever gave Dawes. "It was in connection with a pardon matter," Dawes recalled. "Jacob Wolfson, of New Orleans, had committed an offense against the banking law. The defalcator was in collusion with a bank teller who allowed him to overdraw his account. Later, he was allowed to enlist, and fought bravely in the Philippines. One particular act of heroism was swimming a river to perform a dangerous mission. A petition for his pardon, signed by his superior officers and 1,000 soldiers who served with him, was sent in.

"In cases against the banking law, both the Attorney General and the Comptroller of the Currency were asked for recommendations. I felt that the man had sinned against society but had atoned. I recommended mercy; Griggs recommended against it.

"As the heads of the two recommending agencies had disagreed, I went to see Griggs. I used the word 'mercy' in my talk with the Attorney General. Griggs, a man with a steel-trap mouth, objected to that word. 'The Department I head is the Department of Justice, not the Department of Mercy,' he said, with such an air of finality that I never mentioned it to him again.

"There the matter stood on April 9, when the man was to surrender to a United States marshal and begin his seven-year prison term. Wolfson, believing his case hopeless, came to me. As he came into the office, Abner McKinley, the President's brother, was with me. 'I am never going to take off this uniform and put on stripes,' he said.

"'Don't be too quick,' I told him, and promised to see the President. 'You be back here at two o'clock.'

"I went over to the White House with Abner. The President began to scold me when I brought the matter up. It was the first time he had ever done that.

"'You know perfectly well this man enlisted solely for the purpose of putting himself in a position to ask for a pardon,' the President said.

"When I started to remonstrate, the President smiled and signed a paper and tossed it across his desk to me. It was the pardon. He had not wanted to offend Griggs who, at noon that day, went out as Attorney General. The pardon recommendation had been the first act of Philander C. Knox as Attorney General."

Early in 1900 Dawes became involved once more in the campaign which was to put McKinley in the White House for a second term.

"*January 29:* Spent a time with the President, who is celebrating his fifty-seventh birthday. He reviewed the past few years of his life and his prospects. It would be a great personal relief to him not to receive again the nomination for the Presidency."

Dawes listened while McKinley gave his reasons. The petit mal from which Mrs. McKinley suffered had grown much worse during the year. His administration, he thought, would be counted successful. He had fought a successful war. He had the treaty with Spain, and John Hay's triumph, the open door in China.

In Congress, the legislative program had been a heavy one. Hawaii had been annexed and given a territorial form of government, and we had valuable Pearl Harbor. No action had been taken on the Philippines or Cuba, but that could wait. Congress, for the time, would leave to the President the duty of maintaining American sovereignty and providing a government for the Philippines. A form of government had been provided for Puerto Rico, with the proviso that, whenever its legislative assembly enacted a system of local taxation to meet the needs of the Islands, the Puerto Rican tariff would be removed. An Isthmian-canal bill had passed the House as the first step toward joining the Atlantic and the Pacific.

Gold was firmly established as the monetary standard of the nation. Every dollar was a gold dollar, or its equivalent. There was the greatest volume of money in circulation in the nation's history, and foreign trade was at its greatest peak.

Antitrust legislation had completed its journey through committee and was on the congressional calendar for action at the next session. Congress had appropriated the huge sum of seven hundred million dollars to run the Government in the next year, but the country was prosperous and could afford it.

Future admirals would not have to fight with revenue cutters and other nondescript ships, as Dewey had at Manila. Congress had voted the McKinley naval-expansion bill, and the country was on its way to a big navy. The authorizations were for two battleships, three cruisers, three protected cruisers, and five submarines, the new underwater craft of naval warfare.

McKinley had gladdened the heart of labor by asking an extension of the eight-hour day. There was better feeling between the North and South. He had made, too, a move which, it was hoped, would forever prevent outbursts of yellow fever which, at various times, had plagued Philadelphia, Boston, New Orleans, Charleston, Norfolk, New York, and Memphis. Major Walter Reed, of the United States Army, would soon depart for Havana in an effort to find out whether the disease was transmitted by the mosquito.

But the Republicans had no one on the horizon as formidable as McKinley. Hanna thought Bryan would be stronger than four years before. He wrote to Dawes that winning will "be no boy's play this year."

Chapter Seven

❁

DEATH OF A PRESIDENT

*W*hen Dawes swung the Illinois delegation to Garrett A. Hobart in 1896, it had given Mark Hanna everything he wanted: Presidential nomination, Vice-Presidential nomination, and platform.

With Hobart dead and the Vice-Presidency vacant in 1900, Dawes was again to play a decisive part in the selection of the nominee for that office, a part which was to have a profound influence on the course of American history. Hanna was not to do so well; Platt and Quay were to do better than four years before.

There was no doubt of McKinley's private preference for a running mate. It was Senator William B. Allison, of Iowa. But on June 10, on the eve of the Republican National Convention, a vastly important entry was made in Dawes' journal. McKinley, Hanna, Allison, and Dawes met in the White house and discussed the Vice-Presidential nomination. The result Dawes gave in a dozen words: "Allison persists he will not accept the nomination for the Vice-Presidency." Three days later, Allison made it official with a public announcement: "I will not have the Vice-Presidency; it cannot be forced upon me. If I should be nominated at Philadelphia, I will decline, will refuse to run."

Theodore Roosevelt had also announced: "I will not be a candidate for Vice-President. My statement is absolute."

Dawes favored then Representative Jonathan P. Dolliver, of Iowa, as McKinley's ticket partner, but assumed that the President and the President's friends would keep hands off and allow the

88

convention to choose whomsoever it wished, provided the man chosen was not objectionable to the administration. Hanna openly backed Secretary of the Navy John D. Long, of Massachusetts.

Despite Roosevelt's statement, Platt arrived in Philadelphia beating the tom-toms for the New York Governor. When Quay protested that "A man as combative and impulsive as Roosevelt is the worst type of Vice-President," Platt replied that the best long-range thing which could happen to the Republican Party would be to elect Roosevelt Vice-President and depend upon him to do the things which would come naturally to him to wreck himself. Then the party would have a troublesome man out of its way for future Presidential nominations. Moreover, Platt undoubtedly wanted Roosevelt out of the state house in Albany.

There was another impelling reason for Quay to go along with Platt. The old boss was waiting for a chance to give Hanna his come-uppance. Only six weeks before, Hanna, temporarily bed-ridden with rheumatism, had refused to release Chauncey Depew from their pair so that Depew might vote for the seating of Quay as United States Senator from Pennsylvania. Thus Hanna was decisive in the unseating of Quay by a one-vote margin.

When Dawes arrived on Sunday, he found Roosevelt very much in the race, despite his disavowal. He wrote in his diary: "The sentiment here is clearly for Roosevelt for Vice-President." On Sunday Quay announced that 58 of Pennsylvania's 64 delegates would be for Roosevelt. "And," he added, "we will cut the comb of Mark Hanna."

When an upsurge for Roosevelt came from the Western delegations, McKinley had other worries than his Vice-Presidential candidate. The gravest crisis in the Boxer uprising had come. All that Sunday he was in constant communication with General Arthur MacArthur, at Manila, to ascertain what troops the Philippine commander could spare from the pacification of the archipelago for duty in China. When MacArthur told him he could send his favorite regiment, the seasoned Ninth, McKinley went to bed.

That Sunday night, too, Roosevelt was wavering. He told a caller: "A man cannot be too big for his party. If a call comes, he must accept."

Dawes believed the situation had reached the point where only one man could issue a fiat and bring about his choice for Vice-President. That man was McKinley; and the President, having kept his hands off until now, could not jump into the fight.

Still, Hanna had not given up. He believed he could stem the Roosevelt tide. He announced, at a news conference, that Long would be nominated. Then came the famous Monday break in the situation long unrecorded.

"At about noon, I was in Hanna's room with H. C. Payne, of Wisconsin; Senator J. C. Burrows, of Michigan; and others," Dawes noted. "Much enraged at the fact that Quay had started a stampede for Roosevelt, Hanna seemed about to line up the administration forces for Long.

"He said that, if Roosevelt were nominated 'by Quay and Platt,' he would refuse to be chairman of the National Committee. Hanna and I had almost an altercation, since I insisted, with all my power, that any interference on his part, for Long or anybody, would start a stampede in the West for Roosevelt; and thus, he (Hanna) would be playing into Quay's hands; that it was simply a trick of Quay's to take advantage of the Roosevelt sentiment, and make it appear that he was a factor in it.

"Hanna was in such a state of mind that I arranged to have Cortelyou at one telephone and the President at another (at the White House), so that I could talk with Cortelyou and have the President hear what I said. I outlined the situation to them, and received an ultimatum from the President for Hanna which, at his dictation, I copied and took to Hanna. It read as follows:

"'The President's close friend must not undertake to commit the administration to any candidate. It has no candidate. The convention must make the nomination. The administration would not if it could. The President's close friend should be satisfied with his unanimous nomination, and not interfere with the Vice-Presidential nomination. The administration wants the choice of the convention, and the President's friend must not dictate to the convention.'

"After the session of the convention, I took this to Hanna. He had already called a conference at Bliss' rooms at the Stratford at 10:30 P.M. to decide whether to make an effort to unite the convention on some other candidate than Roosevelt for Vice-President. Hanna said, however, he would follow the President's instructions.

"I was greatly relieved at the outcome, as nothing could have stopped the Roosevelt movement, and the only result of Hanna's interference would have been his humiliation, and embarrassment to the President."

Ten days later:

"*June 30:* I discussed politics with Roosevelt. He evidently knew much of what took place regarding his candidacy between the President, Hanna, and myself, and was very much interested to know something more."

The Republican campaign, under the slogan "The full dinner pail," was fought against the background of a Chinese uprising and a widespread coal strike at home, which found Hanna, the former coal operator, on the side of the miners against the mine owners.

On November 6, the McKinley-Roosevelt ticket defeated Bryan who, this time, had sixty-five year old ex-Vice-President Adlai E. Stevenson as his running mate.

The Dawes and McKinleys celebrated their twelfth and thirtieth wedding anniversaries a day apart, the Dawes January 24 and the McKinleys the twenty-fifth. Dawes wrote on January 24, 1901:

"Our twelfth wedding anniversary. The children presented us with original drawings representing two punctured hearts, and surrounded with forget-me-nots. Had lunch at the White House with President and Mrs. McKinley. . . . I took my dear wife a bunch of violets, and spent one of the happy evenings of a very happy married life. We also received some beautiful flowers from the White House."

For Dawes, there was a particular additional reason for his wedding-anniversary happiness:

"I gave Will Dawes $3,300 to retire the last of the preferred stock of the Dawes Business Block Company at par and accrued dividends at 8 per cent. That makes $47,300 which I have retired at the same terms. He then brought me a deed transferring all the property of the company to me as an individual. . . . The company was a heavy load to me during the panic. I allowed no friend who had invested on my judgment to lose a cent of principal or interest on it.

"Only one man, an old German in Marietta, objected to turning his stock over. He replied:

"'I think I will keep mine. Anything which is good enough for Charley Dawes is good enough for me.' He was a very surprised man when he found I had been taking the money out of my pocket to pay the dividends.

"When I married, I was twenty-three years old. I barely had money enough to pay my railroad fare from Lincoln to Cincinnati for the wedding. At the time the panic struck, I was twenty-eight. A community in Ohio had backed my judgment, and I owed $200,000."

Other members of the family were doing well, too:

"Received annual reports of Evanston and Ottumwa gas companies, demonstrating the ability as manager and financier of my beloved brother, Rufus. He is a great man in every respect, and only his modesty holds him back.

"Bemen's business ability is winning him prestige and fortune. He has come into control of the Little Rock (Arkansas) gas plant, and is president of the company, having about one third himself. His success at Lansing and Little Rock has been over great obstacles placed in his path.

"Henry is, as Tom Ochiltree said, 'not only my brother but my personal friend.' I am sensible of the good fortune of having such brothers and sisters as mine; for they are not only successful, but good and unspoiled by success."

He was backing his friend Walter Wellman on his polar expedition. He also had been one of the originators of the idea to build the Lafayette Monument in Paris, and it had been successful:

"We held a meeting of the Lafayette Memorial Commission in my office. Archbishop Ireland, Reverend Edward Everett Hale, Robert J. Thompson, and myself were present. . . . When the bills for the Lafayette monument in Paris are paid, we will have quite a surplus left. I suggested that each member of the Commission be communicated with, seeking his opinion upon the advisability of asking Congress the authority for devoting the surplus of the funds voted us for duplication of the monument in the United States."

Dawes noted that George W. Perkins had come and spent the

night at his house to discuss "J. Pierpont Morgan's offer of a full partnership. He is guaranteed $300,000-per-year profit. Morgan wants a man in his firm who can maintain its prestige after he is gone. Perkins will accept. He has high ideals and believes that the solution of industrial problems must be approached, first, by the distribution of stock holdings of industrials among the people, then by honest management without inside rings."

Dawes had thoroughly reorganized the Comptroller's office, and was ready to retire and make his long-contemplated race for the Senate in Illinois.

"*June 23:* I decided, this day, to resign my office as Comptroller of the Currency, in view of the fact that I am a candidate for the United States Senate in Illinois. My term does not expire until January 1, 1903, but I cannot be a candidate and perform properly, next year, the duties of my responsible office. In doing this without solicitation or suggestion, I am influenced by the plain properties of the situation; but it is also wise, in politics, to have courage to burn bridges behind you when their existence may give aid to the enemy.

"The President would be glad to appoint me at the end of my term, without doubt; and, in seeking the Senate, I am giving up a congenial and responsible place. But if a man clings to the pleasant things, he will miss the higher ones. He may miss the higher things anyway, but it should not be for lack of courage to attempt them."

"*June 24:* I went over to the White House and told the President what I had decided to do. He was much surprised with the conclusions at which I had arrived. He asked me several times if I had fully considered it, and requested that the matter remain between us two until the proper time for announcement. Later in the afternoon I went driving with the President. He asked me if I had fully determined upon the step, and spoke of how his wife and he would miss Caro and myself.

"*June 25:* I was with the President again. He asked me if I had not reconsidered which, of course, I had not. We discussed briefly the matter of my successor. On reaching home, I read in the *Century Magazine* for this month the article by Woodrow Wilson, 'When a Man Comes to Himself.' When my children reach middle life, if God spares them—and it is for my children that I am writing these journals—I want them to read this article, which I have pinned between these leaves.

"I have never read these journals of mine through since starting them; but I remember some of my plans for reforming things wrong in society, when I was younger, and that I used to write of them in my journal. I do not think I am any more tolerant now of governmental and industrial wrongs than I was then. But, as Mr. Wilson says, 'It is the discovery of what they cannot do and ought to do which transforms reformers into statesmen.'

"The practicability of every reform is determined solely and absolutely and always by 'the circumstances in the case,' and only those who put themselves into the midst of affairs, either by action or observation, can know what these circumstances are, or perceive what they signify. I am far from being transformed into a man who more clearly perceives the limitations of usefulness of those who constantly preach radical doctrines. As someone said to me once (I think my brother Rufe, perhaps), 'Think radically, but speak conservatively, if you want to command influence.'"

And finally:

"I saw the President and formally tendered my resignation as Comptroller, to take effect October 1, for the reason that I will be a candidate for the United States Senate from Illinois. Suggested Cortelyou as my successor. The President immediately called Cortelyou in and left the decision with him. While the appointment would mean a loss to the President of the most efficient secretary a public man ever had, it seems plainly an opportunity for Cortelyou, and I think he so regards it."

There had been another development of which only a handful of people knew at the time. On August 2, 1900, in the midst of the Presidential campaign, Hanna had written to Dawes:

"I enclose a statement from one of my Secret Service agents which, I think, is reliable as to the fact and intent; and, while I cannot see the sense of their having any reason to attack the President of the United States, I cannot but feel it is my duty to suggest caution. It is unfortunate that this should have come at a time when the public's mind is excited over the coming election, and the class issue is again being revived. There are many diseased minds in the country. Therefore I wish you would show this to the President."

The enclosed memorandum, gaining significance from the fact that King Humbert I of Italy had fallen at the hands of an assassin only four days earlier, read:

"The purpose of the following information is that proper safeguards be thrown about the person of the President, and the information following may be corroborated by reference to the Intelligence Bureau of the Government.

"About two years ago, an Italian-American resident of New York City, named E. Moretti, furnished to the Government information relative to a Grotto of Socialists located in Paterson, New Jersey; and, on the strength of that information, Moretti was employed by the Government for a short time and, during the time of his employment, furnished the following particulars to the officer employing him:

"The Anarchists or Socialists, through their various organizations, resolved to rid the earth of a number of its rulers, and the following selections were made: first, the Empress Eugenie of Austria was to be dispatched; then the King of Italy; then the Czar of Russia; then the Prince of Wales or his mother, the Queen; then the President of the United States; and, lastly, the Emperor of Germany. As the first two calls made by this information have come to pass as predicted, this informant, impressed with the possibilities of the situation, asks that the information furnished by him to the Government two years ago be gone over, with a view of corroborating it.

"It may well be that the man, Breschi, who killed the King of Italy, was the second man selected to do the work, the first one selected being killed by his fellow members because of his failure to do the work which had fallen to him by the rules of the Grotto. Then another drawing was had; and, the slip falling to Breschi, he kept his oath. Appreciating that the President and his best friends do not feel apprehensive for his safety, the party responsible for this statement of facts, prompted only by what he *knows* to be *true*, as far as the informant's part is concerned, believes that proper and prompt steps should be taken to protect the person of the President; and, for that purpose, suggests that his secretary, Mr. Cortelyou, be communicated with and requested to triple the guard now surrounding the President. There is but one man now doing the duty."

Dawes' own notes continue the story:

"Though not unusually disturbed by the many vague warnings of this nature so often received, this was surrounded by so many evidences of reliability, as compared with others, that I was much worried, and saw the President and showed him the papers and insisted with all my power on less indifference on his part to his personal safety. Saw Cortelyou about it, and he saw Chief Wilkie, of the Secret Service, in connection with the matter. The guard was increased. The detective claims that the plot includes the assassination of all the leading rulers of the world, and originates at Paterson, New Jersey, where Breschi, the assassin of Humbert, came from."

On April 27 Dawes spent an hour, late at night, with President McKinley, and bade him farewell as the President prepared to leave for a six-week Western trip. McKinley talked over his plans for the summer.

The journey would accomplish three purposes. The President was anxious to make another solidifying trip into parts of the South he had been unable to visit. He had fostered good will between the sections with his earlier trip to Nashville, his speech before the Georgia legislature, and his trip through the Shenandoah Valley. He had put a Southern man, Mobile-born and Nashville-reared Ethan A. Hitchcock, in his Cabinet; and two of the first four generals he appointed in the Spanish War were Fitzhugh Lee and Joseph E. Wheeler, former Confederate Army officers.

Three of the fighting naval war machines he had asked for (the Battleships *Maine, Missouri,* and *Ohio*) were ready for launching. His presence on one of these occasions would give him an opportunity to emphasize the necessity of an adequate two-ocean navy, now that the United States had become a world power. He chose the ceremonies in connection with putting the *Ohio* down the ways at San Francisco.

At the end of the trip he would open the Exposition at Buffalo, then go with Mrs. McKinley to Canton for the summer in their remodeled home. As it turned out, only the southern part of the trip passed off without mishap.

In Alabama, Tennessee, and Mississippi great throngs, among them thousands of Confederate veterans, turned out to honor the President, one of whose close friends was General John B. Gordon, then the commander of the United Confederate Veterans. At New Orleans, which had never been visited by a President of the United States before, eight spirited white horses, with yellow-satin harness, drew the President's carriage in a parade before hundreds of thousands of people.

In gaily-decorated Houston the parade route of the President was strewn with roses; and aged Mrs. Anson Jones, widow of the last President of the Republic of Texas, came to greet the first President of the United States she had seen since James K. Polk.

This triumphant trip continued through Texas, New Mexico, and into California. Then occurred something which caused McKinley to postpone his Buffalo trip from July to the ill-fated September date.

"Mrs. McKinley is seriously ill at San Francisco," Dawes noted on May 14. "All are much worried she may not recover. I wired President McKinley."

Mrs. McKinley rallied sufficiently for the President to participate in the launching of the *Ohio*. He then canceled all further engagements and, ten days later, started the hurried trip back to Washington with her.

As the President reached Colorado on his journey to Washington with the stricken Mrs. McKinley, the Supreme Court handed down its decisions in the first of the consolidated Puerto Rican cases. In perhaps the most involved reasoning by the Court, with the exception of the gold decision rendered by a successor bench thirty-four years later, the Court, in two opinions, decided, in effect:

"The Constitution follows the flag, but not to the extent that tariff laws in the territories must be uniform with those of the United States.

"Puerto Rico and the Philippines became integral parts of the United States upon ratification of the Treaty of Paris, but Congress has power to govern them according to their needs, without reference to the excise limitations of the Constitution."

While the decision generally sustained the insular policy of the administration, both decisions were by 5-to-4 decisions; and one Justice, swinging from one line-up to another, wrote both majority opinions.

The Court's strangely arrived at consensus brought forth Peter Finley Dunne's famous quotation of Mr. Dooley:

"No matter whither th' Constitution follows th' flag or not, th' Supreme Coort follows th' illiction returns."

On July 10, McKinley sent for Dawes and discussed with him a personal matter:

"We walked for an hour in the White House lot, and the President discussed the third-term interviews given out by Depew and Grosvenor, which he regards as unkind and uncalled for, though possibly well meant. He spoke of the best method of stopping it, and of his thought of making a public statement that he would not accept a third term if tendered. In the evening he had a Cabinet meeting to consider the form of his statement. Mrs. McKinley is improving, and the President was feeling very well."

On the following day Dawes wrote:

"The President read me his statement which he gave to the press, finally disposing of the third-term talk. The President's announcement is only what the people of the country who have come to know his high purpose expected. To his friends, his view upon the third-term question has always been freely expressed. It is not generally known, but nothing but a sense of duty led the President to consent to his second nomination. Personally, he felt he had little to gain and much to lose by a second term. The President is a domestic man; and, in the midst of the anxieties and perplexities of his high office, his mind has constantly turned to his Canton home, a return to which both he and his wife look forward with great anticipation."

McKinley's rejection of a third term was the most pointed and specific ever made by any President. He said:

"I regret that the suggestion of a third term has been made. I doubt whether I am called upon to give to it notice; but there are now questions of the gravest importance before the administration and the country, and their just consideration should not be prejudiced in the public mind by even the suspicion of a thought of a third term. In view, therefore, of the reiteration of the suggestion of it, I will now say, once and for all, expressing a long-settled conviction, that I not only am not, and will not be, a candidate for a third term, but I would not accept a nomination if it were tendered me."

Vice-President Roosevelt lost little time getting into the Presidential race. On the day following McKinley's announcement, Roosevelt wrote to Dawes, asking for a meeting as soon as possible. In mid-July, Dawes, in New York en route home from Boston to Washington, noted his first visit to the home of Theodore Roosevelt:

"*At the Waldorf Hotel in New York:* In response to a repeated invitation from Vice-President Roosevelt, took the train to Oyster Bay and spent the night at his house. I had a long talk over the political situation and in connection with his prospects for the Republican Presidential nomination in 1904.

"Roosevelt fears that Governor Odell, through the machine, will control the New York delegation against him. I told him I thought this would greatly strengthen him if it happened, just as Cleveland was strengthened by the successful local opposition of Tammany. I told him that, in my judgment, Illinois would be for him. Professor Nicholas Murray Butler was also a guest at the house. Met Mrs. Roosevelt and the children.

"Roosevelt and I spent two hours in conference, and I told him I was for him, and should be unless the sentiment of our people should change against him, which I did not anticipate. I explained that we were fighting in Illinois to make our organization responsive to public sentiment, which therefore would make us his natural allies in the coming contest.

"When I arose in the morning, there had been placed in my room an unattached tin tub filled with the coldest-looking water I ever saw. Beside the tub was a huge bathing sponge. I decided I would forego a bath until I got back to New York. Took breakfast with the Roosevelts, and a walk with the Vice-President, and left for New York.

"Back in Washington, worked on recommendations as to laws to be passed in the Philippines regulating banking, and sent them to Governor General William Howard Taft."

On August 11, Dawes received a telegram from Cortelyou at

Canton, saying that President and Mrs. McKinley wished Mr. and Mrs. Dawes to come to Canton for a visit. Later, Cortelyou telephoned, asking that they bring Mrs. Rixey, wife of the President's physician, along with them.

"Cortelyou met us at the train with the President's carriage," Dawes wrote in his journal of August 12, 1901. "We had a jolly evening, with Cortelyou playing the Cecelian, a kind of piano. The President was in his best mood. Mrs. McKinley is very much improved in health. The President has greatly enhanced the appearance of the house; and both he and his wife are planning a quiet and pleasant summer. The callers are many, but not so pestiferous as when they came bent on getting office."

At the end of three days Dawes, accompanied by Cortelyou, left for a visit to his old home in Marietta. Mrs. Dawes went to Chicago to find a house where they could move in October. When Dawes went to tell him good-by, McKinley said:

"I am going to sit down and write my Buffalo speech. I think it will be the most important one of my life."

Back in Washington, Dawes found this letter from Vice-President Roosevelt, dated August 20:

"Would there be any chance of Mrs. Dawes and yourself coming here (Sagamore Hill) for a night with us in September? Almost any date after the 8th would suit us. I want to tell you in full about the Colorado, Missouri, and Kansas situations and, also, to get some advice on Illinois again."

Another letter from Roosevelt, dated August 28, read:

"I had rather a succession of mild calamities in my family, which resulted in two of my children going to the hospital, and Mrs. Roosevelt is going to take them to the Adirondacks soon. I shall want to see you after my return from the Adirondacks. Perkins will be back by that time. Cannot I arrange to see both of you together? I had a letter from Cullom I want to tell you of."

Dawes had not replied to Roosevelt's letters when an unexpected tragedy made it unnecessary to do so.

The speech which William McKinley delivered on the Esplanade at the Pan American Exposition at Buffalo on September 5, 1901, was addressed to an audience all over the world.

"We must encourage a Merchant Marine built, owned, and

manned by Americans," he said. "We must build the Isthmian Canal. The construction of a Pacific cable can no longer be delayed. After all, how near, one to the other, is every part of the world. God and man have linked the nations together. No man can long be indifferent to another.

"The period of exclusiveness is past. The expansion of our trade and commerce is a pressing problem. A policy of good will and friendly trade relations will prevent reprisals. Reciprocity treaties are in harmony with the spirit of the times; measures of retaliation are not.

"Let us ever remember that our interest is in concord, not conflict, and that our real eminence rests in the victories of peace, not war."

McKinley's speech excited keen interest around the world. "It is the utterance of a man," said the London *Standard,* "who feels he is at the head of a great nation with vast ambition and a newborn consciousness of strength. Her national life is no longer self-contained or introspective."

At four o'clock on Friday afternoon, McKinley, accompanied by John G. Milburn, President of the Exposition; his secretary, Cortelyou; and two Secret Service men, arrived at the domed Temple of Music for the public reception. He was greeted by thunderous cheers and applause. There is no doubt that McKinley was beloved by his fellow countrymen as few Presidents have been. Visitors stood in line to shake the President's hand.

While the great pipe organ was playing Bach's *Sonata in F,* the President reached out to grasp the left hand of Leon Czolgosz, whose right hand was bandaged. As he shook it, the anarchist Czolgosz fired two bullets from a .32-caliber revolver which he held concealed inside the bandage. The President fell back into the arms of Cortelyou. The muffled sound of the shots was drowned in the organ music. Few people had noticed what had happened.

"I was sitting, about 5:30 P.M., at my desk in the Treasury Building," Dawes recorded in his journal, "when Sam Small, Jr., a newspaper correspondent, hurried in with the news that the President had been shot. I immediately made arrangements to leave for Buffalo. Upon arrival there, I went to the house of Mr. Milburn, where the President was lying.

"Cortelyou told me of the condition of the President. I then saw the President's sisters, Mrs. Duncan and Miss Helen McKinley; and Mary Barber, who was trying to comfort Mrs. McKinley. I did not see Mrs. McKinley. Miss Duncan and Senator Hanna came in.

"Cortelyou described the wonderful calmness and courage of the President after he was shot. His first words were of his wife, then of mercy for the miserable wretch who had shot him and who would have been killed by the crowd, had not the President saved him. The President had said, 'Let no one hurt him.'"

Three days later, when doctors had pronounced President McKinley out of danger, Dawes told of his conference with Vice-President Theodore Roosevelt on the 1904 Republican Presidential nomination.

"Roosevelt met me at the Milburn house and asked me to lunch with him at the house of Mr. Wilcox, where he is staying. He said he wanted to talk to me privately, and would ask Mrs. Wilcox to arrange it so that we would not be interrupted. Colonel W. C. Brown took Mrs. Abner McKinley, Mary Barber, and me driving; and, afterward, I went to lunch with the Vice-President. He drew me aside to discuss 1904 Presidential politics for an hour. I told him his prospects seemed good in Illinois. Roosevelt thinks Cullom has the Presidential germ, though the latter has written him a friendly but rather evasive letter.

"After lunch I went back to the Milburn house, and Mrs. McKinley sent for me to come upstairs, where she was sitting with Mary Barber and the nurse. She broke into tears when I came in, but soon recovered herself, and I talked with her for some time. She says, 'The Lord is with us,' and her husband will recover. She sent her love to Caro and the children, for I told her, now that the President is out of danger, I was going to Washington. Said good-by to Abner and Cortelyou, and all. The President tells Cortelyou he is getting rather lonesome. Even Abner has not seen him yet; nor have any of the family, except Mrs. McKinley, only the doctors and nurses, and occasionally Cortelyou. The President, however, is cheerful, as he has been ever since he recovered from the operation."

Dawes returned to Washington; Roosevelt went to the Adirondacks; and members of the Cabinet left Buffalo. Then came the relapse. Of the death of the President, Dawes wrote:

"*September 13, and Saturday morning:*   At four o'clock in the morning (September 13), Caro and I were awakened by the continued ringing of the telephone bell; and Captain B. F. Montgomery, of the White House, notified me of the sinking spell of the President. I hurried to the White House, where Montgomery was in communication with Cortelyou by wire. At 5:30, Secretary Gage came, and we awaited the sad news of increasing danger. At 7:50 A.M. I left for Buffalo, reaching there at about 8 P.M., and drove immediately to the Milburn house. Latta, of the White House staff, met me at the sidewalk. He was in tears, and said to hurry or I would be too late. I went hurriedly upstairs and was taken to the room of my dying friend, the great President of the United States. He was surrounded by the family group. Mrs. McKinley was sitting by his side, with her face near his. He had one arm around her and was smiling at her. He had ceased speaking some time before this, but he seemed conscious, and he looked at me in the kindly way which was so natural to him. Some little time before this, he had repeated a portion of the hymn, 'Nearer, My God, to Thee, e'en though it be a cross that raiseth me.' He had bade those present 'farewell,' saying, 'It is God's way; His will, not ours, be done.'

"Silently, we stood by his bedside. Abner took my hand in his. His sister, his nephew and nieces, and others were there. Cortelyou stood at the foot of the bed. Mrs. McKinley made no outcry; her grief was past words. Finally she was led away, to see him no more alive. Before she went to rest, she was told the President would not awaken in this world.

"Through the long, weary night, we waited. The Cabinet was on the lower floor; but, from time to time, they and others of the family and near friends would pass in and out of the room, the door of which stood open. As I watched him in the earlier evening, the President did not seem like a dying man to me. He moved his limbs freely, and did not seem to breathe with difficulty. He seemed to want to hold Dr. Rixey's hand, and would reach out to him like a child in the dark. Once he said, 'Oh, dear,' as if in distress. Finally, at 2:15 A.M., the end came. The President lay with head near the side of his bed. The faithful Dr. Rixey, who had been by him through long hours, sat by him then. Around him were the President's sisters: Mrs. Duncan and Miss Helen McKinley; near the head of the bed, Sallie Duncan, and Mary Barber, Jim McKinley, and William Duncan; Mrs. Abner McKinley, Mr. Osborne, and John Barber were present. Besides those of the family were Cortelyou, Webb Hayes, Colonel W. C. Brown, and myself; the nurses, Miss McKenzie and Miss Hunt; and some other attendants.

"The President was breathing mechanically and audibly. Finally, he ceased to breathe, and it seemed he was gone. Then he drew another breath, after a time. Then all was still. Dr. Rixey placed the stethoscope on the President's chest and, in a little time, said simply, 'The President is dead.' The great life was ended.

"The little group around him passed out of the room. It was thus that I looked upon him last. He had died as he had lived, in fear of his God and in his faith in His mercy and goodness. As I left the stricken household and walked out into the darkness, my thoughts were of my own dead father, and of this friend who had now gone forever, and who had been as father was to me; then of the wife who lived only for the President and who, in her suffering and lifelong illness, clung to his strong nature as a vine clings to the oak."

On the morning of September 14, 1901, Vice-President Theodore Roosevelt left his camp in the Adirondacks and, in a swinging, bouncing buckboard, was driven down the mountain passes to a train waiting to take him to Buffalo. Of that day Dawes wrote:

"Went with Senator Fairbanks to the Milburn house at eleven o'clock. I was present at a meeting of the Cabinet with Senator Hanna, Judge Day, Senator Fairbanks, Myron Herrick, and Abner McKinley. Arrangements for the funeral were decided upon.

"I tried to be helpful during the day, and made up a list of people for the funeral train, and was also with President Roosevelt, taking him the text of a proclamation which John Hay had wired, setting aside Thursday as a day of mourning in the country. Roosevelt, however, did not follow Hay's form, but prepared one himself, which he read to me. This Cortelyou sent out. All the old family and political friends whose faces had grown so familiar during the past six years were present at the Milburn house at different times during the day."

Subsequent entries in Dawes' diary tell of the first funeral services in Buffalo, of the immense crowd which passed the President's bier in Buffalo City Hall, and of the trip of the funeral train to Washington.

"At every town, the whole population seemed gathered along the tracks," he wrote. "People were often in tears. At almost every place the school children were standing in line. The Grand Army posts were there with their flags draped in black. Long lines of laboring men, civic and military organizations, stood in silent order. At many points, the people sang 'Nearer My God, to Thee,' as the train passed slowly along. The singing, the tolling of the bells, the sad and silent gatherings made the deepest impression of all.

"Poor Mrs. McKinley was so bowed in grief that she could not bear to look out of her car window. At Harrisburg a tremendous crowd gathered, and so at Baltimore. An immense concourse of people had assembled at Washington. With Captain and Mrs. McWilliams, I was driven to the White House, where we entered a rear door. There I met Caro. In a short time the body of the President was brought in and taken to the East Room. Caro and I had been at the White House when the President and Mrs. McKinley left for Canton. How little did we expect such a home coming. Mrs. McKinley went into the East Room for a short time after reaching the White House, and remained there for a time alone."

In the remainder of his entries, Dawes told of the funeral services in the great rotunda of the Capitol, attended by President Roosevelt and ex-President Grover Cleveland, of the lying in state in Canton City Hall, and the final services.

"For the last time there was gathered in Canton the old McKinley following, and familiar faces were everywhere. Yet how different than ever before was the spirit in which we gathered together. The Chief was gone."

Chapter Eight

❁

CHICAGO BANKER

*W*hen Dawes' resignation from the office of Comptroller of the Currency became effective, he returned to Chicago to carry on his fight in the 1902 Illinois Senatorial campaign.

In 1900, Senator Shelby M. Cullom, discouraged at his chances for re-election, had offered to withdraw in favor of Dawes. Governor Richard Yates, who had been the beneficiary of Dawes' second history-making assault on the Illinois machine, had also tendered his support.

"With the rejection of Yates' proffer of support it would seem that altogether, including my refusal of support from Cullom himself, Fred Busse, Dan Campbell, and Charles B. Rannels, I have come near to a declination of the Senatorship itself," Dawes wrote. "Yet under the circumstances no other course was consistent with self-respect."

Dawes' defeat of the Illinois machine in the 1900 state convention had been spectacular.

He had gone to Peoria to attend what he regarded as a routine state convention. When he arrived he found Governor Tanner and Congressman Lorimer in control. Cullom and the antimachine element admitted defeat. He proposed:

"If you, Senator Cullom, and your friends will do just as I say and fight to the finish absolutely without compromise, I will stake everything on the result and lead the fight. You will either whip the machine now or it will win and hereafter be invincible."

At the end of a turbulent, nose-bloodying two days Dawes had administered a resounding defeat to Tanner and Lorimer, routed the machine candidate for governor, brought about the compromise nomination of Yates for that office, and assured Cullom's re-election.

Back home on the eve of the 1902 Senatorial race, Dawes had little taste for politics. His business interests in Chicago and elsewhere were making ever greater claims on him. Word from Washington did nothing to augment his desire to return there. Most of the old McKinley inner circle cared little for Theodore Roosevelt. There came letters such as this from Secretary of the Treasury Gage:

"The death of McKinley and the occupancy of the White House by a man of acknowledged ability but of a temperamental quality so different, your departure from the government scene, and the changes which if not actualized yet are within the range of possibility, give those of us here a feeling of depression and chronic sadness."

Tanner's rout in the 1900 state convention had eliminated him from politics. But Dawes would still have to contend with Lorimer. And when now in 1902 he learned that Yates, whom he himself had been principally responsible for putting into office, had joined forces with Lorimer, he could be certain that the battle for the Senatorial seat would not be an easy one. "The fight will be clean-cut," he noted, "and either Lorimer or I must be counted out when it is over."

English-born Lorimer had a paramount personal stake in the defeat of Dawes. He coveted the highest American elective office to which he was eligible, that of United States Senator. But in 1902 he did not believe he had the strength necessary to win it. If he was to secure the office in 1908, he would have now to put in a man weak enough to be pushed out six years later. Dawes was not such a man. Eventually Lorimer chose Albert J. Hopkins, a long-time Illinois Congressman. With Dawes and the sitting senator, William E. Mason, it would be a three-man race.

Dawes' principal ally against the machine was Lawrence Y. Sherman, a downstate lawyer and speaker of the Illinois House of Representatives. In February, 1902, Dawes packed a suitcase and embarked on what to him was very distasteful personal campaigning. He took along the book of a Roman historian.

"I got up early as usual, washed in ice water as usual and wiped my freezing face with a towel the size of a hand," he wrote during the first week of the tour. "I then made ready for the daily dive into the pettiness and littleness of a machine-bound Southern Illinois county. At Harrisburg I was met by a large committee and was agreeably surprised to find a lot of high-grade men in politics there. Perhaps my more favorable impression of them was influenced by their kindness to me. I am reading Tacitus in my spare time as I campaign."

Except for such aid as he received from Sherman, Dawes waged a lone fight against a machine which financed itself by a "shake-down" assessment of Republican officeholders. "It may be that I will go down in ruins; but I have at least helped the cause of clean politics in Illinois as much as any other man; for the result will be the adoption of new and honorable methods in party management in the State hereafter."

But things were not what they had been. In the public mind, Dawes had become identified as a man close to President McKinley. "I got an inkling of things to come when my personal mail began to drop off after the death of President McKinley," Dawes recalled. "It was at that time well known that I would be a candidate for the Senate."

In March Dawes noted: "Roosevelt has created the impression that he is against me in this fight. This, I think, he has done unwittingly, for I believe he intends to be impartial." In that same March it became increasingly clear that the strength of Lorimer's candidate Hopkins was growing, while that of Dawes and the incumbent, Senator Mason, was declining correspondingly.

How the likelihood of defeat affected Dawes' frame of mind can be seen in a diary entry of March 10: "Took train for Bloomington. Senator Mason and Congressman Hopkins were on the train. We talked over the campaign. Had hard work in suppressing my sense of the humorous. Some time ago Mason was hilarious and Hopkins gloomy—now Hopkins wears a broad smile, but Mason has stopped brushing his hair and looks like a moulting chicken. Am endeavoring on my own part to maintain equilibrium."

And three days later:

"*March 13:*   The gains made by our political opponents in certain sections have created an impression that we are defeated. Accordingly, we are temporarily deserted if prospects improve, permanently if they do not. Such is politics. I am making arrangements, therefore, to light on my feet in business if the political tiger throws me."

Thus, when the battle had finally been lost, Dawes could write with equanimity:

"I write this on May 11. It is a record of my political defeat. . . .

"Having anticipated the outcome for a long time, my feeling was only one of relief. I turn again to active business life, grateful for the fortune which took me into politics and now takes me out. When I decided to become a candidate for United States Senator, I supposed I would have the friendship of the state administration and of the national administration under McKinley. I had the promise of the support of the Sherman-Busse element of the party also. The assassin's bullet took away my best friend, President McKinley, and from that time my interest as well as my strength in politics declined. President Roosevelt, while endeavoring to be impartial, created the opposite impression, and greatly injured me.

"While I have lost, yet my original plan was well conceived, and as go human projects, was wise. But none of us knows what is to come to us. All we can do is to do our best, and with gratitude to Providence accept that which happens to be wisest for us. All that has heretofore happened to me has been for the best—and I know that my defeat must now turn out for the best. I turn to business with the keen joy of a man entering from a political atmosphere to one where promises are redeemed and faith is kept."

Thus, Dawes left politics. But he had vowed to destroy the Illinois machine, and continued to give his support to Lawrence Y. Sherman. How much Sherman needed Dawes' support can be gathered from an entry in Dawes' diary at the end of that year:

"Against Sherman is being used all the state and national and county patronage possible," Dawes wrote. "The odds are against him. We are confronted in Illinois by a machine of the strength of Tammany. They give no quarter. They hesitate at nothing. To our knowledge they offer cash for legislative votes. They have unlimited resources at present on the surface; but they are rotten inside."

And after a few days, when Lorimer's forces had won out once more, Dawes added:

"Sherman met with defeat but it was a defeat which has strengthened him in the hearts of the people. To the public official public respect is the only enduring reward. This, defeat cannot take from some, nor victory give to others. I take off my hat to this faithful and courageous man."

As Dawes' political prospects darkened, his business outlook brightened. During the winter and spring he had declined the presidency of a newly founded bank in St. Louis, and had consolidated his holdings in numerous gas companies. The latter transaction had been profitable—and, as always, not only to Dawes himself, but also to his friend Banker John R. Walsh and his brothers Rufus and Beman Dawes. In April of 1902 he noted in his diary: "I am now worth, in my judgment, something over $400,000, above all my liabilities."

For a man who was then barely thirty-six years old, and who less than ten years before had owed $200,000, yet had paid off all his creditors in spite of the nationwide panic, this was a satisfactory performance. It is not surprising, then, that the officers of the International Bank, which was being organized in New York with a capital of six million dollars, invited Dawes to accept the presidency and name his own salary.

Months earlier, Charles M. Schwab, president of the United States Steel Corporation, I. N. Perry, a capitalist, George W. Perkins, and Frank O. Lowden and others had urged him to head a new bank and trust company in Chicago. Dawes got off the train from what was to prove his fortunate defeat in the Springfield Senatorial nominating convention, went to Lowden's office, and had Lowden draw up organization papers for a $5,000,000 trust company to be called the Central Trust Company of Illinois. Subscriptions to the stock of this company quickly exceeded the proposed capital. On July 8, 1902, the new bank opened its doors with first-day deposits of more than four million dollars. Planned from the beginning to be a "big bank for small people," it and its successors were to be known for more than a half century as the "Dawes Bank."

"My blood no longer thrills to the call of political trumpets as in the olden days. I have learned the happiness of peaceful business life. The great bank which, with others, I have founded is steadily growing in strength and prestige. Under my feet I feel the rock of established business position and no longer the shifting, treacherous sands of politics."

For the next decade, Dawes was to find nearly unbroken happiness in this life which he called peaceful, but which most other men would have considered uncommonly active. His efforts to put the national currency on a basis which would allow it to weather a possible panic—efforts he had been carrying on since 1898—continued. Within the span of a few months, he found time to address the bankers' associations in eight states, although he had to decline invitations from five more states. In the autumn of 1903, he felt that he had made his first dent.

"The American Bankers Association has pronounced in favor of a heavily taxed emergency currency. Thus the world 'do move.' "

He took a growing interest in civic affairs, and among other things promoted a proposal which then sounded fantastic but has meantime become a reality: that of his friend D. H. Burnham "to build a park on grounds at present submerged in the lake extending from Jackson Park to Lincoln Park, leaving a canal between the new park and the present shore line to be crossed at intervals by bridges." He was, however, not gullible according to 1903 standards: "I talked to Abner McKinley for a long time about his affairs," another note reads. "He is determined to invest some money in a scheme to make artificial rubber. It is a scheme in which he thoroughly believes, but which seems to me must be a fraud of the first water."

He seems to have been a consultant of many of the leading businessmen in Chicago. Various diary entries told of advising with C. H. Deere, whose company would have been the largest in a proposed amalgamation of the leading plow manufacturers into the proposed National Plow Company. Charles Deering consulted him about the details of a merger with McCormick. The plow negotiations stalled, but the amalgamation of Deering and McCormick companies into the International Harvester Company was completed. There were entries of discussions with Judge E. H. Gary of the United States Steel Corporation and James J. Hill, the railroad builder. The young president of the Central Trust Company was moving into the top financial circles of the nation.

Dawes went to New York to discuss currency reform with J. Pierpont Morgan and found that he and the great financier were on the same side of the issue: "Morgan's face is one of the strongest I have ever seen. His hair is iron-gray, and his big moustache coal black. He looked straight at me with the most piercing eyes I ever saw, except perhaps those of President McKinley. He is a fascinating conversationalist.

"Morgan very calmly told me how he kept John W. Gates from acquiring control of the Louisville & Nashville railroad: 'I did it because Gates was interested in profits and not in the proper operation of the railroad. A man interested only in profits is a dangerous factor anywhere in the railroad world.'"

Dawes scrupulously avoided Washington. Mark Hanna had been victorious in his fight for the Panama Canal. In June, 1903, both Senate and House completed action on it and Roosevelt signed it. Dawes had a part in getting Hanna interested at a time when it appeared that the Nicaraguan route would be chosen. Sir Edwin Dawes, who lived at the Dawes ancestral home, Faversham, in 1901 wrote a letter of introduction to Comptroller Dawes and handed it to his business associate, Captain Phillipe Bunau-Varilla, formerly engineer-in-chief of the unfinished Panama Canal, who was coming to the United States to urge the practicability of that route.

Dawes introduced Bunau-Varilla to President McKinley and to Senator Hanna. Hanna invited the Frenchman to come to see him: "I shall always be glad to talk to you about the greatest question of the day, the Isthmian Canal."

Bunau-Varilla's arguments were convincing and Hanna was soon arguing so strongly for the Panama route that its enemies called it the "Hannama" Canal.

But in his hour of triumph, Hanna was lonely in Washington. Of all the original McKinley crowd only he remained in the national capital. He wrote to Dawes:

"Dear Charlie: I was glad to get your kind letter. It seems like a breath of fresh air to get words like yours from one of the 'old guard.' I want to congratulate you, Charlie, upon your splendid business enterprise which I am sure you will make a great success."

Henry C. Payne of Wisconsin, a confidant of Hanna, visited him in Washington, and the next day Dawes made this diary entry:

"I had lunch with Henry Payne. He predicts trouble between Roosevelt and Hanna."

For a short time yet, Dawes, lover of horses, was to resist the new means of transportation which was catching the fancy of the nation. For his first contacts with it were unfortunate.

"*October 22:* Charles Deering called with his automobile to take me to Evanston. We had a strenuous ride—when the machine would go at all. It broke down at Washington and Monroe streets and there for half an hour we were surrounded by a curious crowd. Finally when we did go the chauffeur seemed crazy to make speed. The experience was calculated to wreck the nervous system. We broke down twice before reaching Evanston. We went to Deering's house but rode home behind horses, declining further association with the automobile."

And: "In Philadelphia Lawrence McCormick took Caro, Knowlton Ames, and me out riding in his automobile. After a number of escapes, more or less narrow, we finally broke down in Fairmont Park and after installing the machine in an adjacent stable we went home in the street cars much to my mental and nervous relief."

It was not until a year later that Dawes would buy his first automobile.

His house, of course, was always open to his friends. There are notes of a dinner he gave to Captain John J. Pershing who had returned to the United States after making a name for himself in the campaign against the Moros. And another entry tells of a visit to William Jennings Bryan at Lincoln: "With M. M. Kirkman and S. H. Burnham I called on William J. Bryan at his country home. Bryan greeted us cordially and took us over his new home. He says the newspapers exaggerate everything he does. He said that the publicized $2,500 mantel cost $150—one-half of that in advertising in the *Commoner*—and the $1,500 team of horses really cost him $600. One of the latter fell down in his stall while we were there and at the call for aid we all adjourned to the stable where the horse was soon righted."

There are also numerous other entries in Dawes' diary, in a very different vein. One of them tells of a short visit to New York City:

"Alexander H. Revell, Max Pam, Gus Hanna, and I had dinner and afterward went to the opera. After that Gus took us to the Beaux Arts, a restaurant of extremely high prices and filled with theatrical people as patrons. A fine quartet sang and the scene was an animated one.

"It was midnight when we started out to drive to the hotel. Noticing one or two tramps sleeping on the seats in the park in the rain, they got on my mind and after going to bed at the Waldorf I decided to get up and look them up. I drove back in a cab and got the park policeman to accompany me. Instead of the three or four whom I had happened to see, I found about thirty in the park, all but one of whom I am happy to say I was able to provide with enough for lodging and breakfast. I went back to bed some time in the early morning. I was much impressed by one poor unfortunate man who was sleeping in the rain upon a park seat and who, when he was awakened with a proffer of help, said that he could not consent to take it and that he would find work the next day. Nor could I—though I begged him to do it—get him to accept help. I 'uncovered,' so to speak, before this noble man and bade him 'Godspeed.' "

As the year 1903 drew to a close, Dawes bade it farewell with the words:

"My life seems smoother than for many years. It is no longer full of distractions or anxieties, but for that matter I have never allowed myself under any circumstances to worry greatly about the matter of business or politics. I have been able to help many by the wayside during the past year, and hope to be able to help many more in the future. In that is one of life's greatest compensations."

The opportunity to help for which he was hoping was not far off.

In April, 1903, Theodore Roosevelt had come to Chicago to deliver his celebrated speech on the Monroe Doctrine. Dawes, who thought this speech "quite the best address he has delivered since he became President," took the occasion to record his impressions. They add up to a revealing pen portrait of the President.

"Not being a part of this Administration and, therefore, not

harassed by the sycophants and other visitors, as used to be the case
when I accompanied President McKinley, I watched the proceedings in his suite with both interest and amusement. Roosevelt met
his callers often with an apparently affectionate enthusiasm which
seemed for the moment greatly to please and inspire them. At the
first greetings the face of the caller beamed with mingled gratitude
and hope. After taking his seat, however, and watching for a time
the continual flow of the same affectionate enthusiasm on the part of
the President toward others, the face of the caller with ambition
becomes more thoughtful and finally a shade of sadness appears.

"I confess to some feeling of pride when the President deemed
my advice of some consequence. But, when upon meeting Secretary
Shaw, I discovered a number of others bearing their burdens of
advice upon similar Presidential instigation, and, greatly impressed
with their burden's weight, the humor of the situation became a
source of enjoyment. Having no ax to grind myself, the defectiveness
of the Presidential grindstone did not cause me the anxiety which I
thought I detected on the face of my friend H. H. Kohlsaat, and
some other cocallers with advice for Secretary Shaw. In the President's room, as fast as people came they were invited to stay and
take tea. I noticed that Senator Hopkins and Kohlsaat, like myself,
probably fearing that the tea supply might prove to be deficient,
early joined the procession of those giving advice to Shaw who was
at the time at a room in the old Auditorium Hotel.

"I have a great admiration for Roosevelt. All that happened
really increased my respect for him. His hearty greetings are simply
the natural result of his own good spirits and splendid vitality. But
while his greetings express only what he feels, yet what he feels is
not that which the stranger or casual acquaintance would infer from
his manner. He is too robust in his nature not to confuse one at first
in the attempt accurately to judge of his real feelings by his action.
He has no blind side. He has no sense of reverence, so to speak. He
is fair in his dealings and just in his decisions when he has heard
both sides. He has no sense of fear or inherent love of peace. He
seeks to wield power—not to avoid wielding it. He apparently loves
everybody and nobody—both at once—everything and everybody
being subordinated to his desire to keep the approbation of the public—not simply for the sake of that approbation but for the sake of

that rightdoing as well, which brings it. He is a good President but not as great as McKinley. While he has the same strength of purpose as McKinley had, he has not the power of self-control and self-conquering that McKinley had. And then his strength is not tempered, as was that of McKinley, by the real tenderness of heart and kindness of instinct which characterized McKinley's smallest actions."

Neither Dawes nor his audience gave at the time much notice to a portion of the speech which became the most famous of any attached to T. R.'s name. It was something to which even Roosevelt made no claim to authorship.

"There is," Roosevelt said, "a homely adage which runs: 'Speak softly and carry a big stick; you will go far.' If the American nation will speak softly and yet build and keep at the highest pitch of training a thoroughly efficient navy, the Monroe Doctrine will go far. I ask you to think this over."

Cartoonists leaped to their drawing boards to draw Teddy and the Big Stick. He was implored to get out his Big Stick against enemies, foreign and domestic. No one long remembered any of the balance of his speech.

The subject most discussed by Republicans as the 1904 Presidential contest approached was the relationship of Roosevelt and Hanna. Dawes of all men was the most competent to give testimony on that. Dawes heard their feelings from the lips of each. He talked to Hanna twenty-four days before his death, and the next day after he saw Roosevelt, and immediately wrote a synopsis of his talks with each of them.

Mr. and Mrs. Dawes had arrived in Washington on January 17, 1904. It was their first return to the national capital since October, 1901, just after McKinley's death. Hanna was not in town on the cold January day of their return. Only the day before he had been re-elected Senator by the legislature of Ohio, receiving the largest majority ever given a Senator in Ohio. The afternoon newspapers carried dispatches that Lieutenant Governor Warren G. Harding had brought Hanna before a joint session of the legislature after the balloting, to receive an ovation from the Ohio lawmakers.

Hanna came back from Ohio on January 19 and Dawes went to

the Hanna suite at the Arlington for an hour's talk. For a man who had just won an overwhelming re-election, Hanna seemed strangely depressed. He said that he would be national chairman through the June Republican national convention and expected to exercise all the authority and prerogatives of that position.

"I told him," Dawes wrote in a journal entry made that day, "that I hoped he would not make the mistake James G. Blaine made when he became a defeated eleventh-hour candidate against Benjamin Harrison. Hanna said he did not intend to become a candidate. He was very bitter against Roosevelt; called him untruthful.

"Hanna said he had refused to become a candidate despite the solicitation of J. P. Morgan, George F. Baker, J. J. Hill, and other magnates whom he named, but he had promised them that he would not advocate the nomination of Roosevelt before the convention, thus giving them the opportunity to endeavor to get another candidate.

"Hanna said he did not think Roosevelt could be defeated for the nomination.

"Morgan and Hill, Hanna told me, threatened to support a Democrat against Roosevelt if he was nominated, provided the Democrat was not a too radical socialist or Bryanite. Hanna was emphatic that he would not head the National Committee for the next campaign. He said that if he did and won, Roosevelt would claim all credit, and if he lost, Roosevelt would accord him all the blame."

Next day:

"While Mrs. Dawes remained with Mrs. Roosevelt, I had a long talk with the President," Dawes wrote. "Roosevelt spoke with his customary frankness. I did not seek his confidences but he gave them freely. He talked about his renomination chiefly.

"Roosevelt said that on the porch at Senator Hanna's house at Cleveland, at the time of his daughter Ruth's wedding, Hanna had promised to support him for renomination and that they both regarded it in the nature of a contract for cooperation along that line. Now he said that as convention time approached Hanna receded instead of advanced—that he (Roosevelt) did not care so much so far as the general situation was concerned, although he recognized the fact that the negative attitude of Hanna gave some sort of a nucleus for his enemies in the party to gather around.

"That did not trouble him so much, Roosevelt said, as the fact that Hanna's attitude in Ohio seemed to force him into an alliance with Joseph B. Foraker in Hanna's own state against him."

On the trip, Dawes noted, Fairbanks had told him he wanted to run for Vice-President with Roosevelt. Beveridge wanted to be the 1904 keynoter: "As in the olden days Albert confided all his plans and aspirations for the Presidency for which he expects to be a candidate in 1908."

Dawes told no one what Hanna and Roosevelt had said to him. Into his diary he wrote:

"While our whole trip was enjoyable, I realized after it all the more that I was through with politics, and that my ambitions and associations were permanently changed. A short visit to Washington is enough for me. The air is one of intrigue and striving and change. To have listened to the comments of Roosevelt on Hanna and Hanna on Roosevelt; of Beveridge on Fairbanks and Fairbanks on Beveridge, and of Cortelyou and Justice Day on the whole situation is to have heard a great deal of comprehensive and epigrammatic information."

On the night of January 30 Senator Hanna attended the winter dinner of the Gridiron Club. He had always been that newspaper club's favorite guest and now, as the possessor of another six-year term in the Senate, he got a great ovation. In an affectionate mood the Club's quartette sang his favorite, "The Song That Touched My Heart."

On the following day, a Sunday, Hanna took to bed. A typhoid epidemic was raging in Columbus during the ten days he had spent there, and Hanna had contracted the fever.

In the hushed lobby of the Arlington some of the nation's best-known men waited for news from the Hanna suite upstairs. Theodore Roosevelt called daily at the hotel. Ten thousand miles away the first blows of the Russo-Japanese war were being struck. The Slavs and the Nipponese traded punches on the Yalu River and the Russians retreated from Seoul as the Japanese came ashore at Inchon. Forty miles away in Baltimore raged a $150,000,000 fire, the second greatest holocaust in the nation's history. But nothing took the attention of the political world from the darkened bedroom in the Arlington where Hanna lay in a coma, conscious only at intervals. At times his pulse was so feeble that it was hardly detectable. In all the lurid lexicon of vituperation there was scarcely an epithet which Hanna had escaped. But by now he had lived to be one of the best-loved and most highly esteemed men in American public life.

Just before seven o'clock Monday evening, February 15, Mark Hanna died. In the hushed lobby below, the famous Dr. William Osler announced:

"The end was peaceful. The Senator died as a child goes to sleep."

Notification of Hanna's death came to Dawes in a telegram from Elmer Dover, the Senator's secretary. In the library at his Evanston home that night, Dawes wrote his evaluation of the businessman turned statesman:

"*February 15:* I received a telegram from Dover saying that Senator Hanna died at 6:40 P.M. I went to the telegraph office and sent a message of condolence.

"Thus ends the life of one of the greatest political organizers— probably the greatest—this country has ever had. For many years I was in close contact with Hanna and enjoyed his confidence. He was aggressive and masterful—save with McKinley, to whom Hanna owed his success in chief part. And yet the services Hanna rendered McKinley were well-nigh indispensable. Hanna was sincere and frank above all things. He hated hypocrisy. His political standards were not as high as McKinley's—but what they were, he never apologized for them. In his later life he sought in an unusual degree to be useful to the public in the settlement of industrial disputes, and he rendered most signal service in the settlement of labor troubles. He was a kindly, generous man. He was always natural and always helpful and intensely loyal to his associates. He was often indiscreet when acting under impulse, but seldom unwise in any of his matured plans.

"He was so approachable and so sympathetic that he possessed an army of friends who felt a deep attachment for him. When Hanna once gave his friendship, he seemed unable to believe that friend capable of wrongdoing. This often led him into embarrassing contests for unworthy men; but so great was the public confidence in the rectitude of his intentions that such contests did not seem to injure his standing, but rather to aid it.

"In his relations to McKinley, in which, as intermediary when campaigns were on and Hanna was at a distance, I was at times intimately involved, he was always a loyal and faithful ally. At times he would complain to me bitterly of McKinley who was always unwilling to allow the Government's attitude upon any essential matter of department business to be affected by political considerations, but notwithstanding his disappointment at what he termed McKinley's lack of cooperation, he would always faithfully labor away to do the best he could under the circumstances.

"Hanna was personally scrupulously honest. As the man, however, who raised the campaign funds in 1896 and 1900, he felt it his duty when contributors appealed to him for assistance in the matter of contracts, etc. to do what he could for them. This never led him to my knowledge to ask anything which he believed was unfair or wrong—but it was a most harassing burden which he had to bear. His growth in public esteem was wonderful and his career demonstrated the value to a public man of unjust abuse. The reaction came, and vindicated him, as it always will in similar cases.

"All in all, he was a great man and his death is to be regretted as a national loss. He was a most useful Senator. He was largely responsible for the change in the public attitude in favor of the Panama, as against the Nicaragua route. He was eminently practical in his public services. Had he lived longer he would have been still more conspicuous in his public usefulness—for Hanna had a sincere desire to be helpful. Peace be with him!"

Dawes went to Cleveland for the final funeral service:

"The services were most impressive. Great crowds lined the street. There were many evidences of sincere grief from every source, save in the Hollenden Hotel, where crowds of ghoulish politicians fought and talked the livelong day over the open grave of the great leader."

The peace meeting between Roosevelt and Hanna, for which Dawes had hoped so ardently, had never come. But there was the note which Hanna had sent to Roosevelt from his sickbed, on February 5: "You touched a tender spot, old man, when you personally

1. *Charles G. Dawes as a schoolboy in Marietta, Ohio.*

2. *Charles G. Dawes as a student in law school in Cincinnati.*

3. *The General Rufus R. Dawes home in Marietta, Ohio, birthplace of Charles G. Dawes.*

*4. Portrait of Mrs. Charles G. Dawes painted in London in 1931
by John St. Helier Lander.*

5. *The six children of Rufus R. and Mary Gates Dawes: left to right (in front): Bessie (Mrs. Harry Hoyt) and Mary Frances (Mrs. Arthur G. Beach); Rufus C., Beman G., Henry M., Charles G.*

6. *Meeting of the Allied Supply Board at their headquarters, Combest, December 15, 1918, left to right: General Merrone, representing Italian Army in France; General Dawes, representing American Army; General Payot, chairman, representing French Army; General Ford, representing English Army; Major Cumont, representing Belgian Army.*

7. *Allied Supply Board in meeting: Generals Dawes, Ford, Payot, Merrone. Other members unidentified.*

8. *Generals John J. Pershing, Charles G. Dawes, and James G. Harbord.*

9. John T. McCutcheon's cartoon (January 31, 1939) in the Chicago Tribune of "The Three Musketeers," Generals Dawes, Pershing, and Harbord.

10. Reparations experts arriving in New York on the SS Leviathan, left to right: Owen D. Young, General Dawes, and Henry M. Robinson.

11. August 7, 1927, dedication of the Peace Bridge at Buffalo, New York, where General Dawes delivered the principal address. General Dawes, on the American side, reaching across the ribbon to shake the hand of the Prince of Wales, future King Edward VIII.

12. June 11, 1927, Captain Charles A. Lindbergh returning from first nonstop flight from New York to Paris, is welcomed as a colonel by President Coolidge and Vice-President Dawes, Washington, D.C.

13. *Dawes and Secretary of State Stimson take their seats preparatory to affixing their signatures to the 1930 London Naval Agreement.*

14. *The Vice-President and Speaker Nicholas Longworth begin the canvass of the Electoral College results which showed the victory of Herbert Hoover over Alfred E. Smith in 1928 presidential campaign.*

15. *Dawes leaving the White House after accepting his last appointment to public office—the presidency of the Reconstruction Finance Corporation in 1932.*

16. *President Herbert Hoover and Ambassador Charles G. Dawes.*

17. *Ambassador Charles G. Dawes and Prime Minister J. Ramsay MacDonald.*

18. *Dawes making his "Helen Maria" appearance before the Graham World War I Investigation Committee.*

came to see me early this morning." And Roosevelt had replied in the same vein. Perhaps no more was needed.

The Republican caravan moved into Chicago in mid-June of 1904, with the nomination of Theodore Roosevelt for President and Charles W. Fairbanks for Vice-President assured in advance. Henry Cabot Lodge brought the main platform planks which had been drafted in Washington by Roosevelt and himself. There was to be no employment other than ratification for the more than one thousand convention delegates.

But if the lot of the delegates was a tranquil one, such was not the case in the party hierarchy—the Republican National Committee. Behind the scenes, a bitter battle was being fought over the question who would succeed Hanna as chairman of the National Committee. President Roosevelt had selected Cortelyou, but when Dawes arrived on the scene, he found the bulk of the Committee in open revolt against this selection. Dawes informed the President by telegram of the situation and received the characteristic telegram in return:

"Explain to the opposition that if I am to run as President then Cortelyou is to be chairman of the National Committee, and that opposition to him is simply disloyalty to the Republican Party and covert assistance to the Democrats."

Dawes pocketed the bristling telegram. "Since the backbone of the opposition was in my judgment broken and the effect of the telegram would be to reinspire opposition, I did not show it save to one or two of the loyal friends."

A few days later:

"Cortelyou will be chosen and given full power. Cortelyou's selection marks the final transition from the rotten conditions of management as it was before Hanna's day to an absolutely clean basis. Hanna was distinctly an improver of conditions. Cortelyou will further perfect them since he will even more strenuously than Hanna insist upon clean methods of campaigning."

There were just a few commitments before Dawes could leave the political scene. He rendered what aid he could to his friend Graeme Stewart in a close but losing race for mayor of Chicago against Democrat Carter H. Harrison. Harrison's razor-thin edge came from West Side wards controlled by Billy Lorimer. It did not suit Lorimer to have in City Hall a Republican who might give him trouble.

The 1904 Republican gubernatorial situation was complicated for Dawes by the entry of three of his close friends, Frank O. Lowden, Charles S. Deneen, and Lawrence Y. Sherman against the Lorimer-backed incumbent Yates. In a record-setting seventy-nine-ballot convention, Deneen was nominated.

At Roosevelt's request Dawes acted as trustee and supervised the spending of all funds for the Republican campaign in the West. Dawes saw Roosevelt just once during the campaign. The others present were Cornelius N. Bliss, treasurer of the National Committee, and Cortelyou.

"Roosevelt discussed things in his usual robust way," Dawes recorded. "Said he wanted publicity of campaign funds. Bliss told him he could not get contributions if he made the names of the donors public. Roosevelt said that at this stage of the game he supposed we 'needed contributions worse than publicity.' That settled it."

The campaign which returned Theodore Roosevelt to the White House, waged at a cost little in excess of two million dollars, yielded three hundred and thirty-six electoral votes for the Republican candidate, and a popular majority in excess of two and a half million. Closing his Chicago headquarters, Dawes noted:

"The returns were so one-sided that they were received quietly at Republican headquarters. I received word of Beman's election to Congress in Ohio. Deneen's majority in Illinois was about 200,000. Chicago went Republican by a tremendous majority. This victory against a Democratic party controlled by conservatives indicates coming contests by the Republicans with Democracy controlled by radicals. It means the removal of the center of coming political controversies to the West."

Chapter Nine

✸

TRUSTS, PANIC, AND BREAD WAGONS

*W*ithout in any way diminishing his fight for currency reform, Dawes in 1905 became the most articulate private citizen in the nation on another very live issue—antitrust legislation.

The Sherman Antitrust Act was loosely drawn and vague in its definitions. In the decade and a half it had been on the statute books it had failed almost completely to check or even retard the combination of industrial concerns aiming at the establishment of monopoly.

President McKinley, in his message to Congress of 1899, had urged the lawmakers to correct the increasingly intolerable situation.

"There must be a remedy for the evils involved in such organizations," the President had said. "If the present law can be extended more certainly to control or check these monopolies or trusts, it should be done without delay. Whatever power the Congress possesses over this important subject should be promptly ascertained and asserted."

But no action was taken during the short time the national legislature was in session before President McKinley's death. Nor had the subject received any attention during the nearly four years of McKinley's second term which Theodore Roosevelt completed.

Early in 1905 Dawes published in the *Saturday Evening Post* an article asking for antitrust legislation. He followed up with another article in the *North American Review*, and with a number of public speeches.

Dawes contended that if the Sherman Antitrust Act "is to be useful hereafter, it must be made to define what kinds of agreements are illegal." As the main objections to the law in its present form Dawes mentioned the fact that "its principal section makes criminal, without further definition, an agreement in restraint of trade. It leaves to judicial determination the definition of the crime, and it has not yet been defined, but will be defined only as each case arises. The business community, therefore, is left in doubt as to what constitutes a crime under the law.

"Being indefinite in its definition of the crime, and introducing into business an element of doubt and uncertainty as to trade agreements, it operates to the disadvantage of the scrupulous businessman and in favor of the unscrupulous one.

"The enforcement of this law—giving, necessarily, through its general terms, such wide latitude and discretion to executive officers in their right to proceed against corporations and individuals—is bound to create the appearance at least of favoritism in its application, and to result in lack of uniformity in the treatment of cases arising under it.

"The Sherman Antitrust Act is today encouraging the crushing out of competition, and is encouraging the formation of larger corporations all the time, because they can legally do by consolidation what they cannot legally do as separate corporations through a trade agreement."

Even while Dawes was advocating the clarification and strengthening of the antitrust laws, Theodore Roosevelt decided to revive and enforce the Sherman Act. He requested the Department of Justice to obtain injunctions under the Act against a number of corporations, among them Chicago meat packers, in an effort "to prevent combinations to raise prices."

Since the Sherman Act had long gone unenforced, it was understood that there would be no criminal prosecutions for prior violations. The injunction served merely to put the packers on notice that there would be prosecution if the injunction were to be disobeyed.

In October, 1904, James R. Garfield, commissioner of corporations in the Department of Commerce and Labor, called on the Chicago packers for their books. Skeptical of the purpose for which the books were wanted, a committee of packers, headed by Ogden Armour, went to Dawes for advice.

"Have you lived up to the terms of your injunction?" Dawes inquired.

"We issued the strictest order to our employees to carry out the terms of the injunction and we have seen that it is done," Armour replied.

"Then let the government have your books, but if you want reassurance I'll ask Garfield about the purposes for which they are to be used," Dawes said.

"Garfield assured me the information was only for a cost study by his department, and that the information obtained would be used only by it," Dawes noted. "The packers then turned over the books. Later the packers came to me and alleged that contrary to the agreement the Department of Justice had gained possession of the data. If it had been a matter between the Department of Justice and the packers when I was first apprised of it, I would have had nothing to do with it, but as the intermediary between Garfield and the packers, I was in a sense held responsible. I agreed to go to Washington and make inquiries about the matter."

On October 20, another entry:

"I went to the Department of Commerce where I talked to Secretary Metcalf and Commissioner Garfield. The Department of Commerce people denied strenuously that the information had been misused. I went to the White House where I saw the President who sent for Moody, the Attorney General. Moody also denied that the Department of Commerce had furnished him the information, stating that he was making this independent investigation to ascertain whether the injunction against combination by the packers to raise prices was being violated. I was satisfied that both Metcalf and Moody told the truth. The President kept me for lunch."

In midwinter the District Attorney's office in Chicago announced that an effort would be made to indict the packers for violations of the law committed prior to the injunction imposed by Federal Judge Peter S. Grosscup.

Indignant, Dawes went back to the White House on March 7, 1905. He arrived in Washington at the end of the three days of festivities attendant on the inauguration of Roosevelt and Fairbanks.

"Presidential Secretary Loeb called me at the residence of Justice Day where I was staying and told me to be at the White House at 12:30," Dawes wrote. "Upon reaching there I found that the President had decided, at the Cabinet meeting just finished, to go to the funeral of Senator William M. Bate of Tennessee, and was making his preparations. I was, therefore, taken to him as he was stretched out in his barber's chair. That was the best possible way I could have found him if I was to make a consecutive statement. In his own office it was Roosevelt's habit to do most of the talking. I was also aided by the fact that the barber was old and very slow.

"The President had greeted me so cordially that I began with a conciliatory statement. I said: 'Mr. President, you have taught your friends when they have complaints to make or cases to state to come to you for a square deal. I want to say to start with that I do not come here as a critic of anything which has been done thus far in this case, but of what the District Attorney's office at Chicago says it *may* do. If I speak strongly it is with the expectation that speaking with justice, I shall receive justice.'

"Roosevelt sat up straight in his chair and said:

"'You are always honest and I want to hear what you have to say.'

"I talked with all the force I could command and at intervals he sat up, with the lather on his face. I said:

"'At my former interview with you and Attorney General Moody, you outlined to me your policy in regard to the reforms you hoped to inaugurate under the Sherman Antitrust law, and your method of accomplishing them. I understood from that interview: *first,* that you would not as a policy seek to secure industrial reform by the humiliation of individuals through indictments under the Sherman Antitrust law which for over ten years has been a dead letter on the statute books, and that you would proceed by injunction against the corporations to improve industrial conditions; *second,* that you had with the fullest deliberation proceeded against the packers in an injunction suit, which, being successful, amounts to a restatement in a concrete way of the Sherman law; that this action constitutes fair notice to the packers that if *after* this injunction there are violations of it, and of the Sherman Antitrust law, then they would be subject to indictment and arrest for such violation.

"'With this understanding I went away. My friends among the

packers had already issued to their employees the strictest orders to obey this injunction. They tell me it has been obeyed. I believe them.

" 'But, however that may be, the District Attorney's office at Chicago now publicly announces that it will indict the packers for violation of the Sherman Antitrust law antedating the injunction, and that they will not limit their investigation to alleged violations of the injunction.

" 'Now I come here demanding equal administration of the law —that enforcement of the law shall be uniform. That I have a right to demand.'

"The President again sat up straight in his chair and interjected: 'You have a right to that, you shall receive it!' 'Well then,' I said, 'I demand that along with the effort to indict the packers of the West for unproved offenses against the Sherman Antitrust law, you now proceed to indict James J. Hill and J. Pierpont Morgan and the officers of the Northern Securities Company for their *proved* infraction of that law in the already adjudicated *Northern Securities* case.

" 'Garfield's report shows that the packers make about two per cent on their gross business, and I have just read in the Philadelphia *Record* that if they do $800,000,000 per year business then the $16,000,000 profit is too large. And yet the United States Steel Corporation, with its advertised billet pool in existence, made last year about $50,000,000 on a gross business of about $440,000,000. Why is there to be one rule for the East and another for the West? Or is there but one rule? I believe that whatever policy you eventually pursue will be a fair policy but I warn you that your subordinates in office may create policies and problems for you before they have your personal consideration.

" 'In every city there are retailers' pools—on sugar, on ice, on meat—on almost every commodity—formed for mutual protection and for arranging what might be called the rules of the trade. The men in these pools are not all scoundrels. They seek to avoid a competition that may absolutely destroy them. Most of the evils of which the country complains are the outgrowth of unrestrained and unregulated competition. A large corporation will sell below cost in a particular locality in order to destroy the local competitor, and thus enable it later to exercise a monopoly.'

"The President at this point rubbed the lather off his face and sprang out of the chair. We went back to his office. He said to me: 'Dawes, I want you to go down to the Department of Justice and make that speech to them. The Attorney General is in Virginia, but Hoyt, the Solicitor General, is at the Department. I have to be pretty careful in what I say, but I want you to know that I give great weight to what you have said.' He asked me to remain for lunch with him the next day, but I had to leave that afternoon."

Back in Chicago, Dawes told Armour and P. A. Valentine about the White House conversation.

"Armour is very much alarmed and worried over the matter," Dawes wrote. "He said to me in the most dejected tones:

"'Dawes, I am living and recently have been living the darkest hours of my life. I believe the intention is to indict the packers. Everyone eats meat and a suit against the packers would be politically popular. Roosevelt wants popularity. I am an accident in this business which I inherited from my father who was a great leader. I am not a criminal and if I am indicted as a lawbreaker it will be a great grief to me and my family.

"'I have endeavored strictly to obey the injunction. I have wanted to obey the laws always. All my life I have tried to be a good citizen. I have in this world only my mother, my wife, and my daughter. If I left my business to my little girl it would be a curse to her. I have felt almost as if I would like to quit the worry and stress of business life and sell out. Yet I have a sense of duty to the men who have grown up with the business and who would lose their places that has led me to abandon the plan. I have long since lost the desire for money and I feel I have few friends.'

"While Armour was speaking he was so much agitated at times that I thought how different a man he really was from the man he is painted in the press. As I grow older, I realize more and more that there are more than two sides to every question—there are two sides to every view. I hope I may be just. I can see, too, as I grow older, how great is the influence of environment on one's mind. In my younger days I was a radical in many ways. I wonder sometimes whether my views are changing because I am coming really into larger knowledge of men and affairs, and the underlying conditions of life.

"This I am coming to see: There is too little charity in the world, too little sympathy for the weak and suffering, too little of the giving to others. But I do not find the givers among the critics of conditions or of men. Nor do I find the critic much different from other men, save in his complaining. I know the world is getting better, but it is a slow growth. The altruistic spirit is growing, but the selfishness of men and the intolerance of men are barriers which for ages have endured—and will."

Dawes went to Washington once again on June 5. He had another talk with Roosevelt on the proposition of indicting the packers for infraction of the Sherman Act, and recorded:

"The President stated that Attorney General Moody and District Attorney Morrison at Chicago claimed that the spirit at least of the injunction has been violated, and that if there was a case they would indict. Contrary to his policy heretofore of proceeding against the corporations, Roosevelt is determined to proceed against the person of the packers. I am firmly convinced that the packers have not violated the spirit of the injunction, and I so told him. If they have, I have been deceived by men in whom I trusted. I do not believe it, and I stated my belief in strong words. The President promised to reopen the discussion with Moody and District Attorney Morrison of Chicago, who is in the city, the next day."

On July 1, less than a month after Dawes' second visit to Roosevelt, an indictment was returned by the Grand Jury of the Northern District of Illinois Federal Court, charging the packers with "conspiring in restraint of trade and commerce among the states and with foreign nations, and with an attempt to monopolize such trade and commerce, in violation of the Antitrust Act."

On March 21, 1906, Judge J. Otis Humphrey held that the record showed that the information obtained by Garfield from the packers "was demanded by the Department of Justice for the purpose of this prosecution, and that Garfield declined to give it, as he had promised the defendants it would not be so used; that later, upon repeated demands of the Department of Justice, and upon the order of the President, he turned it over to that department. It is contended that as to all such evidence the defendants are entitled to immunity, and I am of the opinion that they are so entitled. The immunity pleas filed by the defendants will be sustained as to the individual defendants, the natural persons, and denied as to the corporations, the artificial persons, and the verdict will be in favor of the defendants as to individuals, and in favor of the government as to the corporations."

Dawes had hoped that Roosevelt "with his great popularity will, before this period of general interest in corporation matters is passed, take leadership in having Congress perfect this law and by clearer definitions make it enforceable. Any agreement for the purpose of extorting an unreasonable price ought to be put under the ban of the law. The American businessman wants the law clarified so that he can pursue his business without the fear of molestation and criminal prosecution when he is not a criminal.

"As a matter of experience we know in this country no law is tolerable if enforced, or useful if unenforced, which designates good and bad acts alike as criminal. You don't put the whole community in the pest house because some members of it have the smallpox."

There had been, Dawes soon asserted, an appearance of favoritism in the cases instituted by the Department of Justice.

"In the *Northern Securities* case," he said in an address before the Conference of the National Civic Federation, "a limited action was taken against the corporation only, and no attempt was made to hold the officers criminally. In the case against the packers, the effort was made to hold them criminally liable. In this latter case, the Government found itself in the attitude of announcing through one department, Commerce and Labor, after a thorough investigation, that the business was not a monopoly and that its profits were reasonable, and of seeking at the same time, through another department, Justice, to put its owners in jail as public malefactors.

"The *Northern Securities* case was so presented to the courts that the reinstatement of the Chicago, Burlington and Quincy Railroad as a competitor of the Northern Pacific and Great Northern Railways was not involved in the decree. As a consequence, when the Northern Securities Company was dissolved by the decision, the same interests remained in control of the railway situation in the Northwest. They had that control, represented by two separate stock certificates instead of one single Northern Securities stock certificate as formerly. No patron of the Great Northern or the Northern Pacific knows, except as a matter of history, that the government won its great antimerger decision.

"The proper remedy should have been sought in an effort to restore the old condition of competition, not in changing in the hands of the same owner a piece of white paper for a piece of red paper and a piece of blue paper. It must have been known at the time when the case was brought up that it could result in nothing practical when no attempt was made to bring into court that which was the very cornerstone of the whole transaction."

But the filing of antitrust suits became more and more a matter of fits and starts, while trusts were multiplying by leaps and bounds. Dawes thought "the chief endeavor seems to be to satisfy the public mind through selected civil and criminal cases.

"Another thing: the fact that attacks upon men of prestige and men of supposedly high character and men of position is made possible under this law, and that attacks upon the men who do outstanding things attract public attention, has resulted so far in an inability of the Department of Justice to refrain from trying their cases in the newspapers prior to instituting the case."

Some government actions, Dawes thought, had all the appearance of being made to keep the muckrakers content. He paid his respects to them too.

"They have done some good—and they have done harm. Much of the writings of the muckrakers is one-sided and superficial. Some of the muckrakers cover up their superficial knowledge by the use of sharp phrases. They know, too, that a fine way to engage the public attention for any political party or any young man or any idler— and the critic is often an idle man—is to assault somebody who is doing something. For it is the doers and not the drones in whom the people are interested. The muckrakers cannot see the grass for the snakes. They point to a hole in the sidewalk and claim the whole town is going to fall through it. Whatever may be written about him, the man who nails himself to the right principle will in the long run be vindicated."

Dawes saw Theodore Roosevelt less than a half-dozen times after the packer episode. Thus it came as a surprise to him when in

December of 1906 President Roosevelt sent him the first draft of a message relating to currency reform with a statement that he desired Dawes' criticism.

"I criticized it rather severely since it leaned toward the authorization of an increased bank currency, subject to only a small tax, which would allow the notes to be used in normal times and to that extent prevent their use in time of panic.

"It is distasteful to me to criticize the President, and I do not intend to do so further. Although urged to do so by Justice Day, at whose home Caro and I were visiting in December, I did not call on him when in Washington. I could not, after having criticized him as severely as I have to a few of my friends, bring myself to meet him as an apparent friend. And yet—he has appointed my dear friend Cortelyou Secretary of the Treasury, and I can almost forgive him everything for that."

Black headlines in the Chicago newspapers of Monday morning, December 18, 1905, jolted the city as it had not been jolted for years. The three banks of John R. Walsh had failed. Excited citizens grabbed the papers to read with apprehension. Would the closing of the Chicago National Bank, the Equitable Trust Company, and the Home Savings Bank carry down the whole Walsh empire?

In the dominion built up by the one-time Irish immigrant lad were utilities, newspapers, railroads, quarries, coal, wharfs, warehouses, real estate, amusements. Walsh did nothing that was not prodigious. His success had been sensational, his failure surely would be no less so. It could mean loss of jobs, shutdown of business. Might it not also plunge the country into a panic and bring catastrophe to other cities?

But the details were reassuring. There had been an all-night session of 50 Chicago bankers and a few of the city's leading merchants and manufacturers, representing altogether $500,000,000 of Chicago's wealth. The conferees, just before daylight Monday, had come to an agreement on an unprecedented cooperative action. The other banks in Chicago would take over the assets and guarantee the deposits of the three Walsh institutions, and if there were losses the guaranteeing banks would prorate them. The bankers had perceived that the failure of Chicago's most colorful man, who was also

one of its richest and most highly respected citizens, might precipitate a financial crisis that could not be confined to Chicago.

Behind this simple announcement, there was concealed the
story of a dramatic clash of wills between Marshall Field and Dawes,
from which Dawes had emerged victorious and with added stature.

All day Sunday Comptroller of the Currency Ridgely from
Washington and a committee of six bank presidents had been in
session with Walsh and his Board of Directors. At nightfall a call
had gone out for all bank presidents in the city, routing them out
of their homes, churches, or clubs. Dawes had been fetched from
Orchestra Hall where he was presiding over a memorial meeting
for Graeme Stewart.

Assembled in the lofty marble hall of the First National Bank
on Monroe Street, the bank presidents heard from James B. Forgan,
head of that institution, that Walsh had loaned to his own enterprises and invested in their securities some $15,000,000 of the funds
of his banks, and that they were in an insolvent condition. Forgan
then promised the assembly that a committee, meeting in the Walsh
Bank, would soon report with more information and with recommendations to meet the situation.

The assembly waited for several hours. Finally, a messenger
arrived from the Walsh Bank and asked Dawes to join the committee
meeting there.

Again the assembly waited. Dawes and Marshall Field, over at
the Walsh Bank, had their tug-of-war which deadlocked the committee for hours.

The disagreement came over the question whether the bankers'
guarantee should cover only the private deposits, or both them and
the public deposits of Chicago, Cook County, and the State of Illinois. Field insisted that only private deposits be guaranteed. Dawes
held out for a full guarantee.

Imperious, blunt as a hippopotamus, Field pressed his point.
There were few men who could cross Marshall Field. Seventy years
old now and in the last year of his life, he had come to Chicago forty-
nine years before as a Yankee store clerk. First with Potter Palmer
and Levi Z. Leiter as his partners and then by himself he had built
up his great mercantile business. The nation's most successful merchant had the highest respect of Dawes and of all the other conferees

—but Dawes came from the same New England stock as Field and could be as inflexible. And he felt his plan was the more equitable.

Behind Field stood such big Chicago bankers as Orson Smith of the Corn Exchange Bank, Byron Smith of the Northern Trust Company, and Ernest A. Hamill of the Illinois Merchants Trust Company. But Dawes' argument won the backing of James B. Forgan. Rising dramatically, Forgan said: "I will never agree to the guarantee unless Dawes' point is conceded!" An accord seemed impossible. Then John J. Mitchell, president of the Illinois Trust Company, agreed to Dawes' plan. The impasse was broken. Marshall Field, the two Smiths, and Hamill capitulated. Dawes, in his record of the session, said:

"To John J. Mitchell belongs the chief credit for one of the greatest acts of public-spirited cooperation known in the banking history of our country, probably the greatest. I left at 5:40 A.M. It was necessary for me to take the position I did. I felt it was my duty to my own institution and only true equity. That it was conceded, however, was an inexpressible relief to me."

On Monday there were runs not only on the Walsh Bank but on other Chicago banks also. But confidence soon returned.

"*December 20:*   I called on John R. Walsh with whom in the old days I had so much business. He told me he had been a damn fool. He showed great self-control. He said he had not spoken to me on the night of the conference at any length, for he would have broken down if he had done so."

Dawes thought back to a day ten years before when Walsh had told him the greatest of his ambitions was to own a railroad. That ambition had become the chief reason for his downfall. Of the fifteen million of the bank funds he had invested in his own enterprises the biggest chunk had gone into three ill-starred short-line railroads.

There was no evidence that Walsh had intended to deceive or defraud anyone. But he had run afoul the national banking laws—and a jury gave him a five-year sentence in the Federal Penitentiary at Leavenworth. The white-haired Walsh served a year and nine months of his term, was paroled because of failing health, and died in Chicago nine days after his release.

The disaster which might have come at the time of the Walsh

failure, but was averted then by the cooperative action of the Chicago bankers, hit the nation twenty-two months later, on October 22, 1907. The Knickerbocker Trust Company of New York failed.

The Knickerbocker was the city's "society bank," its clientele the most fashionable in town. It had been involved in the efforts of F. Augustus Heinz to corner the copper market, and when copper dropped from twenty-six to twelve cents per pound in six months, the fate of the bank was sealed. Long lines formed at the tellers' windows on that Tuesday morning. By noon $8,000,000 had been paid out, and the windows slammed shut.

On the stock exchange, prices plunged to new lows. A number of brokerage houses failed. False rumors ran regarding the solidity of other banks. There was a run on the Trust Company of America, and the Union Trust Company in Providence, Rhode Island, closed. At Pittsburgh, Westinghouse Electric Company failed, the Southern Steel Company at Birmingham closed its doors, and business institutions all over the nation toppled.

Never had a financial panic come so unexpectedly. It came at a time when the country was harvesting bountiful crops and selling them at good prices; mines, mills, and manufacturing companies were busy; railroads had more freight than they could haul. Labor was fully employed. Almost at the very moment when the Knickerbocker was failing, President Roosevelt, in a speech at Nashville, boasted of the strength of the nation's financial structure.

The effect of the New York failure was felt throughout the country. For nearly a decade, Dawes had been advocating an emergency currency for just such a situation. Nearly seven years earlier, during his days as Comptroller of the Currency, he had written: "Things are running smoothly now, but the next panic will carry down a lot of these new banks." Now the panic was upon the country, and the country had no more means to fight it than it had had in 1893.

Dawes' diary gives a blow-by-blow account of the effect of the cataclysm on Chicago. It quickly became evident that the government in Washington was concerning itself principally with New York. But the West continued to call for money in steadily increasing amounts—and the West did business mainly with Chicago. There was no cessation of these outside drains as Chicago financial institutions strove to keep the city's own industrial situation somewhere near normal.

"*October 25:*   Cortelyou has been putting large sums of money into New York banks in an attempt to stem the panic. As I came down Adams Street in my automobile Friday morning, I saw express wagons being loaded with specie from the Sub-Treasury in the Post Office Building and I realized the money was going to New York.

"I interviewed J. B. Forgan on the matter, and found that his bank, the First National, had applied for $1,000,000 government deposits from the Treasury and had been refused.

"Through Comptroller of the Currency Ridgely, whom I called long distance, I had Cortelyou on long distance from New York at midnight. He said he had practically exhausted his funds with the demands of New York banks, but would let me know if he could help the Chicago banks tomorrow. I told him that Chicago was already in as bad a fix as New York; that we were certainly going on a clearing house basis, and that for his own record as well as the banks' sake he should find us the money. I told him the New York banks were refusing to ship us the currency while the West was taking $5,000,000 a day or thereabouts from us."

Chicago was in desperation.

"The drain of currency on each Chicago bank is something fearful. I met with the Clearing House and remained there until 6 P.M. It was a memorable meeting. It developed that probably every bank in Chicago would be compelled to close next week unless clearing house certificates were issued. From the meeting I went to Evanston where Cortelyou called me by telephone from New York.

"Cortelyou told me he had placed still more money in New York during the day. He said he would leave for Washington at midnight and there check up his remaining cash and let me know by Sunday afternoon whether he could help us. Men desperately in need of money called me at home as well as at the bank. On the other hand, a number of my friends with surplus funds have called to ask if I had need of them. Vice-President Fairbanks sent his son, Warren, to ask if I could use $60,000 personally."

As Chicago banks fought for their lives, the heads of the institutions went to their desks on Sunday morning. Dawes remained at his bank all Sunday night. At four o'clock Sunday afternoon

Comptroller Ridgely telephoned Dawes that Cortelyou would order the Sub-Treasurer at Chicago to deposit $3,000,000 cash with government national bank depositories in Chicago—$1,000,000 a day for three days.

"I announced this to the assembled bankers at the clearing house meeting, and insisted that the trust companies should be given a share of this money, furnishing to the national banks a portion of the bonds required to secure the deposits. The matter was referred to me for my determination of what was fair, and there in the clearing house meeting I arranged some trades between national banks and trust companies, which made a more equitable distribution of the relief afforded by the cash. I did not ask any for my bank, the Central Trust Company, which made me a fairer judge of what was right between the others."

By this and other government actions, Chicago banks managed to stay open. Another panic had been met. But in New York all the old stand-by props, such as optimistic statements by President Roosevelt, Pierpont Morgan, John D. Rockefeller, E. H. Harriman, and Andrew Carnegie had failed to lift the gloom.

Charles A. Coffin, who had been President of the General Electric Company during all its existence, conceived the idea that the best psychological effect could be achieved by reorganizing the very bank whose failure had precipitated the crisis. Funds to make it stronger than ever were quickly subscribed. Coffin and a reorganizing committee met with J. Pierpont Morgan in the Morgan Bank.

"The first thing I would do would be to try to get Dawes away from Chicago," Morgan told the committee.

Dawes agreed to talk it over and met with the committee at the Plaza Hotel. He was told that if he would head the bank he could name his own terms. This was the most attractive offer anyone had ever made him, he assured the committee, "but," he said, "I have thought it all over; what my Chicago association means to me, what life means there and here, and I find that my heart has mastered my head. I am going to stay out West."

For most of the first twenty years in which Dawes kept a diary, it had been his custom to sit down at the end of the year and write a progress report, telling of what he had sought to accomplish and how far he had succeeded. These summings-up were intended only for the eyes of his children. At the end of 1906 he had written the next to last of these yearly summaries. It is the longest, and also the last written piece of advice he gave to his children. He had said:

"It will be interesting to me and should be to my children to go over the record of a fairly active life. This is my forty-first year of life. As I look back I can see how little worthwhile it has been, except in so far as I have made it useful to others. I can safely say to you children now, that the greatest pleasure I can have is in thinking, as I am tonight, of the people I have helped or helped to help themselves.

"So order your life that as the years pass you can look upon them as having afforded you the chance to help the struggling, who without your aid might have sunk. I want you to know that to me charity has always seemed the greatest virtue. Help people and then you will be helped, perhaps, when the Lord settles your accounts and you sorely need it. To charity add the other virtues; but remember that without charity there can be no salvation and no real character that will avail. Remember at all times the poor, the sick, the discouraged, the forsaken. I know there are some people in the world whom I have saved, and that if I am saved it is that and that only which will be the cause. This I know—the one thing as surely as the other. To give aid to the utterly helpless—there is nothing finer in life."

Now a year later, at the close of 1907, he wrote:

"On this day, realizing the distress that walked our streets as a result of the existing business situation, I arranged at my own expense to feed the hungry. I put the matter in charge of Malcolm McDowell. I called Mayor Busse and he arranged for the cooperation of Dr. Evans, the health commissioner of the city, and others. Got Ogden Armour to furnish the horse and wagon.

"Each night we feed from four hundred up to eight hundred and fifty people. Medill McCormick of the *Tribune* heard about the matter and took up the movement through the *Tribune*. I sent him my check for $500. All in all, starting from this little movement, thousands will now be cared for each of these cold nights with food and lodging. I have kept my name out of it, of course, but I feel a deep satisfaction in the matter. I will keep my wagon going until the other arrangements will fully take its place."

Some days later, he added:

"P.S.: We fed from our bread wagon, in the ten days before the *Tribune* took up and founded the lodging house, about 11,000 men."

The depression dragged on. For years, the bread wagons reappeared every winter. In 1910, Dawes took Ogden Armour and James A. Patten into partnership, but in the winter of 1911 he ran the enterprise again entirely at his own expense. That year he noted:

"Have run my bread wagon with Malcolm McDowell. The suffering is very great in the city. We will have fed between 30,000 and 40,000 during the winter. Thank God I am able to do it."

Chapter Ten

❁

ONE MAN IN A HUNDRED,
AND A MELODY

On March 17, 1908, Senator Robert M. LaFollette rose in the Senate to denounce the "one hundred men who are running the country." While Senate rules in effect at the time prevented LaFollette from giving the names on the Senate floor, he issued his list for publication in the country's newspapers.

It was a formidable group, including John D. Rockefeller, J. Pierpont Morgan, Andrew Carnegie, James J. Hill, E. H. Harriman, John Jacob Astor, August Belmont, H. M. Flagler, William Rockefeller, Henry C. Frick, Cyrus McCormick, Jacob H. Schiff, Levi P. Morton, Clarence W. Mackay, H. H. Rogers, C. M. Schwab, W. K. Vanderbilt, Harry P. Whitney, E. H. Gary, and eighty-one others.

The Senator was selling the nation short. No one hundred men or, for that matter, no one thousand men had ever been able to run the United States at any period of her history.

The names of Rockefeller, Morgan, Carnegie, Hill, and Harriman had been heard for at least forty years, those of Astor, Vanderbilt, and McCormick for nearly half a century. The youngest man on the list was Charles Gates Dawes. He was a mere forty-two years old—and he was to outlive all the other ninety-nine.

No one was more surprised than Dawes himself to be mentioned in such mighty company. He was a wealthy man in 1908, to be sure, yet he was still far from the peak of his wealth which he was to reach perhaps ten years later. The Dawes Bank was only six years old. And since he had avoided publicity not only in connection with his charities but in all other respects, his name meant nothing to the vast majority of Americans.

As ardent McKinleyites in 1896, Dawes and LaFollette had been rather close friends, but that closeness had long since ceased to exist. Dawes never felt the need to make any public comment on LaFollette's speech. He had already made what amounted to a rather pat answer on the subject of the personal power of captains of industry in a speech to a group of businessmen:

"You see articles as to the tremendous power of certain men because of their great wealth. This is a favorite way of creating the impression of the existence of a sinister power. You see these men credited with the aggregated resources of a group of banks or railroads or industries that are actually owned by hundreds of thousands of people. How do these men gain that influence over the property of thousands of other people who willingly entrust it to their guidance? As a rule they exercise leadership and power because their exercise of it is wise, temperate, and just. Inert wealth has no power. Wealth in motion is power. Many of the greatest leaders in finance today are not men of vast wealth, but those who through their qualities of care, initiative, and justice keep large bodies of wealth in useful motion.

"And let me tell you something: In my observation the man who follows the leadership of another man with his money demands a much stricter accounting than the man who simply follows a political leader with his vote. How many men would last as leaders of financial power through their influence over the investing class of the country, if they appealed to the prejudices of the people instead of their reason as do many of the demagogic leaders of today? I would not include all politicians in this indictment, as I would not include all financiers in this eulogy. The demagogue is to the statesman what the "get-rich-quick" mining promoter is to the kind of financier I am discussing."

Dawes was to be much occupied that year with his effort for emergency currency legislation. He was president of the Chicago Bankers' Club in 1908 and caused some consternation among its

membership when he chose as its annual banquet speaker the un-
likeliest person conceivable: William Jennings Bryan.

Bryan, less than two months away from a practically unopposed
third-time Presidential nomination by the Democrats, appeared at
the dinner on May 23 and made it a momentous occasion for himself. He unexpectedly unveiled the paramount issue on which he
would campaign—the guarantee of bank deposits. Whether Bryan
knew it or not, Dawes had suggested this insurance for depositors
in his book published back in 1894.

Bryan also urged emergency currency legislation in his Chicago
Bankers' Club speech. It was an entirely different plan from that
which Dawes had advocated. In reality it was the multiplicity of
plans that held back any legislation now. Two groups, the backers
of the Aldrich bill on one hand and those of the Vreeland bill on
the other, were deadlocking the issue in sullen disagreement.

In the spring of 1908 Dawes appeared before the banking and
currency committee of the House of Representatives in Washington. Hostile at first, the committee rose and applauded him when
he had finished his statement.

"The absolute impossibility of the financial doctors of this
country uniting upon any one measure has been demonstrated,"
he told the committee. "No plan of any one man will become law.
With our diversified interests, our diversified opinions, and the great
breadth of the country, any bill passed will be a composite—a compromise."

"There are defects in the Aldrich bill and you should make
every effort to correct them. Fifteen years ago there was a panic and
there was no legislation afterwards. Last year we had another panic
and we came nearer than many people realize to going over the
brink. We are confronted with the necessity of remedial legislation
of some sort. Only at a time like this when the catastrophe is fresh
in the minds of the people can you get action. I am never a sym-
pathizer with the postponement of the correction of an evil. It does
not make any difference if it is fifty years before we need to use
this legislation; it should be passed now."

The Aldrich-Vreeland law which resulted remained on the
statute books for six years before it was replaced by the Glass-Owen
Federal Reserve Bank measure. In its short life, Dawes believed, it

averted a panic in 1913 when for the first time in this country there was an unprecedented liquidation of deposit credits and at the same time banks increased their loans to business and industry instead of constricting them.

In an interview given at the time of the passage of the bill, Dawes said:

"It is an imperfect law. It has defects which future Congresses will have to cure as they appear. But it will enable banks in reserve cities to pay their debts in times of panic. It is not a guarantee against financial panic. No law can be."

Dawes' part in the 1908 election was to be smaller than in previous years. Joseph G. Cannon seemed slated to hold the Illinois delegation as a favorite son. Dawes' friend, Vice-President Charles W. Fairbanks, who yearned to move into the White House, came to see him a number of times. But it was obvious that Theodore Roosevelt intended to pick his own successor, and that his favor would go to Secretary of War William Howard Taft.

Dawes recalled a luncheon with Taft and Secretary of State William R. Day many years before, shortly after McKinley had chosen Taft to head the Philippine Commission. Taft had bemoaned the fact that he would have to leave the circuit judgeship which he liked. But Dawes had said: "If you do a good job in the Philippines you are likely to be President of the United States."

Dawes himself, for the last few years, had hoped that Roosevelt would appoint Taft Chief Justice to succeed the aging Melville Weston Fuller. He supported Taft after the nomination but did not accede to Taft's request that he become treasurer of the Republican National Committee.

Once again, both the Republican and Democratic nominees were Dawes' close personal friends. He had shared many a lunch and dinner at Losekam's in Washington with his former law school mentor William Howard Taft. And Bryan had been close to him ever since the days in Lincoln when Bryan's gargantuan appetite had been accused of rendering the operation of Don Cameron's restaurant unprofitable.

"Whoever is elected this year," Dawes commented, "the country is in for a big board bill. It will be a lush four years for the White House grocer!"

While Dawes' long-standing battle for currency legislation had thus finally been successful, the outlook for his efforts to bring about clean party politics in Illinois had to grow much worse before it grew better.

William Lorimer had won a triumphant re-election to the House of Representatives. But his eye was still on a seat in the United States Senate.

Illinois held its first Senatorial preference primary in 1908. Lorimer did not enter it, and the choice went to Hopkins. But the primary was only an advisory one and the Illinois legislature would elect. The unwary Illinois reform element could hardly credit the reports which began to come out of Springfield in January. Lorimer was determined to put Hopkins aside and take the seat himself.

Few more loathsome scenes have ever been enacted in a state legislature than those which occurred in Springfield during the 125 days from January 20 to May 26, 1909. In that time, ninety-five ballots were taken. Hopkins had started with 90 votes, 13 short of a constitutional majority. On the ninety-fifth ballot, Lorimer, amid widespread charges of naked bribery and corruption, got 108 votes, 5 more than a majority. This vote was made up of 53 Democrats and 55 Republicans, the first time in history that an almost equal alliance of Democrats and Republicans had elected a Senator. There was scant doubt of the methods used to bring the needed final votes to the Lorimer side.

Dawes was shocked that Lorimer could be elected a Senator from Illinois. He made a rather gloomy memorandum on the political outlook:

"The United States has become the wealthiest nation the world has ever known. Its form of government is now undergoing severe tests. The discontent, which prosperity seems to foster in the people almost as much as extreme poverty does, is diverted largely now toward large corporations as well as toward the widespread corruption in politics.

"The attractions and profits in business life are such that, unlike fifty years ago, our strongest men seek business instead of public careers. As was once the case in Rome when it was difficult to find good men who were willing to take public office, it is now almost impossible to get the best class of our citizens interested in office holding. Our state legislatures are largely corrupt. Many of our municipal governments, through reforms, are seemingly making more progress toward better conditions than any other of our governing agencies."

Although William Lorimer's right to his seat in the Senate was under fire from the day he took the oath of office, it was not until July 13, 1912, that the Senate adopted a resolution declaring that "corrupt methods and practices were involved in his election, and that the election, therefore, was invalid."

In 1909 Dawes had purchased a large straw-colored brick house in Evanston. Aged oak trees threw their cooling shade over the tile roof and the round corner towers that were popular in the nineties. The lawn, smooth as a putting green, reached to the shores of Lake Michigan. The ample stables housed only the riding horse of Mrs. Dawes. Dawes' automobile stood in the adjacent garage.

It was the second home he had owned, and while the little house on D Street in Lincoln had been rather tight, the Evanston home was large for his present needs. His son, Rufus Fearing, was ready to enter Princeton, and his daughter Carolyn was about to depart for the Misses Masters School at Dobbs Ferry. But it gave him space to house and expand his fine library and to offer to his friends the musical entertainment of which he was so fond.

Dawes' unquenchable love of music had involved him in another "good steady job without pay"—that of raising money for the Chicago Grand Opera Company. How it came about is told in his diary for the year 1910:

"I went to a luncheon where a few Chicago people met Phillip M. Lydig of New York. It seemed that Clarence H. Mackey, Otto H. Kahn, and Lydig had expected Chicago people would subscribe for $300,000 in a new grand opera company, New York to take $200,000. J. C. Shaffer had raised $100,000 in Chicago but the enterprise was at a halt and the New York people, having on the face of their Chicago expectations entered into contracts involving over

$200,000, were in an embarrassing situation. This is why I have had so much to do with opera. Harold McCormick and I raised enough money through stock subscriptions to put the enterprise on its feet, when added to what Shaffer had already raised.

"This naturally put us at the head of the business, and McCormick, Shaffer, and I have certainly had an experience. Nobody here pays much attention to its business except us. It has been enjoyable work in many ways. The Company lost about $260,000 the first season—only about $60,000 was lost in Chicago, the rest in the East. We had to raise $134,000 to try it again the next season. We have to average $7,500 per night to break even, which thought consoles me for having failed to take up the business of impresario for a life's work."

In 1911 Dawes entered the musical world also as a composer. He wrote his "Melody in A Major" at one sitting, with no thought of publication, as a simple piano score, cobbled it some more for the violin, and thought perhaps he would, if a leisure time ever came, make an orchestration of it.

At Marietta, at Lincoln, and later in Chicago and Washington he had many friends among musicians. When they came to his house Dawes would take part with them in trios, quartets, and quintets. He had taken a particular interest in Francis MacMillan, the violinist, and sponsored his first appearance in this country before an enraptured audience in Orchestra Hall in Chicago.

When MacMillan was next in Chicago after Dawes had composed the "Melody," he played it and thought it excellent.

"It's just a tune that I got in my head, so I set it down," Dawes told MacMillan, "I never gave the thing a name. If you want it you can have it. It has served its purpose as a diversion for me."

Dawes was under the impression that MacMillan sold it to a publisher for $100. His first feeling when he became aware that he was an acknowledged composer was one of chagrin.

"No one told me it had been published," he said. "I was walking down State Street and came to a music shop. I saw a poster size picture of myself, my name plastered all over the window in large letters and the window space entirely filled with the sheet music.

"My business is that of a banker and few bankers have won

renown as composers of music. I know that I will be the target of my punster friends. They will say that if all the notes in my bank are as bad as my musical ones, they are not worth the paper they were written on.

"I never studied music at all, never received instructions on any instrument. I think my parents were afraid I might become a musician, so they discouraged my taking lessons. I always had an intense love for music and what little I know I taught myself. The flute was the smallest of the instruments so it was the easiest to smuggle into my room and then, too, it was not as noisy as most of the others. So that was the instrument I learned to play."

The original "Melody" copyright was followed by eleven others. They included a piano music-roll arrangement by Milton Suskind, an arrangement for the piano by Marie Edwards von Ritter, a pipe organ version, an arrangement by Adolph G. Hoffman for large orchestra, another for small orchestra, and one by Sydney Baynes of Great Britain, also for orchestra, an arrangement for a waltz by Harry L. Alford, for an alto saxophone by Rudy Wiedoeft, and an adaption called "Let Me Dream"—words and arrangement by Don Wilson. Dawes himself helped Carleton L. Colby to make an arrangement for a military band.

Fritz Kreisler, in January of 1922, added the Dawes composition to his repertoire.

In 1923, Kreisler explained to Dawes how it was chosen:

"When I was on tour it was my custom to try out new music, with Mrs. Kreisler playing the accompaniments. This piece came to me in a great bundle sent by a publisher for my consideration. When we tried it out, Mrs. Kreisler exclaimed:

"'This is a good one.'

"I was glad to hear her say so as it had also taken my fancy because of its tunefulness and its strong musical value. I had no idea the author was a famous man."

But Dawes replied:

"I was not but you are making me famous."

As a phonograph record, Dawes' song, in the month of its greatest popularity, sold 30,000 copies. And in 1951 the "Melody in A Major" was revived and had a run on radio, television, and records under the name "It's All in the Game."

Bread wagons and operas were but a few of the many extra-curricular activities Dawes undertook either on his own initiative or because they were saddled upon him by others. With Carter H. Harrison he was receiver for the Chicago, Milwaukee Electric Railway, with D. Forgan receiver for the Illinois Tunnel Company which had made the first grandiose effort to build a Chicago passenger subway. He also was president of the Home for Destitute Crippled Children, a job which took more of his time, he said, than any other chore, "in settling, or endeavoring to settle, various rows in regard to management between a very able staff of physicians and a very able house committee of women."

Dawes read a great deal, made numerous speeches, and occasionally wrote on invitation articles for the *Saturday Evening Post*, *Pearson's Magazine*, and the *National Magazine*. At the same time, he was in 1911 absorbing several other banks into the Central Trust Company, and buying and selling utilities from the Pacific Coast to the Gulf of Mexico. Yet the notes in his diary for that year are written in the debonair tone of a man half at work and half at play:

"Palm Beach—February: I took a flight in a hydroplane with my friend Walter Brookins, the aviator." Considering the frail aircraft of those days, this showed real courage.

There is also a record of a leisurely visit to Supreme Court Justice Day in Washington. Day was giving a dinner for his eight brethren on the Supreme Court Bench, and Dawes was the only outsider present.

"There was at the time as there seems always to have been in this country a public discussion of the ages of the Judges," he wrote. "The dinner turned into a humorous discussion of senility and an effort to assess the mental infirmities of the various members of the Court. Most of the Justices gave very candid estimates of their mental powers or lack thereof. Holmes explored his own mental vigor with great self-insight and objectivity and much wit. It was the consensus (as near as the court ever comes to unanimity) that McKenna was the most senile.

"Chief Justice White delivered the opinion of the Court. McKenna dissented. He admitted senescense but denied senility.

There is a bond of mutual affection between the portly Chief Justice and agile little McKenna. None of the Justices appeared to me to be suffering from mental or physical fatigue. They seemed to eat what they wanted. They have a great variety of interests and all put in long hours at work. I was impressed by Chief Justice White, a man of immense vitality and understanding. Charles Evans Hughes has a fine mind and is more sociable than I had heard."

At the time of the dinner, Harlan, the oldest member of Court, was 80, Holmes 70, McKenna 68, White 66, and Hughes 49.

For months before Lorimer's expulsion from the Senate, Dawes had been deep in behind-the-scenes activity in the campaign of Lawrence Y. Sherman, who sought to unseat Shelby M. Cullom. It was no soft undertaking, for Cullom had represented Illinois in the United States Senate for thirty years.

"Sherman has been going around the state with a change of clothing in a paper gripsack," Dawes wrote. "He was my staunch ally when I sought the Senate seat and I owe him a ten-year-old debt of gratitude. Sherman has written more progressive legislation for Illinois than any other man. No one has remained in public life at a greater sacrifice to himself. I am going to do everything I can to help him."

Thirty days before the primary election of April, 1912, Dawes left his bank desk, organized Sherman's campaign for a rousing wind-up tour and raised enough money to put him on the same kind of special train as gubernatorial candidate Deneen was using. Sherman defeated Cullom for the advisory preference by 40,000 votes. But in 1912, Republican nomination did not mean certain election. It would be nearly a year before Sherman knew whether or not he was to have a Senate seat.

Dawes declined election as a delegate-at-large from Illinois to the 1912 Republican national convention, giving as one reason that it seemed at that time Theodore Roosevelt would be the nominee for President.

"I would not," he wrote, "be a member of a convention whose probable nominee I would not later support at the polls."

During the 1912 convention Mr. and Mrs. George B. Cortelyou, who had come to Chicago from New York, were guests at the Dawes home. Cortelyou now resided in New York and was president of the Consolidated Gas Company.

"Together Cortelyou and I watched the proceedings from the outside," Dawes wrote, "though we both were invited to participate in the respective conferences—Cortelyou by the Roosevelt managers and I by the Taft managers.

"The convention and the factions were led by noisy men of small mental caliber. As I went over to the hotels where the leaders congregated and saw them and reflected upon the greatness of the occasion and the vastness of the country whose interests are at stake, I was reminded of bats in a deserted church."

After a bitter conflict the convention nominated Taft in the fetid heat of the Coliseum. With the announcement of the ballot's result, a band somewhere in the rafters of the vast hall struck up, "Waltz Me Around Again, Willie." There was a faint ripple of applause. The delegates were perfectly sure that William Howard Taft and the party of the Elephant were not going to waltz to victory this time.

In September, after the Republican schism and the entry of Roosevelt into the Presidential race on the Bull Moose ticket, Dawes wrote a memorandum:

"I suppose in after years, it may be interesting to me to note my present feelings as to the political prospects. I early had an admiration for Theodore Roosevelt, believing him to be all that was commendable in public leadership. Believing in him and his motives, as my personal contact with him and his associates gradually opened my eyes, I was shocked and surprised long ago as many have been since. Vast multitudes still believe in him, but I do not think he can be elected. There would be no logic in his election. If he proves anything but one of the leaders in a political faction hereafter I shall be surprised. But a leader of some kind he will always be."

The Republican split put Woodrow Wilson in the White House. Edward Dunne, an able Democrat, moved into the State House at Springfield. The legislature was so closely divided between Republicans and Democrats that for a time it appeared Illinois would have no United States Senator. It was only through the prestige of Governor Dunne that the deadlock was resolved. Dunne brought about the election of James Hamilton Lewis to the Cullom vacancy for which Lewis had the Democratic, Sherman the Republican nomination. Thus Lewis got a six-year term in the Senate, while Sherman, completing first Lorimer's unexpired term, began eight years of service as a Senator. Dawes' long-standing battle for clean party politics in Illinois had at last been won.

Chapter Eleven

❁

GRIEF, AND A MEMORIAL

$\mathcal{I}$n 1912, tragedy struck the home of Mr. and Mrs. Dawes. On September 5, their only son, twenty-two-year-old Rufus Fearing, was drowned in Lake Geneva, Wisconsin.

Young Dawes had foregone his summer vacation to work in the Dawes gas plant at Chicago Heights. He was to spend one more year at Princeton and then, after an apprenticeship, assume the management of one of his father's utilities. Eventually, Dawes had hoped the quiet, serious youth would succeed him in all his business enterprises.

"I had told him," Dawes wrote, "that I had decided, in view of his industry and his abilities and character, he was fitted to bear heavy responsibility early in life and yet, for the proper development of his qualities, he must early have the opportunity to work out, without the sense of assistance from me, the achievement of his higher success and standing. He would thus feel that he must rely upon himself and, in the advance of a business for which he was solely responsible, find the measure of his capacity."

Rufus Fearing had been a star athlete at Lawrenceville. He had, however, suffered an attack of typhoid fever while with a surveying party in South Dakota in 1908, which left him with a weakened heart. As a result, he played neither baseball nor football at Princeton, but was captain of the fencing team.

The death of his son was the great sorrow of Dawes' life. On the night after his death, Dawes wrote an estimate of the boy's character, to be read by Rev. Frank W. Gunsaulus at the funeral.

The tribute attracted wide attention, and hundreds of thousands of copies of it were distributed by the YMCA.

In addition to this widely circulated tribute, he had put down in his diary an eulogy of his son, written for his eyes alone. They evoke an echo of the words with which Rufus Dawes had bid farewell to his son Charles back in 1887: "Charles, I think you are possessed of a sufficient sense of values not to confuse the false shadow of fame or the acquirement of wealth with the substance of solid achievement. You may some day win both fame and wealth, or you may win neither. I can only say to you what I have said to you before: The only success in life is the development of character!" A quarter of a century later, Charles Dawes' farewell to his son Rufus Fearing shows how much that Dawes family tradition had been kept alive through two generations:

"My son's life was noble and useful. I will put down some of the salient points of his character. His mind was most unusual. It was thorough and quick. He was a thinker and philosopher—an exact investigator. He had a retentive memory. He formed just conclusions. His opinions I found at all times to be sound and original. He had remarkable self-discipline. He never complained, no matter what hardships he was enduring. He was of a very cheerful disposition and had a fine sense of humor. He abhorred arrogance. He stood unflinchingly by his principles. He was exact in money matters yet extremely generous. He counted wealth as little, recognizing the true nobility of labor. He was kindly. He had taken me, asking me to help them, among the poor and lowly of the earth. In all his life I found nothing to regret. He died with all the noble illusions of a high-minded youth undisturbed and undispelled."

As the last entry in the little stack of journals in which he had recorded happenings or impressions in his new home in the West, as a young married man and as a lawyer, industrialist, public official, and banker, Dawes put down this notation:

"I bring this journal to a close by writing of my son even though my broken heart must suffer much in doing it. I have kept this journal for nearly twenty-five years. In reality, what I have put down for the past twenty years was intended entirely for him to read, and now that he has gone I have no heart further to continue it.

"My boy lived long enough to win out. Whatever the years added would only be material. In a man's character is his real career. All that my dear wife and I have ever found in him has been joy and pride and splendid hope. This hope we have in each other that we will do as he would have us do—that we will live for others than ourselves; that through us and our strength the weak shall be lifted up; the hungry and cold cared for; the suffering comforted.

"We must work, but we must do it only to give the more. We must fight our grief in order that with unhindered powers we may strive in larger and more generous ways to be useful. May God give us the strength and the will and the love and the power to help in the years left to us in greater measure those less blessed than ourselves. *Finis.*"

In the tribute to his son, Charles Dawes had extended a lasting invitation to all of his son's friends. "He loved his friends," Dawes had written, "and but recently told his mother that our house was all through the coming years to be the stopping place for his college friends passing through the city. How grateful our lonely hearts will be to them now if they will only accept this invitation and sleep in his room and fill for a little time the empty chair." The first of Rufus' many and close friends to come was Roger W. Straus, his Princeton classmate.

But now Charles Dawes, who within a year after his son's death had adopted a son and a daughter, was to extend hospitality on a much vaster scale.

Chicago was the showcase of the bustling, fast-building West. The more the West grew, the more Chicago grew. Just as Chicago factories furnished the material that went into the building of the West, so also did Chicago furnish a great part of the human catalyst for the surging development of the West's raw wealth. It was the barracks of the largest seasonal labor army in the world. These migratory workers created for Chicago a problem of which Dawes quickly took notice. Annually, about May 1, that army would move into a dozen Western states to lay railroad tracks, grade roadbeds, dig drainage ditches, aid harvesting. When cold weather came around November 1, it moved back to Chicago. It had nowhere else to go. There it would get along as best it could until the next spring, when employers would come again to dip into the man-power pool.

Perhaps one alcoholic spree after the return would take the earnings for a man's summer of hard work. Few of the laborers managed to get through the winter on the summer's savings. In bitter winter weather, they found shelter in Chicago's flop or "scratch" houses on South Clark, South State, and West Madison Streets. There was the year-around problem that the West and even Chicago's seasonal demand never absorbed all of the workers. The unneeded found a day's work in Chicago when they could. When Dawes returned to Chicago after five years of public service in the McKinley administration, he found conditions among this class of laborers more distressing than when he left.

The bread wagon he ran in Chicago for the next few winters to dispense hot coffee and sandwiches to long shuffling lines of shivering men he did not feel was enough. He was providing food but no shelter. His fortune by now had reached the point where he could build and assure the continued operation of a place which would provide both food and shelter.

The Rufus F. Dawes Hotel for Men, Chicago's first endowed home for the unemployed, opened on January 2, 1914, with 300 guests. It had 303 beds and was the Ritz-Carlton of the unemployed. Charles Dawes had set up the endowment and spent $385,000 on the building of the institution which, in his own words, was intended "as a memorial to my son who had shown deep interest in the conditions which this hotel is designed to meet."

Many people had warned him against the enterprise. First of all, the cautious voices had said, he would have trouble with drunkards. Dawes replied:

"A drunken man can freeze to death just the same as a sober one. I would hate to be the man who made the decision on admittance with the thermometer ten degrees below zero."

The new hotel opened in a blinding snowstorm. It never had any trouble with drunken people. Since the guests turned their clothes in to be fumigated, and received nightshirts in the meantime, it was impossible for them to carry liquor. Dawes' instructions to the hotel staff were plain: "The purpose of this hotel is to take care of people whom no one else cares to take care of. They are our guests just as people are guests at any hotel. They must not be made to feel that they are objects of charity. The bills are small, but our guests pay them, and they can depart with their self-respect unimpaired."

The bills were indeed small. A bed cost six cents. For ten cents, a guest got a separate room. A menu posted at the hotel's opening gave these prices:

Meat hash and beans	3 cents	*Mutton stew with*	
Coffee, with milk and		*bread*	3 cents
sugar	2 cents	*Soup with bread*	2 cents
Roll	1 cent	*Doughnut*	1 cent
Macaroni and bread	3 cents	*Baked beans and bread*	3 cents
	Pie, all varieties	3 cents	

In the cheery lobby of the hotel was a huge painting of the Battle of Lake Erie, and Lawrence's legend:

DON'T GIVE UP THE SHIP.

Dawes' hotel, "a ladder for the down and out," was successful from the first. It took business away from Hogan's Flop and other places along Chicago's filthy, dreary, cruel Skid Row. Even the IWW rooming house nearby charged ten cents for sleeping on the floor.

There was a game room in the basement of the Dawes Hotel, and a reading room with newspapers, magazines, and books. The hotel provided a place where guests might shave and shine their shoes. "A clean face and well-blacked shoes create confidence." The only rule enforced by the hotel not enforced by standard hotels was that it required guests to take daily baths.

Many of the seasonal laboring men who went to jobs in the West made arrangement on their return for winter hotel accommodations. For eighteen dollars a comfortable room could be obtained for six months.

In its first two years, the hotel furnished 294,222 lodgings with bath, at five cents each; 62,770 baths with lodgings in separate rooms at ten cents each; meals running into the hundreds of thousands at an average price of six cents. Its free employment agency found jobs for thousands.

So successful was the hotel that it led to the organization of the Rufus F. Dawes Hotel Association "to own and operate hotels, restaurants, and lodging houses whereat the needy, the unemployed, and men of impaired means may procure food and lodging at prices within their ability to pay; and if, as a result of its operations, any profits shall accrue to said corporation, the same shall never be distributed among the members of the corporation but shall be forever dedicated and shall be devoted to aiding the poor and needy in such manner as the trustees shall from time to time determine."

At the end of the first year's operation, Dawes made the longest statement he ever made concerning the hotel, in which he said:

"The purpose of the Rufus F. Dawes Hotel, as operated by Henry M. Dawes and myself, is to provide men with accommodations at reasonable figures. It is no different from any other hotel except that its charges are lower.

"It assumes that its guests are gentlemen and appreciative of gentlemanly treatment. The fact that in the operations of the hotel a deficit results is not made the excuse by the management for any different treatment of guests than is customary in other first-class hotels. However sympathetic with religious, educational, and charitable work I might be—and I am so—if I went as a paying guest to a first-class hotel and found the management solicitous as to my mental state, religious beliefs, and daily occupation, and insisting upon my listening to unsolicited advice or religious or educational addresses, I would regard it as an insult and an assumption of inferiority on my part and superiority on theirs, unjustified by the nature of our relationship.

"Accordingly, the Rufus F. Dawes Hotel management, proceeding on the idea that its guests are not to be considered as a class or species, or anything but American citizens, has succeeded beyond our best expectations. There are no rules in the hotel different from any other first-class hotel, save those relating to sanitation. I make the assertion that there is no hotel in the country, accommodating anything like an equal number of guests, that has as little trouble with its patrons as ourselves. In fact, we have no trouble at all."

The second Rufus F. Dawes Hotel for Men was built in Boston and opened January 7, 1916. It had double the capacity of the one in Chicago. Over the fireplace in the lobby of this hotel hung the portrait of William Dawes, great-great-grandfather of Charles G.

Dawes. He was the man who rode with Paul Revere on the memorable night in April, 1775.

Not quite three years later, on February 17, 1917, the Mary Dawes Hotel for Women was opened in Chicago. It had 250 rooms at ten, twenty, and thirty cents per night. Meals were seven cents. It was highly successful and, one year, made $5,000. This hotel was named for the mother of Charles G. Dawes. Off the lobby was a cheerful, well-furnished living room. There were living rooms, sewing rooms, and laundry rooms.

Again there had been well-meaning warnings. Dawes was told that good girls would not go to the hotel unless he took every precaution to keep immoral women out. Dawes' reply was characteristic:

"I have seen women of doubtful morality in every hotel I have ever been in. There is a hotel in New York with the best-known name of any hotel in the United States and such women, in diamonds and tiaras, go there. Hotels seem to take them in and welcome them. We will operate on the same basis that the biggest hotels of the country do."

In the twenty years the Mary Dawes Hotel ran, it never had a complaint about the morals of its women guests.

To the manager and clerical employees of the Mary Dawes Hotel, Dawes issued these instructions:

"We are simply hotelkeepers, and the Mary Dawes Hotel is nothing but a hotel run as a first-class respectable place, differing from other hotels only in its cheaper prices. Since our guests pay for our service, we assume no right as hotelkeepers to inquire into their private affairs. There is nothing in the fact that one becomes our paying guest, either in our hotels for men or for women, which should subject him or her to any other restrictions than if a larger rate per day was being charged.

"We wish to assure our patrons that so long as they are orderly and deport themselves properly while in our hotels, their independence will not be interfered with, nor will they be affronted by unasked advice and interference in their private affairs.

"At the Rufus Dawes Hotels in Boston and Chicago in the last three years, we have registered and cared for over 500,000 guests, and we claim that at no hotel charging fifty times their rates is better order observed or greater appreciation of others shown by guests.

"The purpose of the Mary Dawes Hotel will have failed if it does not demonstrate that our women guests, in all the finer essentials, are the equal of our guests at the men's hotels; that they as fully resent unwarranted curiosity in their private affairs; that they as fully appreciate independence; that they as fully appreciate respectable surroundings and the respectable deportment of others —in other words that, as a whole, they will match respectable treatment with respectable conduct."

Things did not come off quite smoothly when the Mary Dawes Hotel in Chicago opened. But Dawes did not give any thought to the threatening disturbance, and how it was conquered, until many years later when he, then Vice-President of the United States, came back to Chicago for a visit.

"As we stepped out of the hotel tonight," he then wrote, "a well-dressed young man was waiting for us. 'I am Joe,' he said, and then all of that first evening when we opened the Mary Dawes Hotel came back to me in recollection. 'Little Joe' (he was then) was a young hoodlum born in the alley behind the hotel, and he was the leader of an active gang of young ruffians of about twelve years of age. On the opening night, these ragamuffins gathered in force and so annoyed the crowds of guests and visitors coming in at the front door that an attendant started to telephone for the police.

"Fortunately, I heard him and, stopping him, decided on another course of action. I stepped out into the yelling crowd of youngsters and said I wanted them to come in and have supper with me. Joe, much embarrassed, accepted for all, and I entered the hotel with the lot. Their procession created something of a sensation. Treated like gentlemen, they acted like gentlemen. Without a murmur, they submitted themselves to Mrs. Dawes and Miss Decker, who scrubbed their faces and hands for them before they sat down at a table with Mother at one end and myself at the other. They were rather subdued, but my how they ate—and especially the ice cream!

"One of the little fellows told me his father had just come home, and when I asked where his father had been, he said, 'In jail.' This was Joe, and Joe told me then that the boys would 'always be nice to the hotel,' and he would do any work he could at any time, 'fur nuthin'.' And so all these years the boys have been 'nice to the hotel,' and the manager told me that Joe has called constantly ever since that time to ask how he could help. For some time I kept track of him, but I had not seen him for years before tonight. He is now a chauffeur—honest, well-behaved, and successful. Why don't we realize more the enormous returns which come from little kindnesses? And these returns come oftenest when we need them most, when the sun is setting and the day's work is almost done."

Also many years later, he noted: "I never visit these hotels without happiness. Since the hotels have opened, many instances have occurred of the most beautiful of all charities: that of the poor for the very poor, of the suffering for those who are perishing. On bitter cold nights, the streets of every great city are a Gethsemane for many of the homeless and half-clad poor, some of them brought to their condition through no fault of their own, but all of them with a right to help if the religion of Christ means anything. On such nights, the Rufus Dawes hotel is filled to overflowing, and then is when it does the most good.

"Late one winter night, when the thermometer stood at ten degrees below zero, and after the doors of the hotel had been closed, John Hanson, the manager, heard a persistent knocking at the door. Opening it, he found a shivering and thinly clad man and, beside him, sitting on a wheeled board that could be propelled by hand, was another man without any legs. The first man explained that his friend, the cripple, was sure to 'go under' during the night unless he got shelter. He said he was all right himself and could stay out.

"To pay for a lodging for the cripple, he held in his hand two postage stamps, which was all he had, and asked John to take them in lieu of the regular charge of five cents. Of course, they were both cared for—but if that one thing had been its only service, it earned its cost that night."

All three hotels continued to be operated for a considerable length of time, even after the Federal Government assumed the burden of relief. In 1939 Charles Dawes gave the Rufus F. Dawes Hotel in Chicago to the Chicago Community Trust which, in turn, leased it to the Chicago Industrial League for one dollar per year and continued to operate it in the same manner as Dawes had done.

The Mary Dawes Hotel in Chicago was deeded to the Trustees of the Dawes Arboretum of Newark, Ohio, in 1938, and was subsequently sold for use as a lodging house. The Rufus F. Dawes Hotel in Boston was given to the Boston Industrial Home and, as this is written, is still being operated on the same basis under the name, "The Rufus F. Dawes Hotel, a Refuge for Unfortunate Men."

In later years, when Dawes, much to his regret, found himself in the limelight, newspaper reporters and even friends would often ask him:

"Tell us something about your charities!"

"Charities?" Dawes would reply. "I have no charities. At times I have tried to help some people—that is all."

Dawes came up to the Republican national convention in 1916 with the possibility that he might play a decisive part in the naming of the party's Presidential candidate. He might even come out of the convention with his long-time ally, Senator Lawrence Y. Sherman, as the nominee. A game apparently was coming up in which any hand well played could be the winning one, and Dawes sat with a good hand. The sixty-six delegates of Illinois were instructed for Sherman. Bewildered by the situation in which he found himself, Sherman asked Dawes to assume command.

Never did a political party gather in greater confusion than did the Republicans when they assembled for their national convention in Chicago in June. There was the certainty that a record number of names (nineteen) would be placed before the convention for its Presidential nomination. The man whom the majority of the party obviously wanted to lead it was Charles Evans Hughes. Dawes then had only a slight acquaintance with Hughes, who sat untouchably on the United States Supreme Court, and no one had the answer to the question of whether he would accept if nominated. The man who wanted most intensely to be nominated was Theodore Roosevelt, and he was the one Republican Dawes would not support in the fall election if he were nominated.

The Republicans were not to have the stage alone. As the GOP met in the Coliseum, the Bull Moose met downtown in the Auditorium, ready for a coalition if the Republicans nominated Roosevelt, ready to go it alone if some one other than Roosevelt carried the day in the Republican convention.

An unpublicized preview of the convention was run under the heavily beamed ceiling of the 40-by-100 living room of the Dawes home in Evanston on Sunday, June 4, with most of the candidates other than Roosevelt and Hughes represented. In the long discussion, the most important statements were made by Dawes and Senator James W. Wadsworth of New York.

Dawes told the conferees he believed Hughes, if nominated and elected, would be a great President, but he thought he would be hard to elect. Dawes believed either Sherman, Cummins, Theodore E. Burton of Ohio, or perhaps Fairbanks would make a better candidate.

"Wilson will be no easy man to beat," Dawes told the gathering. "In the Middle West, a case will have to be made that he ought to be beaten. Any Republican candidate will carry the East, but the election will be won between the western border of Pennsylvania and the Pacific Ocean, and I think a Western man will do better in this great area. I do not believe Theodore Roosevelt can get, under any conceivable situation which can arise in this convention, as many as 150 votes, so it will be Hughes or one of the men represented here."

Wadsworth interjected: "I represent the New York delegation, which is for Elihu Root, but Charles E. Hughes is its second choice. If conditions arise where Hughes can get the nomination and Root cannot, New York will break to Hughes."

Wadsworth's statement ended the meeting. With the New York delegation ready to support Hughes, there could be no fusion of the other candidates. The convention's outcome was foreshadowed.

On Friday word-weary delegates heard more than a dozen Presidential candidates nominated. The biggest noise-making came when Senator Albert B. Fall of New Mexico put Roosevelt's name before the convention, but the cheers were from the galleries and not the delegate sections. On the first ballot even favorite son Sherman outpolled Roosevelt by one vote, 66 to TR's 65. To Hughes went 253, a fourth of the total convention strength. Only Weeks with 105 and Root with 103 exceeded the 100 mark.

On Saturday, June 10, the third ballot gave Hughes 949½ votes.

Roosevelt got 18½. Charles W. Fairbanks for Vice-President completed the ticket. The Bull Moose got word of the Republican outcome and nominated Roosevelt for President and Governor John M. Parker of Louisiana for Vice-President. Denied the Republican nomination, Roosevelt declined the Bull Moose proffer. He had no taste for another third-party race.

Dawes' June prediction that Hughes would have great difficulty in the central and western farm belt was borne out. Such Republican dependables as Ohio, Kansas, Nebraska, and North Dakota were in the Democratic column in November and Indiana and Minnesota were barely saved. California also deserted the G.O.P. Wilson won another four years in the White House by the narrowest of margins.

Chapter Twelve

❁

WAR

On June 28, 1914, Archduke Francis Ferdinand of Austria fell to the attack of a Serbian assassin. Within less than three months nearly a dozen European and Asiatic nations had become involved in the great slaughter of World War I.

The effects of the conflagration were felt at once in the United States.

"The old landmarks by which we could guide ourselves and formulate our plans have been swept away," Dawes said in an address at the Chicago Union League Club in November, 1914. "A large part of the world has reverted to barbarism. How much this war will affect us as a nation, or whether we will be drawn into it, no one can now tell. If it is much prolonged, it is extremely doubtful that it can be kept within the limits of Europe, Asia, and Africa. There must be preparedness in this nation which wants no war. There must be national preparedness and individual preparedness. I do not, for instance, know what the day's work may be for me. The world may be on the threshold of an elemental convulsion of humanity which will last for a century. Certainly the loss of life and the waste of wealth which this war will bring will profoundly shake the world."

On May 7, 1915, a German submarine sank the Cunard liner *Lusitania*. President Wilson sent a warning to Germany on May 13, another one on June 9. Secretary of State William Jennings Bryan, unwilling to support the President's second note to Germany, resigned his office. Later he came to Chicago and visited Dawes.

164

"Bryan asked me to introduce him to the Chautauqua audience in Edgewater," Dawes wrote. "I could not refuse, yet I felt a little ashamed that a man who so lately had held the high post of Secretary of State should be so engaged. I was somewhat more ashamed of both of us while we waited backstage for our appearance before the audience. We were surrounded by tumblers, and there were a bear and a bear-wrestler next to us. It was a hot day, and Bryan and I were the only ones of the gathering who had on many clothes."

Dawes was once more in disagreement with Bryan. Bryan opposed the Anglo-French loan. Dawes was the first banker in Chicago to back it. On September 16 he announced that the Central Trust Company would take a half-million-dollar participation.

Other sinkings of American vessels by German submarines followed. In April of 1917 the nation went to war.

Theodore Roosevelt hurried to Washington and asked Wilson for permission to lead a volunteer army division overseas. Instead, Wilson made the dramatic surprise announcement that there would be an American Expeditionary Force to Europe, commanded by Major General John J. Pershing. William Jennings Bryan made headlines by announcing he would try to enlist as a private, something he never did, however.

Charles Gates Dawes, in May of 1917, closed his desk in his bank and put on uniform.

As a youth, Dawes had run levels for a surveying party of the Marietta, Columbus and Northern Railroad in Athens County, Ohio. The proceeds had helped him to pay his way through Cincinnati Law School. Now, thirty-three years later, that experience furnished his qualification for service in the Western European shooting zone. Engineers, he knew, would be the first, or among the first, American troops to reach the battle front, and that was where he wanted to be.

At fifty-one, and with an ankle separation that frequently put him on crutches, Dawes did not appear too promising a candidate for an Engineer's commission. He had, however, potent friends, among them the Commander in Chief of the American Expeditionary Forces, John J. Pershing. In May Pershing informed him that a commission as major in the Corps of Army Engineers would be forthcoming.

"Charley," Pershing said, "I once thought I would follow you into law, but I never imagined you would follow me into the Army."

While Pershing was merely surprised to see Dawes in uniform, others were dismayed. Among them was forty-three-year-old Herbert Hoover, who had just been selected as the United States Food Administrator. Hoover urged Dawes to abandon his military career at once and head a new organization to control grain prices in the United States.

"Hoover talked to me for an hour or so and was very emphatic in his invitation. He said: 'I can find a hundred men who will make better lieutenant colonels of engineers, and I want you right here.' Hoover is an extremely able man. He will succeed if anyone can in the difficult task that confronts him."

But Dawes stood firm. Late in May he joined his regiment, the 17th Engineers, for training in Atlanta. The regiment was made up of 750 engineers from the South and 350 from the North, under the command of Colonel John S. Sewell. Dawes had personally recruited forty of them at Marietta, and others from among railroad friends. It was just the kind of an outfit he liked. Moreover, there was reliable information that, come August, the 17th Regiment would be in steel helmets and gas masks, building narrow-gauge railroads behind the French lines.

Dawes organized a band out of the enlisted personnel of the 17th Engineers, and when he found that the Army would be slow in getting instruments, he purchased them himself and presented them to the musicians. His ankle gave him no trouble. He soon reached the rank of lieutenant colonel.

"The tactics became a little hard for me, but I was soon drilling a battalion and feeling thoroughly at home in it. Hoover gave me a great scare by wiring: 'Would you bear me implacable resentment if I asked the President to assign you to me?' I wired back: 'Under no circumstances do such a thing. It would be unfair and cruel, and I know you would not consider it.'" That was the last Dawes was to hear from Hoover for some time.

The 17th Engineers reached New York on July 28 and embarked on the *Carmania*. The *Carmania* arrived in Liverpool on August 11, after zigzagging its way through the submarine zone. Dawes had not been idle on the way over. Colonel Sewell placed him in command of regimental boat drill. Dawes slept with his clothes on, in the after wheelhouse near the after island, which was to be his post if there were a submarine attack. He devised a method of getting men on deck most expeditiously opposite their boats and rafts. He figured the time required to get men from the hold into ships of all sizes. Learning that no drill manual existed for the landsmen who would follow, Dawes wrote one and sent it to Pershing. It was adopted as standard by the United States and used on all the transports. Those ships carried two million soldiers to Europe.

The 17th Engineers were the first American troops to reach London. Through cheering throngs they marched past Buckingham Palace and were reviewed by King George, Queen Mary, and American Ambassador Walter Hines Page.

Dawes was giving a dinner for the officers of the regiment at the Ritz when a sudden order came to embark immediately for France. The 17th crossed the channel to Havre on a cattle boat.

"We officers slept on a floor so crowded that if anyone left his place in the night to go on deck, the natural expansion that ensued made it impossible for him to get back and find space enough to lie down in. As a result, he slept thereafter on deck. It was a contrast to the Ritz in London."

The 17th went to St. Nazaire, supposedly on its way to the front. At St. Nazaire, Dawes occupied his time by making a study of the facilities of that base and what ought to be done to prepare it for the immense number of American troops and the large amount of freight that would be unloaded here. He prepared and sent to Pershing a preliminary report recommending reconstruction of railroad facilities, additional wooden docks, the use of machinery instead of manpower for boat unloading, and other improvements. Pershing was to adopt all of them.

But no orders came for the 17th to move. It heard that the 13th Regiment was at the front building the narrow-gauge railroads the 17th had expected to build. Dawes went to Paris to carry to Pershing the protest of the indignant 17th against being held away from the front. The Commander in Chief of the A.E.F. lost no time in telling Dawes he intended to detach him from his present duties and assign him as head of an organization, to be known as the General Purchasing Board of the Army, which would coordinate, control, supervise, and direct all purchasing for the United States Army in Europe.

The way Pershing had plunged into his job impressed Dawes. He wrote:

"Pershing is the man for this emergency. He has a great faculty for disposing of things. He is not only a great soldier but has great common sense and tremendous energy. He has made me the head of a board of ten officers, representing all the purchasing departments of our Army, including also the Red Cross and the Army YMCA. He gives me practically unlimited discretion and authority to go ahead and devise a system of purchasing; to organize the board; to arrange liaison connections between the French and English army boards and our own; to use any method which may seem wise to secure supplies for the Army in Europe, thus relieving the American transports of a considerable part of their tremendous burden. I have been put in a position relative to our Army supply and purchase operation in France that has no counterpart in the armies of England and France. He gives me authority to select my assistants within or without the Army. In other words, he makes me an important element in this war."

The last sentence was a masterpiece of understatement. Everyone with whom Pershing discussed the idea of such a board with Dawes at its head had advised against it. Even Colonel James G. Harbord, Pershing's Chief of Staff, felt the A.E.F. Commander was making a mistake and placing too much authority in Dawes, who was admittedly Pershing's closest friend. Indeed, it is doubtful that Pershing would have established the board if he had not felt that he had in Dawes the man who could accomplish the task he had in mind.

Pershing immediately took Dawes to M. Painlevé, French Minister of War.

"Dawes," Pershing told Painlevé, "will centralize all our Army purchases in Europe, take control of these purchases, and will organize a system for locating and transporting supplies."

Painlevé expressed his satisfaction with the arrangement, the first man who had. Thus was born the board which was to buy everything possible in Europe, in order to save precious ship space and to offset to a great extent the effect of hostile submarine activity. How well Dawes did his job was shown by this war's-end report. He had bought more than ten million ship-tons of supplies in Europe, compared with less than seven million tons shipped from America.

Pershing explained to Dawes privately why he had overruled his advisers and created the board with Dawes at its head. He had discovered that the Allies were far weaker than he had believed, and was of the opinion that Germany would have been the certain winner if the United States had not joined. The war was going to be won, but the bulk of the job might fall to America. If the Allies collapsed, the surest safeguard to the A.E.F. would be an unbroken line of communication back to the French ports, maintained by the Service of Supply. The weight of evidence was that the French and British could hold out, but it would be made doubly sure if purchases of supplies for American needs could be made in Europe in sufficient quantities to save as much space as possible for troop transports.

The two old friends continued their conversation over lunch. Pershing was quartered in a house owned by Ogden Mills which had formerly been the palace of Jean Lannes, one of Napoleon's marshals. The great dining room, in which Pershing, Dawes, and some members of Pershing's staff took their meal, was large enough to accommodate a hundred guests.

"John," said Dawes, "when I contrast these barren surroundings with the luxuriousness of our early life in Lincoln, Nebraska, it does seem to me that a good man has no real chance in the world."

Pershing meditatively replied: "Don't it beat hell!"

Pershing left Paris to open his headquarters at Chaumont, while Dawes opened his office in a single room in the Ritz Hotel. Ten days later, he had taken hold so energetically and displayed so much organizing ability that Pershing wrote to him: "Officers here, some of whom opposed the creation of the board, have many good things to say for you."

Dawes, in a memorandum, said:

"In every way, John is using his vast power to strengthen and uphold my hands. Dear fellow and loyal friend, I hope I do not fail him. He has told me how much he relies on me and how gratified he is at what I am doing, and what his officers say of it. He will never realize what these words mean to one in the quiet of the night, when, weary with the work and battle of the day, he takes mental account of himself and his task.

"The executive ability of Pershing impresses me more and more as time passes. Nothing counts with him but results. The law of the survival of the fittest among his officers is at work. In war, no excuses count. Performance alone answers. Conducted as it is, no reputation will be made by accident.

"If I fail in my military career, it will not be because I have failed to grasp firmly all the authority within reaching distance of me."

Yet Dawes' tender-heartedness crept in when some of the men selected for his staff proved inadequate for their tasks.

"Whether it is military method or not," he wrote, "where I find men unfitted to carry on certain ideas or lines of work assigned them, I am trying to change them, without breaking their hearts and spirits, to some work better adapted to their ability. In proportion, as power has come to me in life, I seek to avoid its ruthless use. Its exercise is no less effective—indeed, I have found it more effective— when with it are exhibited patience, reason, and moderation. The law of compensation is ever at work. Unhappy will be the man in power who for one minute forgets it. God keep us all humble in mind."

Although Dawes was determined to keep up with his diary, he found it hard to do so, for several reasons:

"The operations of my office are so vast, the matters of vital importance with which it is concerned are so varied, the demands upon my time are so pressing that it can only be of a general nature. These notes will often be made under pressure, but always with a sense of responsibility and a desire for accuracy. I will not write of war's horrors as I run across them. Others will do that. I will sometimes write of some of the amusing things of which one must train himself to think in times of apprehension."

Dawes was carrying out very important duties with a very low military rank. His opposite numbers from another nation invariably out-ranked him. But he never felt handicapped, no matter with whom he was dealing. "The history of this war will be written around achievements, not shoulder straps." At times, he even found his low rank advantageous. He could perform his duties "without being put in an unnecessarily conspicuous position, which I am anxious to avoid."

By mid-September, 1917, Dawes found that exceeding everything in immediate importance was the problem of coal and its transportation to the American Army arriving in France in ever-increasing numbers. He heard that Admiral William S. Sims, commanding the United States Naval Forces operating in European waters, was in Paris, and went to him in an effort to borrow a collier.

"When I got to Sims' house, he was preparing to go to some social event and was heavy with braid and lace. The minute I mentioned 'coal,' he began a tirade.

" 'There is not a man in the Army who knows his business,' the impatient Sims barked. 'I do not intend to waste time!' "

The man who was a mere lieutenant colonel interrupted the startled Admiral with a still louder bark:

"Damn you, Sims, I am not in the Navy and I haven't been in the Army long. I have been in this coal business just about a week. I didn't come here to be insulted or to listen to you insult the Army; I came to borrow a ship. I am trying to prevent a fuel famine. You say there is no one in the Army who understands his business. If you will listen to me, you will find one who bears a reasonable resemblance to a man who knows exactly what he is talking about."

Sims listened, and Dawes carried his point. Later he wrote:

"I regret that I descended to extreme statement but, immediately after I had spoken, the gold lace dropped away and a clear-headed, helpful man emerged. Sims could not give us a ship, but gave beneficial suggestions and kindly encouragement. We eventually got coal moving in all the supply needed."

After the coal, there came the labor problem, involving the task of finding 50,000 men for the building of military railroads.

"General Pershing has placed upon me the responsibility of procuring labor in Europe for the work of the A.E.F., which will require, in the aggregate, 100,000 men. He says he soon will begin ordering to the front men trained for combat duty and now used for labor, depending upon me to fill their places by rapidly recruiting labor forces.

"Pershing has suggested to the French that we use some of the Russians now in France as laborers. It has been kept a profound secret, but two divisions of Russian troops on the French line (about 40,000 men) revolted after killing many of their officers. The French have them in barbed-wire enclosures, and are rather at a loss what to do with them."

The labor corps Dawes organized for the A.E.F. started off with two hundred companies, totaling about 50,000 men. Assigned to him were 133 captains, 133 first lieutenants, 134 second lieutenants, 100 sergeants, and 2,000 corporals. As the corps eventually passed the 100,000 mark in personnel, Dawes reported that it was composed of Chinese, Indo-Chinese, Spanish, Italians, Portuguese, French, Senegalese, Greeks, Maltese, Belgians, North Africans, and some German prisoners of war.

Lumber had to be procured, forage, railroad ballast, crossties, steel, barbed wire, picks and shovels, oil, sugar, clothing, chloroform. Dawes got them coming in an unbroken stream. He knew the importance of what he was doing for the men on the fighting lines, and spared neither himself nor others to get the job done. He could plead, cajole, or demand—but if need be, he could also be quite robust.

Once when railroad crossties were urgently needed at the front, an officer wired Dawes: "Exigent we have crossties. Move heaven and earth to get them by Saturday."

It was Wednesday. Dawes telegraphed back the same day: "Raised hell and got them today."

In spite of such undiplomatic language, Dawes soon did the work of a diplomat. There was his deft performance in the case of the Belgian locomotives: Belgium had turned over to France and England 1,100 of them, but firmly insisted on holding its remaining 600 for civilian use at the end of the war. After all efforts of the British and French had failed, Dawes succeeded. Next, he suggested a way to solve the grave money-exchange problem between France and Spain and between France and Switzerland, and straightened out the difficult task of getting railroad ties in neutral countries.

"I feel as if I were exercising the power of one of the old monarchs. Sometimes I negotiate single-handed with governments."

And then, there were the horses and the mules.

War has always been cruel to men. World War I was cruel also to animals. A total of 185,000 horses and 63,000 mules went to the battlefields with the American Expeditionary Forces alone. Of these,

60,000 horses and 7,000 mules were killed in battle, an immensely greater proportion than that of men under fire.

Dawes threw out a dragnet to bring in every animal possible from Western Europe's dwindling supply of horses and mules. In memorandum after memorandum, he told of his quest:

"The French agreed today to let me have 30,000 horses. This is in addition to the 136,000 they have already furnished me. . . . Prospects better for 60,000 animals from Spain. . . . Got 13,000 horses from the British. . . . After being at the front and looking at a German barrage laid down on the front line, I know what horses mean to our men. This is why I keep everybody in a tension. Ever since I have been here, I have tried to visualize military needs to keep myself at the highest pitch of effort. I have tried to see always a private soldier holding out his hands to me, and my beloved Commander smiling when I filled them."

There was a story behind the mules which Dawes "imported" from Spain. Among the many outstanding men whose assistance Dawes had been able to enlist was August Belmont, back in the United States a horse breeder and racer as well as a financier. Belmont had sold his thoroughbreds in order to join the American Expeditionary Force. A promising colt which he sold to Samuel Riddle was called Man O'War, later considered the greatest race horse of all times.

"I don't think you know anything about mules," Dawes told Belmont, "but the Army needs everything that moves on wheels or legs. I think you have got sense enough to manage both the Spaniards and the mules."

Belmont left on his unfamiliar errand while Dawes noted in his diary:

"A man never knows what he can do until he has to. I got businessmen to finding things, and some of them did remarkable jobs." Soon Belmont would be meeting picturesque Spanish smugglers at night in the Pyrenees to buy contraband mules.

Dawes, now past fifty, was working sixteen and more hours a day and liking it. In March of 1918 he had been recommended to President Wilson as the best-qualified man to head the newly created War Finance Corporation. When the recommendation was withdrawn at the insistence of Pershing, Dawes heaved a sigh of relief.

"I do not think I could survive being taken away from this work of mine here, to which I am giving and shall give all that is in me," he wrote. "Compared with it, nothing that I have done heretofore in life seems important."

He now recommended and himself began the difficult negotiations leading up to what was to be his supreme achievement, the creation of the Military Board of Supply. Late in March the Allies had reached an agreement for the consolidated command under Foch. Dawes' conception was that there should be a coupling up of the rear of the three Allied armies, American, French, and British, just as the Foch agreement had coupled them up at the front.

The idea came to Dawes during a visit to his old organization, the 17th Engineers, still at St. Nazaire. He saw the United States building great warehouses there, while French warehouses were emptying. He was certain that such waste existed in many other activities. In effect, the recommendation he sent to Pershing was an extension to the French and British armies of the procurement system which Dawes had established for the American Army.

"For every argument for the Foch command at the front, there exist two arguments for a similar authority for supply and transportation in the rear," Dawes wrote to Pershing. "I mean by this supplies from America, supplies from France, supplies from England, and the land and sea transportation, warehousing, and handling thereof."

Pershing approved Dawes' recommendation on April 17, and cabled to the War Department that aviation, munitions, coal, horses, gasoline, oats, hay, meat, flour, shoes, sugar, wagons, tentage, demountable barracks, lumber, supply depots, and warehouses were the principal items that could be pooled.

Premier Clemenceau of France gave his sanction to the idea at once. "Why hasn't someone thought of this before," he wondered. "It will mean an end to tremendous waste in wealth, manpower, and material."

The first meeting on the pooling proposal was held in Paris. The original intention was to meet at the office of the French Minister of Armament, but Premier Clemenceau was so strongly in favor of the Dawes proposal that the meeting place was changed to the waxed-floor, gilded-mirror council room at the Quai D'Orsay. When

Dawes walked in, he was greeted by Clemenceau and most of his cabinet.

Dawes had been told in advance that the British would probably strongly oppose. He was not long in finding that this was true. Dawes, the sole American representative, took along as interpreter Chauncey McCormick, one of the businessmen who took captain's commissions under Dawes. The British delegation was headed by beribboned, six-foot-eight-inch Lieutenant General Sir John Cowans, Quartermaster General of the British Army. Flanking Cowans were Sir Andrew Weir, the later Lord Inverforth, Sir J. W. Curry, and Generals Atkins and Cannot. Colonel Payot and Messieurs Canne and Jeanneney represented the French.

Cowans obviously expected that General Pershing would be present. "Extraordinary people!" Dawes heard Cowans say as he glanced at the low-rank American representative.

Cowans rose. He asked: "Is General Pershing here?"

"No, General Pershing is not here," Dawes replied tartly.

"What?" Cowans exclaimed in astonishment and exasperation, and with a patent sneer at Dawes' rank.

"Well, I am here and, if you have got half as much authority as I have, we'll get somewhere."

Cowans had been facing Dawes and speaking directly to him, so low that he could not be heard by the others. There were fifty reasons, he told Dawes, why Great Britain could not agree to the plan.

Dawes rose and faced the audience as he spoke to Cowans.

"Here you are sent here by your Prime Minister, who has agreed to this in principle. And you say you can give fifty reasons why you can't agree. You stay here and find one reason to agree to it. We are trying to win a war, and we want to find ways to do things."

After three hours, the meeting broke up without an agreement. The British representatives wished to consult their government.

Dawes later explained his attitude:

"It wasn't my way of dealing, but we were in a war. I knew that on my reply to Cowans would depend our relations in the future. Cowans was a distinguished military man, and military men like to deal with men of equal rank. He had a bed quilt of ribbons and medals on his breast, attesting his service to his country. Men would rather die than surrender a prerogative, and a prerogative was involved for England. Realizing that I must shake the English up thoroughly if we were to land anywhere, I tried to keep the minds of the conferees on the necessities of coordination and to prevent the English from focusing attention on the difficulties of the widespread application of an unquestioned principle."

Clemenceau and Dawes jointly presided over the second meeting on May 16. The British did not appear, but filed a written statement. Pershing and Clemenceau agreed on the pooling plan, whether or not Great Britain took part. Pershing, believing the matter so urgent that the winning or losing of the war might depend on it, dispatched Dawes to London with a plea to Lloyd George to join.

Dawes arrived in London, paid a courtesy visit to Major General John Biddle, commanding the American forces in England, and told him of his mission.

"I'd like to make the arrangement for the appointment and go along with you," Biddle said. Dawes agreed. Biddle went to the telephone and told the British Premier's secretary: "Colonel Dawes is here from General Pershing on what I consider an important mission." An appointment for three o'clock the next day was agreed on.

Biddle came back from the telephone well pleased. But Dawes was astounded: "Why, Biddle, you can't expect me to wait until three o'clock tomorrow!"

Dawes asked if he might call. Biddle agreed, but said that he had never been able to get an appointment even as early as the one he had gotten for Dawes.

Dawes got Lloyd George's secretary on the telephone and was told that the appointment made by Biddle was the best that could be arranged. Any change was "quite impossible, and the request for it most irregular."

"What?" Dawes roared into the telephone. "I come here on a matter of the highest military importance, and you tell me I have to wait twenty-four hours?"

He continued to pour vitriol over the wires, until the secretary asked him to wait. Finally the secretary returned to the telephone and asked Dawes to come over immediately.

Lloyd George was waiting in the hall. Dawes presented to him the letter from Pershing, designating Dawes as the representative of the American Army, and containing a copy of the plan which Pershing and Clemenceau had signed.

"I am for it," Lloyd George said, "but our War Office is against it."

"I believe this statement of the plan is so simple that the British War Office cannot misunderstand it or be against it," Dawes said.

"I'd get the War Council together right now to consider the matter, but Lord Milner is in Paris," the Premier said.

"Isn't Cowans the sticking point? If he is, I would like to talk to him," said Dawes.

"You fix Cowans, and I'll let you write the British letter of acceptance of the plan," Lloyd George replied.

It was Paul D. Cravath, member of the American Mission to the Inter-Allied Council on War Purchases and Finance and a friend of Dawes, who made the appointment for Dawes with Cowans.

"Now don't you go over there and be a bull in a china shop. Remember, Cowans is intensely British," Cravath warned.

"He's no more intensely British than I am intensely American," Dawes replied. "I think we will get along all right."

"Cowans was busy writing when I was admitted to his office," Dawes later recorded. "His back was to the door. I went over un-invited and took the vacant chair by his desk. He looked up sur-prised, but was cordial. We soon worked out a satisfactory arrange-ment. Cravath, Dwight Morrow, and I wrote the British letter of agreement."

And by three o'clock the next day, the time set for the confer-ence, Dawes was on his way to Paris.

Dawes wrote of the agreement:

"It clears the way for common sense. The other day, I saw two trains of sixty cars each, carrying identical freight, passing each other in opposite directions. Not a pound of this freight should have been moved. There should be no more continued piling-up of unnecessary supplies behind one line while another line has a shortage."

Dawes' London visit had also cleared the way for a meeting of minds: Cowans and he became close friends from then on, and his call on the British Prime Minister marked the beginning of a warm friendship with Lloyd George. It was Cowans who later ordered that

Dawes' portrait be hung in the British War College, and Lloyd George who recommended him for the highest British war medal Dawes received.

By autumn of 1917 Dawes had become the talk of Paris. He smoked long black cigars and wanted a big cup of coffee along with his meals where others wanted a demitasse at meal's end. Titles meant nothing to him. The Countess of Pembroke, family name Herbert, wife of Lieutenant Colonel the Earl of Pembroke, was "Mrs. Pembroke," Lady Sarah Wilson, a daughter of the Duke of Marlborough, "Mrs. Wilson." His diary fills in some of the details:

"The French believe in the sacredness of fixed procedure at a dinner. When I told the headwaiter at the Ritz that General Pershing was to dine with me and I was ordering dinner in advance, he was much distressed because I ordered no soup. His protests were polite but extremely insistent. Soup should be served; the General would expect soup. Was I sure he did not want it? He would prepare it anyway and, if the General did not want it, it would not be put on the bill. Was I very sure that the General could get along without soup? 'Well,' I finally replied, 'when the General and I patronized Don Cameron's lunch counter in Lincoln, Nebraska, he was able to get along without soup and nearly everything else I have ordered that costs over ten cents!'

"This remark, designed to arouse the waiter's sense of humor, went unnoticed in his profound depression over my obstinacy, and so I let him make his soup and pass the question directly to the great chieftain himself for decision. When the General, dining at my expense, decided for soup, the waiter's joy was so evident that the threatening sacrilege had not been committed that I was glad for his sake I had raised the question."

He was a roaring, tearing legendary figure who set the stage for important meetings by precipitating acrimonious debate. He held interest by shocking or amusing men as he drove home his point. His strictures on incompetence and ineptitude were worth going miles to hear. His vocabulary was the most picturesque in the A.E.F. He passed out long cigars. Other men liked the cigars and came to like him. He had utter contempt for time-wasting canons. He looked askance at "Allied boards, town meetings, and common-consent discussions." His own board was no debating society. He wrote to Pershing:

"I never had a meeting of the General Purchasing Board, except on minor matters such as the distribution of office space, never on determination of action. Our organization is military. The reason why our Allied boards fail is because action has to be by a board and not by an individual."

Yet the legend did not take account of the fact that Dawes' sometimes unconventional behavior not only served to get things done, but had in fact been adopted for this very purpose. Even when Dawes was seemingly losing his patience, he knew perfectly well what he was doing. A notation in his diary is revealing:

"In our inter-Allied conferences, whenever I happened to represent our Commander in Chief, which was frequently, I soon came to employ certain methods to secure early decision. When the conference was confronted with necessity of agreement on something involving a sacrifice to one of the parties, and a bitter difference was inevitable, I always endeavored to precipitate the issue immediately in the clearest and most distinct way. By smoking cigars, by great emphasis, by occasional profanity, no matter how dignified the gathering or impressive the surroundings, I generally got everybody earnestly in discussion of the very crux of the question in the first half hour. My disregard of the conventions was studied and had a purpose. It served to save precious time by dissipating that atmosphere of self-consciousness in which men so often commence their negotiations. By having the session start in comparative acrimony, the foundation was laid for a natural reaction which brought good feeling later on. This would cause everyone to leave the conference in better humor than if the fight occurred just before the ending.

"If the differences between conferees are vital and important enough, they will be strongly contested. A perception of this at the beginning of a conference, and a courageous meeting of the situation, creates rough sailing for a time—but it grows steadily smoother at the end. Weak men or vain or conventional men, or even strong men at times, by overpoliteness, by overdeference to a nonessential environment or strange and dignified surroundings, carefully avoid ruffling the waters at first, only to ride later into the inevitable storm.

In such cases, all leave the conference annoyed, some by the decision and some by the other conferees. In a common cause and a common emergency, men should come out of a conference not only with a decision, but as friends.

"Among sincere and honest men in an emergency involving the common interest, the quicker disagreeable truth involved in decision is met, the surer will be an honest and a quick settlement of respective duty. In this, I am not speaking of ordinary conferences among ordinary men, but of vital conferences upon which hang great events."

His closer associates quickly came to see that there was method in Dawes' apparent madness. Harbord, who had opposed Dawes' appointment, became one of his staunchest adherents.

"Dawes is one of the finest characters I have ever known," Harbord noted, "generous, high-minded, straightforward, courageous, and very able. Outspoken and apparently impulsive, he generally thinks things over in detail and then puts them out in the impulsive manner. The air of impulsiveness is no indication that his verbal output is not based on due deliberation. He is a winning personality, very much of a special pleader, and the master of insidious approach. Our country has no more devoted and loyal servant than him in the performance of a duty that, in my judgment, could not have been so well performed by any other living man. And the performance of that duty is essential to our ultimate success in the war."

Even Pershing himself seems occasionally to have used the Dawes method. Dawes wrote:

"General Pershing told me of his violent interview with Foch of last Saturday. Pershing said he and Foch called one another everything in the book. While notes were taken of the interview, they will never indicate how important and tense was the issue. At one time, Foch told Pershing he would appeal to the President of the United States. It ended with John's success. Yet Pershing and Foch are great friends and will always be so. Each admires the other. Unusual men take unusual methods of expression at times, but they never misunderstand one another."

How well Pershing was satisfied with Dawes' own performance may be gathered from a cablegram which he sent to the War Department on January 3, 1918, asking that Dawes be promoted:

"Colonel Dawes has performed a service which could not have been rendered by any other officer. He has coordinated the great purchases already made in this command, avoiding competition and raising of prices, and resulting in the savings of hundreds of thousands of tons of shipping. Besides this, he has coordinated our purchases and those of France and other Allies, and is the author of the France-American purchasing agreement. He merits this promotion, and his usefulness will be enhanced by it."

And on a less official occasion, Pershing remarked:

"Dawes to me is a pearl without price, but I don't think I will ever militarize my old friend."

Dawes himself disagreed on the second point:

"I am learning to flop up my hand in receiving salutes. I am going to be a real soldier yet. This morning, I remembered to put on my pants before my shoes." But there is another entry in Dawes' diary, showing that his hope to become a genuine military man continued to encounter difficulties. It refers to a visit of Pershing and Dawes to the headquarters of General Foch.

"With all his grasp of the great things of military operation and organization, General Pershing by no means overlooks the important relation of some little things to a general scheme. His mind is certainly open to details, no matter how impressive the surroundings. My own somewhat pronounced indifference toward certain military conventions, born as often of ignorance as intention (although not always) is a matter of some embarrassment to him. After he had finished his conference with General Foch, he was standing with General Harbord across the road from me and some Frenchmen, waiting for Foch to take his automobile for his trip to Abbeville to see Haig.

"I saw him looking at me, notwithstanding the sound of the cannon, and the general surroundings, with an expression of mingled friendliness, admonition, and concern which characterizes his countenance during some of my interviews with his better-disciplined military associates. It led me to make a hasty self-appraisement in which, however, I could surmise no fault. He spoke to Harbord, and the latter walked across the road to me. As Harbord carefully buttoned up my overcoat, which was opened, including the hooks at the top, he murmured in my ear, 'This is a hell of a job for the Chief of Staff, but the General told me to do it.' Some soldiers told me that, in England, there was a kodak shot taken of John with one breast pocket unbuttoned. For this picture I am going to search that country, to use it for justifiable defense purposes."

The Military Board of Allied Supply had hardly set up shop in the old Chateau at Coubert when, on September 12, 1918, the Americans scored their great triumph at St. Mihiel. For four years that salient had defied the hammering of the French Army. Now it was in American possession.

On the very day that St. Mihiel fell, Dawes had completed an elaborate system of motor regulations to govern, first, road traffic in the zone of operations; second, the hauling of troops by mechanical transport; third, governing troop movements by mechanical transport. Pershing ordered the regulations put into effect immediately. Graduates of a Dawes motor transport school were put on the roads, guiding traffic and preventing jams. As the American Army moved into the Argonne, Dawes somehow got material to extend the normal gauge railroad to Varennes.

Three times during the last two months of the war, Dawes went to the front, bouncing precariously at high speed over badly worn and deeply rutted roads. On October 5 Pershing ordered him to come to Souilly. Again Pershing was to tell him of his battle plan. He intended to attack heavily on October 9 at the Meuse and the Aire. Dawes remained on Pershing's train until the day after the American attack had started at Montfaucon. From there, he kept bombarding his two headquarters in Paris and Coubert with calls for supplies.

On October 21 he went again to Pershing's train at Souilly, and on the following day was under fire at Fleville, near Grandpré. He wrote:

"Everything is in good shape, and I am confident that, as our lines advance, the supplies can be brought up."

By now, Gouraud's right and Pershing's left were out of the Argonne Forest and fighting side by side between Grandpré on the Aire and Vouziers on the Aisne. Ninety-three thousand animals and 3,500 motor trucks, capable of carrying a combined load of 20,000 men with their equipment and supplies, were in operation. Dawes was in an automobile accident on his return from Pershing's train to Paris, but escaped uninjured. He was going back to strong-arm more horses.

In all his shuttling back and forth from his Paris headquarters to the front, and in a half-hundred Paris air raids, Dawes never received a war injury. The only time he was ever knocked off his feet—if we can trust his own recollection in this matter—was in June, 1918, when a bomb exploded near his hotel and threw him sitting into a rocking chair.

Pershing opposed an armistice. He believed a complete military victory would lessen the chance for future war. Dawes agreed with Pershing.

"*October 3:* May the Lord bring this war to a close soon, provided its close marks an enduring peace. But this war must be *fought to a finish, not negotiated to one.*"

At 5:30 in the morning of November 11, 1918, German representatives put their signatures to an Armistice agreement in a boxcar in the Forest of Compiègne. At 11:00 o'clock that day, the guns on the Western Front fell silent.

Chapter Thirteen

❁

HELEN MARIA

*A*s Dawes walked down the Place de la Concorde on his way to his office in the Elysée Palace Hotel that morning of November 11, 1918, nothing would have pleased him better than to pack up bag and baggage and go home to the United States. It is not a usual thing for a man of affairs to leave his desk suddenly and go away to war, but Dawes had done so eighteen months before. He now felt his job was completed. The day for his kind of man in uniform had ended.

Only a part of Paris had yet been given the news of the cease-fire as Dawes made his morning appearance at his desk. He was greeted with the information that General Pershing wished to speak to him on the telephone immediately. Dawes called the Commander in Chief at the Chateau Vals des Escoliers at Chaumont. Pershing, Dawes thought, had accomplished everything he had come to France to do.

"For the first time since I have been over here, I did not anticipate an emergency, but thought his mind might be on the victory," Dawes said in a letter to his mother, describing how the Armistice came to him. "It was characteristic of the Commander in Chief that he was hard at work, and what he wanted was to talk over the plan for a financial section for the General Staff. When I congratulated him on his success, he said that he would not consider that he had succeeded until the Army was safely back in the United States."

Dawes himself had some suggestions.

"I suggested to Pershing that he should issue to the Army chiefs

184

of services an order, stopping immediately construction and purchases not essential to the A.E.F. under the new conditions created by the Armistice. It seemed to me that such a statement, issued on the very day of the Armistice, would not only result in great saving through the prompter action of the chiefs of the services, but would indicate to the American people that the A.E.F. appreciated its duty to save everything possible in view of the enormous sacrifice which our nation had made in order to supply us.

"At the request of the Commander in Chief, I later dictated over the telephone such a suggested statement, first telephoning it to Harbord, who approved it. I am anxious to see how the Commander in Chief will finally issue the statement. In anything important, he usually writes out the matter in longhand, then gives it careful revision. As a result, Pershing's individuality is so apparent in his orders that I can generally tell from reading the ones he has personally prepared. He is a great master of English."

Outside in the streets of Paris, and in its night clubs and ballrooms, there was gaiety and celebrating such as the world had seldom seen. The ringing of bells filled the air. Women in evening clothes and men in the uniforms of a dozen Allied nations filled the public places which only a short time ago had stood empty in fear of air raids. But Dawes had a job on his hands. In constant telephonic communication with Pershing and Harbord, he was busy putting the tremendous business machine of the American Expeditionary Force into reverse.

"One does not know how many tens of millions of dollars saving to the people of the United States depended upon prompt and intelligent action," he wrote. "I only noticed casually the singing and cheering crowds in the streets, and gave myself over unreservedly to the consideration of orders and instructions to the purchasing services under the authority of the Commander in Chief and Commanding General."

Through Dawes' office the next day began to flow transactions reflecting the crisis which the sudden ending of the war had brought to Europe. Dawes, whose waking hours for weeks had seldom been free of the thought of horses, quickly heard of that animal from another angle. Italian General Merrone came to Dawes' headquarters with a telegram from his government that it held 1,000,000

Austrian prisoners, and 200,000 Austrian horses, with no food for the prisoners nor hay for the animals.

Pershing, Dawes, and Harbord had soon worked out their plan for contract cancellation and methods of liquidation of the immense property and plant of the American Army in France. An order by Pershing set up the Advisory Settlement Board of the A.E.F. "to consider and recommend policies connected with the disposition of war supplies, material, and equipment." The members of the Board were Dawes, Edward R. Stettinius, civilian, and Colonel John A. Hull, Judge Advocate and Finance Officer of the A.E.F.

At the same time Dawes, driven by the desire to return home as soon as possible, was preparing his final reports as member of the Military Board of Allied Supply and as General Purchasing Agent of the A.E.F. and Chairman of the General Purchasing Board. When he looked at the final figure of the supplies he had purchased in Europe, even he himself was amazed.

"If anyone had told us at the beginning that this task confronted us, we should not have believed it possible," he wrote. "As David must have kept his mind on his slingshot instead of the size of Goliath, so it must have been with us."

It took him until March of 1919 to prepare the last of his wartime reports, that as American member of the Military Board for Allied Supply. He regarded it as "my most important contribution to the military literature of the war, and the most important document which I have ever prepared." But he wondered how many would read it: "The world is in a crisis, and Europe will remain in one indefinitely, so the minds of this generation will not concern themselves largely with retrospect."

Even before one job was completed, there came calls for Dawes to help in another one.

The first call came again from Herbert Hoover, who wished to draft Dawes as chairman of a military commission which was to go to Berlin and take charge of relief of the German civilian population. Had Dawes been free at that moment, he might well have followed Hoover's call.

"In the great press of work of the last week, my visits and work with Herbert Hoover remain in memory. He outlined his plans for feeding Europe, so far as it has been possible to formulate them.

His present liaison with our Army is through my office. He shared my frugal lunch on the office desk the other day.

"He impresses me more each time I see him. He is clear, distinct, intensely practical, fearless, and possessed of the widest perspective. He is essentially a man of action." Dawes added: "In view of the disturbed conditions in Berlin and the interesting nature of the work, my inclination toward adventure was somewhat involved."

While Pershing had vetoed Hoover's request, on the ground that Dawes "cannot be spared from his present service," he himself urged Dawes to accept when, in February of 1919, Secretary of War Baker asked Dawes to become the military member of the United States Liquidation Commission, of which the civilian members were to be Judge Edwin B. Parker of Texas, former United States Senator Henry B. Hollis of New Hampshire, and Homer H. Johnson of Cleveland, Ohio.

"Here I am," Dawes wrote after he had accepted, "head over heels in a mean and thankless task, but one which I have no honorable right to decline. Had I not long ago decided to sink personal considerations in this war service, I should have avoided this position as I would have avoided the smallpox. The 'going is good' for me to leave the Army now, but to stay as a member of a commission to sell its assets is to work hard without the incentive of a war purpose; to run the risk of making serious mistakes which will result in attacks upon one's motives; in other words, to risk the reputation for success which I now have for no adequate personal purpose.

"However, the way things have been put to me, I should feel like a skunk if I did not do it. There is no patriotism in what I am doing, only a desire not to shirk what I am really qualified to do and what I ought to do. Somehow, it is not so inspiring to work at saving money for one's government as to work at helping save its life. And *this* is what I had looked forward to as the time when I should be leaving for America!"

On the night of his appointment as a member of the Liquidating Commission, Dawes went with Hoover to be decorated Commander of the Legion of Honor by Clementel, French Minister of Commerce, "who inexpressibly horrified me by kissing me on both cheeks before a large audience, of which the American part must have been tremendously amused. As we sat at the table together, I told Hoover our old friends in Cedar Rapids, Iowa, and Marietta, Ohio, who knew us better, would never have made the mistake of making either of us so prominent or of kissing us."

The task of the Liquidating Commission, it soon became obvious, would require six months. There were American war supplies of a nominal value of $1,500,000,000 scattered in all parts of war-ravaged France. At home, the United States had an unneeded stockpile worth $2,000,000,000. Great Britain had approximately $2,000,000,000 worth of supplies in France, and France itself had an immense stock.

"Transportation facilities for this stock in France are limited," Dawes wrote. "Its value is lessening with time. France, as a government, is in financial straits, and yet it is the logical purchaser of our property. Our negotiations are rendered more difficult by the complicated intergovernmental credit situation. It is necessary to deal upon the highest plane and with great energy. Whatever we do will be criticized, but I prefer to be criticized for doing *something* instead of nothing."

Payot, Dawes' French coadjutor on the Military Board of Allied Supplies, had once said sadly: "Both Dawes and I work sixteen hours a day. But Dawes spends all his time fighting the Germans. I work four hours fighting the Germans, and twelve hours fighting my own people." Now again, Dawes would be irked by the fact that the representatives of other nations were unwilling, or perhaps unable, to keep pace with him. But since his work was no longer a matter of life and death, he was able to take a humorous view of his difficulties:

"It amuses me to think what must have been the first impressions of me received by those splendid officers and dear friends (so used to conventional military methods of statements and address) when, breathing fire and brimstone, I made incursions into the system. My mind then was fixed upon the red-hot poker of dire necessity pressed upon the lower part of my back, and I was oblivious to nicety of expression or conventional forms of military salutation. Now I am by degrees relapsing into more placid and dignified ways befitting a banker and businessman."

It was not until early July that the Liquidating Commission received its first firm offer from the French for the purchase of American supplies. On July 24 the Commission accepted the offer. That night, Payot and Dawes had their last dinner together:

"We couldn't talk to each other, having no interpreter, but we just sat around and felt badly about separating."

On March 28, 1919, Pershing had conferred upon Dawes the Distinguished Service Medal "for the magnificent service you rendered the common cause." Decorations from other nations followed in quick succession: On May 4, at Tours, he was made a Companion of the Bath, Harbord and other officers being decorated at the same time. On June 17 King Albert of Belgium conferred upon him the Commander of the Order of Leopold and on July 16 he received the Croix de Guerre. The Italian decoration, Commander of SS Maurice and Lazarus, came next. But to Dawes, who had declined Pershing's offer that he ride as a member of the Commander's Staff in the Peace Parade in Paris on July 14, since "to ride in it means I cannot see it," decorations meant little or nothing.

"One of the most difficult things to do is to refrain from accepting undeserved credit," he wrote. "I have been so accustomed to associating ceremony with nonaccomplishment since, in civil life, it is the chief resource of those desirous of publicity, whether deserved or not, that I confess I was not overcome on these occasions.

"The value of ceremony as a social power is unquestioned. It cannot be dispensed with without destroying one of the great incentives of human effort and one of the useful agencies of proper governmental and social discipline. But in all my negotiations as an Army officer in inter-Allied conferences, I fought it as a bar to progress and understanding. In proportion as men are right-minded and intelligent, ceremony is unessential in their relations."

How much decorations meant to others than himself, Dawes was soon to learn when he was assigned with the duty of making up a list of men to receive the Distinguished Service Medal.

"The craze for decoration among all peoples is an amazing phenomenon," he wrote. "Let a man receive praise from press, pulpit, and everywhere else for service, but fail to give him that ribbon, and he feels as if he has been disgraced.

"The heart-burnings among officers who have not received the Distinguished Service Medal, when they unquestionably deserve it, leads me to question the advisability in our country of any govern-mental system tending toward the creation of classes; the disap-pointment of the unpreferred is apt to be directed toward the government as well as toward its agent in decoration distribu-tion. . . .

"The Decoration Board of the A.E.F. is swamped with thou-sands of requests for reconsideration of disapprovals of the D.S.M. As a matter of fact, it has been impossible, and always will be im-possible, to discriminate justly in the distribution of awards in a large army, because of the very vastness of the task which prevents a consideration of all the cases from the viewpoint of the same minds. An officer of the A.E.F. who has succeeded in his task, has been promoted, has been commended by his superior officers and associates, should not feel himself reflected upon because he has not received one of the few Distinguished Service Medals distributed among millions of men. And yet some of them do, and I greatly regret it.

"The world 'will little note nor long remember' even our names, much less the minor things relating to our personal vanity. I suppose, as one who has received much more recognition than he deserved, it is easy for me to recommend philosophy to those who have been unjustly treated. But, when I find disappointment so keen and rage so blinding that I have to endure patiently an attack on the system and everybody connected with it, including intimations that I have not been duly active for my friends, all because I have failed in strenuous recommendations to have the D.S.M. awarded where it is deserved, I come to realize that the system is questionable.

"How little anyone cares to hear of our failures and grievances. If the world was not cold, human vanity would demand all its time and energy expended in sympathizing with grouches. Realizing, es-pecially this morning, that this is a very cold world after a conversa-tion with some officers who did not get the D.S.M., I suggested to them the following paraphrase: 'Weep, and the world laughs at you; laugh, and you laugh alone.' This did not seem to comfort them, their sense of humor being submerged, along with their other facul-ties, in deep pessimism."

When the Liquidating Commission had completed its work,

Dawes, on August 2, sailed out of Brest Harbor on the freshly painted *Leviathan,* a great contrast to the *Carmania,* splashed and daubed in camouflage, zigzagging through the submarine zones when Dawes had come over. He carried as his most prized possession a sword selected for him and engraved to him by Pershing.

As Dawes returned to Chicago directly from the port of debarkation, he was greeted by a Presidential boom. In an interview William Jennings Bryan said he thought Dawes the man most likely to appeal to both progressives and conservatives in the Republican party. Bryan added: "Dawes' personal character is impeccable." Replying to a letter in which Bryan had also mailed a copy of the interview, Dawes wrote:

"Your letter written to me from Washington did not reach me for a long time. As for politics, I enclose an authentic interview in this morning's Chicago *Tribune* which, I think you will agree, disposes of the question. From the time I left politics nearly twenty years ago, I have never had any idea of re-entering, and will not do so under any circumstances. Just the same, I appreciate your kindly thought of me which prompted your interview and letter."

If the office held any lure for him, still Dawes would not have sought the Presidency. His friend of a quarter of a century, Frank O. Lowden, whose record as Governor of Illinois had been outstanding, was an active candidate with Dawes' full support. Dawes knew also that some Republicans would object to him violently since he had become a vigorous champion of Woodrow Wilson's conduct of the war, and had defended the peace treaty.

"This peace conference," he had written from Paris, "has probably done the very best it was possible to do in the environment in which it acted. When the environment is forgotten and the unconquerable necessities of an actual situation do not confront the critic, there will be much international literature devoted to a demonstration of how much better a treaty would have resulted if the nations had summoned the critics to the conference instead of their greatest men. The highest art of criticism, as a rule, is developed only in those personally incapable of constructive accomplishment."

And in a newspaper article he had added:

"I have faith that the honest judgment of the American people will be forced to the same conclusion as was that of the representatives of all governments signing the treaty, to wit: that, since it was impossible for any of them to have in the treaty all they would desire, they would accept the best treaty possible.

"I therefore look forward to an ultimate rally of American public sentiment behind it, faulty as it may seem to us in certain details, as embodying the hopes of a better future for ourselves and the world.

"As a people who would not evade or shirk the responsibilities which our own sovereign decision to enter the war has brought upon us, we should lift our eyes and efforts from the smaller aspects of our situation, and ratify in its entirety this great treaty of peace in which thirty nations have at last composed their differences after the most terrible war of all time."

He was outspoken against those who had attempted to obstruct the war effort after the United States cast its lot with the Allies. In a speech at Cincinnati, he said:

"There is no better interior decoration for an American jail than those scoundrels who stabbed the country in the back during the war. Hell, when we get Grover Bergdoll in jail, it will be time enough to talk about getting Eugene Debs out."

While Dawes succeeded in squelching his boom, talk of Pershing as the Republican nominee continued and caused him real anxiety.

Pershing had brushed aside politicians who talked to him about the Presidential race. But in Lincoln there lived one of Pershing's University of Nebraska cadets, Mark W. Woods. Grown wealthy by 1920, Woods had made an effort to get his old instructor to make a try for the White House. He got little encouragement from Pershing, but put the A.E.F. Commander's name in the Nebraska Presidential preference primary anyway. In a hotly contested three-way race between Pershing, Major General Leonard Wood, and Senator Hiram Johnson of California, the primary was carried by Johnson.

While Pershing had little interest in the Presidency for himself, he was fearful that the nomination would go to Leonard Wood, for whom he had no great admiration either as a soldier or a statesman. Pershing's Nebraska vote did prevent Wood from carrying a state which had been conceded to him. That result could not have been displeasing to Pershing. It was a painful blow to the heavily financed Wood campaign.

The temperature outside of the Chicago Coliseum, where the Republican national convention was in session, stood at 96° in the late afternoon of the second Friday in June, 1920. Inside, it must have been a good ten degrees hotter. There was not so much as a timid breeze in all Chicago.

After the fourth ballot for the Republican nomination for President, Leonard Wood was leading Lowden by a narrow margin. Harding had received only 61½ votes. Seventeen candidates in all had received votes for the Presidential nomination. The coatless, collarless delegates had sweltered, screamed, and paraded through the aisles for ten solid hours in a field day of oratory and demonstrations. Even "Tieless Joe" Talbert of South Carolina peeped over his high collar to observe it was the hottest convention day in his recollection.

From the Pennsylvania delegation, at the end of the fourth ballot, came a motion to adjourn. Chairman Henry Cabot Lodge put the motion. There was a good volume of ayes, a thunderous roar of noes. Apparently the motion had been defeated, but Lodge declared it carried and walked off the platform. Had the convention continued in session for another ballot or two that day, Lowden might have been nominated. The next day, after the long night meeting in Col. George Harvey's smoke-filled room, it was a different story. Harding, far back in the early balloting, rushed forward to take the nomination.

Pershing, who had believed he would be compelled to leave the Army if Leonard Wood was elected President, jubilantly telegraphed to Dawes his pleasure at Wood's defeat: "Could anything be better? The victory is ours. I die content."

On the morning of February 2, 1921, Charles G. Dawes got off a train in Washington and walked to the Capitol. He had been offered, and it was generally believed at that time would accept, the post of Secretary of the Treasury in the Harding Cabinet. But it was other business that brought him to Washington this day. He was to appear, an hour later, before the House Committee on War Expenditures, a body formed after the Republicans won control of Congress in the 1918 election. The chairman of the Committee was Representative William J. Graham of Illinois.

The Graham Committee had a unique history. It had begun its hearings in 1919 and, by the date of Dawes' appearance, had taken thirteen million words of testimony, bound in twenty volumes of thirteen hundred pages each.

At the beginning of the investigation, a subcommittee of the Graham Committee had gone to France and asked for Pershing's records. When it was found that the records, packed in one hundred and eighty shipping boxes, were aboard the boat on which Pershing was to return, the Graham Committee abandoned that phase of the hearing and summoned Judge E. B. Parker, chairman of the Liquidating Committee.

Parker, famous for his mastery of detail, appeared before the inquisitors, bringing with him three boxes of records, each so heavy it required two soldiers to carry it.

The first question addressed to Parker was:

"Why was this large number of airplanes burned by the Army in France instead of being salvaged?"

Parker went into his box for the records. His answer to the one question consumed an hour. The surprised Committee promptly adjourned with the statement to Parker that his answer had been so complete and satisfactory, they felt justified in assuming that all the business on which he was called to testify had been completed properly and in the best interests of the United States.

The summons to testify came to Dawes nearly two years after the Committee had begun its work. A week before his appearance, Charles M. Schwab had been on the stand. The Committee had been brutal in its questioning, and the industrialist, believing the Committee was reflecting on his integrity, burst into tears.

Dawes resented the Committee's call. He was a busy man. He arrived in Washington on the morning he was to testify, and walked around the Capitol park for an hour, waiting for the Committee to assemble. The longer he walked, the angrier he got. At ten o'clock, he went to the Committee room. There was less than a quorum present. One or two newspapermen sat at the press tables. The audience was limited to two wealthy Washington spinsters, the

Patten sisters, who attended every Congressional hearing to which they could gain admittance.

The scene was to become more animated in short order. In the first thirty minutes of his testimony Dawes had given a sufficient preview of his spirit to bring newspaper reporters scurrying to the press table. By noon, every seat in the hearing room was filled and Capitol police were holding back crowds which tried to get in.

"You were the purchasing agent for the American Expeditionary Forces?" asked Representative Oscar E. Bland, Republican, of Indiana.

"I was," Dawes answered in the only mild tone of voice he used during his seven hours' appearance.

"Is it not true that excessive prices were paid for some articles?" Bland continued.

"When Congress declared war, did it expect us to beat Germany at twenty per cent discount?" Dawes ripped back. "Sure, we paid high prices. Men were standing at the front to be shot at. We had to get them food and ammunition. We didn't stop to dicker. Why, man alive! We had a war to win! It was a man's job!"

"Is it not true that excessive prices were paid for mules?" Bland went on.

"Helen Maria!"

Dawes had jumped from his chair. He strode to the front of the long mahogany Committee table. "I would have paid horse prices for sheep, if the sheep could have pulled artillery to the front!

"Oh, it's all right to say we bought too much vinegar and too many cold chisels, but we saved the civilization of the world! Damn it, our diplomatic system was a failure. Our American ministers would not cooperate with us, even though it was a matter of life and death for our soldiers. They were all tangled up in State Department red tape. This thing of pink-tea diplomatic officials is fatal in time of war. English diplomacy was as bad as ours. Brigade after brigade was without horses. To get vitally needed horses from Spain we had to send men there with money in their pockets. We bought smuggled mules in the Pyrenees in the middle of the night.

"There was nothing pink-tea about the way we handled it. There was no time for conventionalities or unlimited debate. Why, we actually hired an outfit of professional smugglers, the like of which you never saw outside of *Carmen,* to get those horses into France. For weeks, we had these smugglers leading horses and mules up and down the dark mountain defiles of the Pyrenees, delivering them at dead of night with mystic pass words and all of that. They were not nice men, but they got the mules out of Spain and we got them to the front, and the horses dragged the cannon.

"We asked France for horses. We were told: 'If we take these horses off the farms at harvest time, we will have a revolution.' Our argument was that, if we could not put the artillery into the Argonne for our men, the Germans would come through and take their horses and take all France."

By now, Dawes was roaring.

"The American people do not support any such monkey business as is going on here. If you men would spend more time trying to stem the millions of waste going on under your noses instead of trying to put fly specks on the United States Army, we would have a lot better government.

"Long after this Committee is dead and gone and forgotten, the achievement of the American Army will stand in an everlasting blaze of glory. You have tried to make a mountain out of a mole hill. The people are tired of war talk and faultfinding. Thank God, the Army was American, not Democratic or Republican.

"I tell you the people are not interested in this Committee. If I were not here, strutting and swearing, there would be no news in this. I bitterly resent this effort to reflect upon the entire Army because some poor devils blundered in Switzerland. You cannot put a blotch upon the Army. What the Hell did we go in for—to steal money?"

"Were there not grafters who followed the American Army?" a Committee member asked.

"Yes, they were there!" Dawes snapped, "Some of the most despicable characters on earth, trying to help the Army by selling it things it needed at exorbitant figures. There was one man we caught and deported. What's his name? Oh, what's the use! I'm not a muckraker. He was a traitor."

No witness had ever talked in such a way to a Congressional Committee. But the investigators sat spellbound while Dawes continued:

"If members of Congress had been there and their minds had been open and wise, you would have done the same thing as the Army did in the matter of prices," he said. "When it comes to a question of necessity, you never have any trouble with politics.

"I have no reason to hold this Committee in high esteem. I am here today to do what I can to put an end to the detestable official effort to blacken American military achievement for political and partisan purposes.

"Give the War Department some credit. Considering everything, the record of what was done by the War Department in getting ready for war shows a greater accomplishment than that of France or Great Britain for the same period of time. I don't believe you can pick flaws there; and I am not speaking as a Democrat.

"There were hounds in this country who tried to spread the news that Pershing was at the theater the night of the Armistice. He was there like hell! He was at his office, starting the work of canceling vast war contracts to save money."

Dawes' last remark had given one of the investigators an idea. Promptly the question came:

"What about the surplus food and clothing in France? Could the Liquidating Commission not have obtained more than the $400,000,000 it received?"

"I was a member of that Liquidating Commission," Dawes retorted. "You can give me all the hell you want because I sold a lot of junk to the French for $400,000,000 instead of keeping 40,000 soldiers there to guard it while we tried to peddle it. My conscience hurts me sometimes when I think we charged too much! It is just that sort of fool talk that forced Great Britain to hold on to its stock and attempt to drive a hard bargain. The stuff is there today, rotting. England lost billions by listening to that sort of bunk—listening to a lot of people who were afraid of muckrakers at home. They are raising the devil in England now because England did not sell its supplies when we sold. There is no use throwing mud when you were not there to know the conditions."

For seven hours, Dawes spoke his mind in terms that could not be misunderstood. "A man had either to cry or swear," he said when it was all over. "Charley Schwab did the crying and Charley Dawes did the swearing. I accomplished my purpose. I might have done it without profanity, but this is doubtful."

Dawes did accomplish his purpose beyond a doubt. "I think I speak for the Committee," said Subcommittee Chairman Johnson of South Dakota, "when I say we wish there were more witnesses as truthful and unafraid."

Dawes' name leaped to the front pages of the country's newspapers. His printed testimony was a bestseller at the Government Printing Office. But the public was cheated: his speech had been emasculated by deletions and omissions. The deletions were because of the swear words; omissions because, Committee members said, he often spoke too fast for the stenographers to take it down.

Dawes was already on his way back to Chicago. There he received a telegram from Pershing: "All Washington is agog over your splendid testimony, and they approve of it in every detail even to the cuss words."

But more than the cuss words had been eliminated in the official record of the hearing. The expression "Helen Maria," a familiar phrase to him in his Nebraska days, had also disappeared. Even the newspapers had misunderstood it. It was quoted as "Hell and Maria." Thus misspelled, it was to enter the Dawes legend as his favorite epithet.

Chapter Fourteen

❁

SAVE A BILLION

Immediately upon his inauguration on March 4, 1921, President Warren G. Harding asked Dawes to head a committee to investigate and recommend reorganization of the War Risk Board—later the Veterans Bureau—and to formulate plans for the proper care of the veterans of World War I.

There were eleven members on the committee, among them wealthy Miss Mabel T. Boardman, Secretary of the American Red Cross. As the committee sat down to its first meeting in Washington, each member found at his place a note requesting his presence at a social affair at Miss Boardman's house that night.

Dawes walked in and convened the committee in his usual brisk manner. He picked up the note from Miss Boardman, as well as another note telling him that a suite of seven rooms had been fitted out for his use in a new building on the site of the old Arlington Hotel.

"How long do you think we are going to be here?" Dawes asked the War Risk Bureau Director.

"Six or seven months."

"Well, I am not going to be here even six or seven days," Dawes snapped. Then, turning to Miss Boardman, he said:

"Now, Miss Boardman, we are not going to your party tonight, or to any other social event, until we solve this problem. Furthermore, I see the Surgeon General sitting there. We are going to give him just fifteen minutes for his testimony, and that will apply to all other witnesses. If we can't get all we want in that time, perhaps we can extend it slightly, but I don't think we will have to do so."

With a groan, the committee buckled down to work. On the third day its report was in preparation, and Dawes went home. He had given Washington a sample of efficiency and economy as he understood them. President Harding was to ask at once for more of the same.

Harding and Dawes had first met in June of 1920, two days before Harding was nominated for the Presidency of the United States. At that time, Dawes had been doing everything in his power to promote the candidacy of his intimate friend Frank O. Lowden.

"I think," Lowden had said as he and Dawes sat alone in a private room of Lowden's campaign headquarters, "that, as the host governor of the State of Illinois and as a candidate, I should pay a courtesy call on all the other candidates, and I want you to go with me."

With a dozen or more open and receptive candidates, this was a considerable chore, but the two old friends trudged bravely from headquarters to headquarters. Harding was the most affable of all the candidates. He wondered why he had never met Dawes before; had high praise for Dawes' brother Beman, whom he had known for many years; and said he had been much interested in a magazine article Dawes had written: *"How a President Can Save a Billion Dollars."*

After his election, Harding telephoned Dawes at once and asked if it would be convenient for him to come to Marion for a conference. At Marion, Harding said without qualification:

"I am going to offer you the first post I have offered to anyone in the Cabinet. I want you to be my Secretary of the Treasury, and let's save that billion dollars you wrote about."

But Dawes shook his head. The Secretary of the Treasury, he told the President, was not the man to make the savings. The only way in which economy in government could be practiced was through the enactment of legislation providing for an executive budget.

"Only in this manner can you inaugurate a system of coordinating business control over the various departments which for 132 years have been almost completely decentralized.

"The one way the law can be made to work after it is enacted is for the President of the United States to make it work. As long as the President of the United States is not indifferent to his duty, budget law or no budget law, the system will work. But let the impression be created in the business organization of the government that the President's eye and the eyes of his agents are not watchful, budget law or no budget law, the system will fail. Nothing should be allowed to divert the attention of the public from the duty and power of the President to a machine which without him would be as dead as a locomotive without water or coal.

"A Cabinet member cannot do the job. As Secretary of the Treasury and a member of the Cabinet, I could not tell other members of the Cabinet what to do. But, as your assistant secretary or as assistant President or whatever you might call it, I could, if I could sit by your side and issue executive orders. Just because the United States Government is the biggest business in the world, there is no reason why it should be the worst run. But only one man can make it run right, and that is the President of the United States."

But Harding was not quite convinced. He persisted in his belief that the Secretary of the Treasury was the man to balance the budget, and that Charles Dawes would be that man.

In the light of subsequent history, Harding's discussion of Cabinet possibilities with Dawes that day was an interesting one.

"I would like to appoint Fall Secretary of State. I have great confidence in him and respect for his ability. I think Fall's appointment would please the Theodore Roosevelt following, for you know Roosevelt selected Fall to put him in nomination for the Presidency four years ago. Fall is a bigger man than he is given credit for being, but the country probably would not take to his appointment as Secretary of State. I am going to offer the post to Hughes, but he is not my preference for the place. I would much rather have Fall.

"I am determined to have Hoover in my Cabinet. He is going to be the hard one to get. Penrose and Philander Knox are dead set against him. They say he ran for the Presidential nomination, or at least allowed the use of his name, in the Democratic primary in Michigan. They don't like him because they think he is a Democrat and, even regardless of that, they just don't want him."

Harding concluded their Marion talk with the startling statement:

"Dawes, now that this frightening job is in my lap, I don't know why I ever wanted it. I have been very happy in the Senate. I want to be a good President for four years, and that is all I want. Barring a financial panic such as Grover Cleveland had to contend with in ninety-three, the Republicans will have a long tenure in control. I'd like to see you nominated and elected President in 1924. I will do what I can to help you."

Dawes passed over the remark with a polite pleasantry. He never mentioned it to anybody but one or two close friends. In fact the extent of Harding's faith in Dawes did not become public until Vice-President Curtis died in 1936. Among Curtis' memoirs, which he had kept private to the end, was the report of a visit he had paid to the President in 1923, as Harding was leaving on the Alaska trip never to return to Washington. Curtis had urged Harding at that time to run again in 1924, lest Calvin Coolidge should become the Presidential nominee.

"Charley, you are not worried about that little fellow in Massachusetts, are you?" Harding replied.

A moment later, Curtis said, President Harding turned to him, put his hand on his shoulder, and said:

"Charley Dawes is the man who is going to succeed me!"

A month later, Harding was dead, and Coolidge President.

But that was three years later. Dawes left Harding, after their Marion talk, with the impression that the proffer of the Secretary of Treasury portfolio was open to him, but he had not accepted. Harding apparently felt that the matter was settled. When William Howard Taft visited Marion on December 24, Harding told him that he had offered Cabinet places to Hughes, Dawes, and Hoover, and seemed confident that all would accept.

In Florida in January Dawes asked Harding to put him out of consideration for Secretary of the Treasury, saying: "As much as I would like to see your Administration a success, Senator, nothing could tempt me into public life now, except possibly Director of the Budget, if that office is created, and that I would take only a year for the purpose of putting it in running order."

Harding said he agreed with reluctance, but added:

"Please don't let it be known that you have been offered and refused to be Secretary of the Treasury. I still have not been able to remove Penrose's and Knox's objections to Hoover. I would be inclined to make Mellon Secretary of the Treasury if the Pennsylvania Senators would end their objection to Hoover. Mellon probably has too much money for a Secretary of the Treasury. I may get as much criticism over his appointment as I would if I put J. P. Morgan in that place."

When Harding volunteered that he intended to appoint Harry M. Daugherty, who had been his campaign manager, as Attorney General, Dawes protested that it would be a bad appointment, Dawes said. He quoted Harding's reply:

"Well, I wouldn't be here (President-Elect) but for him. He has asked me for the place, and I am going to give it to him. Other people, too, have advised me as you have. But I would not be right with myself if I did not appoint Harry."

When Dawes' decision became known, Pershing wrote him from Washington:

"I think your declining the place of Secretary of the Treasury is the biggest thing you ever did. You are in so much better position to say things that need saying than you would be if you were an official. You know very well your distinct personality was never in subjection while you served in the A.E.F., and you could never have accomplished the splendid work you did had I in the least undertaken to curb or restrict it, which I never thought of doing, as you know."

In June of 1921 Dawes booked passage to Europe for himself and his family. No sooner had he done so than Congress passed the Budget Act and Harding asked him to become the first Budget Director. Dawes agreed, upon the stipulation that "the Bureau of the Budget shall be impersonal, impartial, and nonpolitical." Unless it was and always remained so, it would fail.

"You must realize that you are the first President to tackle the job of a coordinated business control over the departments," he told Harding. "I doubt if you recognize the strength of the 150 years of archaisms which you must fight. 'Delay, linger, and wait!' is the watchword of bureaucracy."

The President promised Dawes to support him with all his authority. Dawes canceled his steamship reservations, came to Washington, and at once began to set up the Budget Bureau.

"Under the law, the Director of the Budget acts under the authority of the President and, after my conference with him, there was left no doubt of the earnestness of his purpose. I knew that all the rest of my life I would be cursed with regret if I did not attempt the work of establishing correct business methods in the governmental administration of our country."

In a city where everyone was demanding mahogany furniture, Dawes emphasized economy by scraping together enough old oak furniture from Government warehouses to equip his office under the eaves of the Treasury Building.

The auguries for success in Government saving, Dawes believed, were good. There was a then-popular President who had been voted into office by the greatest landslide in the nation's history. In the light of later Government expenditures, a billion-dollar saving might seem negligible. But to a nation unaccustomed to debt, the more than twenty-three billion dollar deficit of three years of war budgets seemed enormous. With war taxes still in effect, there was a clamor for a reduction in expenditures and for retirement of the national debt.

Dawes' first step was to meet the Cabinet en masse in the office, and in the presence, of the President, and to explain his concept of his present assignment. The Budget Bureau was concerned only with the humbler and routine business of government; it was concerned with no question of policy except economy and efficiency.

"A Cabinet officer, as I see him," said Dawes, "is on the bridge with the President, advising him on the direction in which the ship shall sail. He is concerned with matters of the highest importance. But, at the same time, that Cabinet officer, under our Constitution, is charged with responsibility for a limited portion of the common machinery of the ship. He will not properly serve the captain of the ship or its passengers, the public, if he resents the call of the Director of the Budget from the stokehole, put there by the captain to see that coal is not wasted. In whatever direction, as a matter of policy, those in higher place and authority may turn the ship, the way the coal is handled and conserved determines how far in a given direction the ship will sail."

In his diary, Dawes explained the purpose and the effect of this meeting:

"The important thing I wanted to do with the Cabinet was to create the impression that helpfully and sympathetically, with common sense and proper appreciation of the rights and sensibilities of others, these principles were to stand now and for all time as the rock of the budget system of the United States. In order to create this impression and to deal with the peculiar psychology of the situation, I started mildly and precisely, gradually precipitating one or two personal controversies which I handled firmly, all with the approval of the President who knew exactly what I had in mind. The entire Cabinet, however, believed, in my judgment, that whatever rights were given to me by the President, I would not be timid about exercising, and that was my principal idea in meeting them."

His most important allies, Dawes knew, would be the many hundreds of bureau chiefs and supervisors who could effect economies each in his own sphere of authority. Accordingly, one of his first recommendations to the President was a system of promotions and salary increases among those bureau chiefs who made savings. This proposal was a subject of Dawes' talk at the meeting of the entire business administration of the government which he had called for the day following his session with the Cabinet.

President Harding, Vice-President Coolidge, General Pershing, the members of the Cabinet, and twelve hundred bureau chiefs and routine officers of the Government tramped into the auditorium for the first such meeting in the nation's history. The chiefs of these routine business organizations were the men who, through all the history of modern government, had been systematically asking for more appropriations than they needed, the old system of asking for a little fat to make sure the appropriation would last the year out.

Dawes used no pyrotechnics. He spoke in a low, earnest, kindly, conversational tone. He had praise for "the tens of thousands of loyal Government men and women who, in this immediate emergency, must be chiefly depended upon to reduce the present terrible cost of governmental administration."

At the end, with a touch of old-fashioned evangelism, he called on all those who would cooperate to rise. The entire audience rose.

"I am glad to say," Dawes noted in his diary, "that an attitude of cooperation exists already so far as the Treasury Department is concerned. Indicating what sort of a man is at the head of this Department, in his conception of the necessities of the present and the future of the Budget Bureau, Secretary Mellon walked upstairs to my office. He did this because he regarded it as necessary in connection with a call from me for information needed by the President of the United States. It will be an historic walk in the annals of the Budget Bureau."

Dawes' attitude would not always remain as amiable as it had been in the first session. At the very next meeting, before an audience as large as that of the first, and again including President Harding, Vice-President Coolidge, the Cabinet, and General Pershing, he felt the need of saying some disagreeable things.

He had learned that the Army was selling surplus supplies at ridiculously low prices to speculators who resold them at large profits to the Navy. Dawes reported this information, then told of the cooperation he had received in some quarters, and also took notice of an underhanded effort to sabotage his campaign for economy. Suddenly he interrupted his speech and called to an assistant:

"Now hand me those brooms!"

Two brooms were brought in. Dawes brandished them above his head.

"This may look like stage play, but it is not, because things like this have got to stop. Here is a Navy broom, made in accordance with Navy specifications. Here is an Army broom, made in accordance with Army specifications. Now, the Army had 350,000 of these brooms surplus. The Navy needed 18,000 brooms. It could have had the Army brooms for nothing but, because they were wrapped with twine instead of wire, the Navy wouldn't take them as a gift. So the Navy went into the market and bought brooms at top prices.

"Suppose a thing like that had occurred in a private business organization. Would it ever be necessary to bring it before the entire body of the organization at a semiannual meeting as an example to be avoided? The mere knowledge of it in the body of a business organization would drive the guilty man out of his position in disgrace!"

While Dawes was driving home his point in this and other ways, he was also concerned to establish the office of Director of the

Budget on a basis from which a man less forceful than himself could carry on. Since this required authority in some respect over the members of the Cabinet, it was a delicate matter.

"The administrative vice-president of an ordinary corporation," he wrote, "becomes a conduit of pressure downward upon the business organization in the interest of unified executive plan and policy. Unfortunately, however, our governmental Cabinets have always been a conduit for the transmission of pressure from the body of the business organization upward for complete departmental independence.

"As advisers of the President in matter of national policy, they can rightfully stand upon their dignity without injury to the country, and, the more independent their advice, the more valuable it may be; but, as the administrators of the routine business, they must be at all times subordinate to the President and to the coordinating machinery now created by him for the transmission of a unified business program.

"I dictated, as a memorandum to the President, the reasons why the Director of the Budget must have the right to summon in conference, when needed, the Cabinet heads, to insure the successful operation of the Bureau. It is absolutely essential for the first Director to get these things settled in custom and as recognized principles, since, unsettled, they will hereafter wreck the system. The force of the *status quo* in Washington is very strong.

"I want to get a *status quo* on this matter of the relation of the Director to the Cabinet heads for the benefit of the system, hereafter as well as now. Some time in the future, as so often in the past, there will come an administration headed by a man not especially trained to the business view of government administration. There will be some new Cabinet officer of forceful methods, great conceit, and inflamed with the desire of impressing his little personality on the history of the country, entirely unmindful of the long line of forgotten predecessors who attempted in vain the same thing.

"This man will see in the machinery essential to control the business methods of the Government a challenge to his individual power and importance. With the Chief Executive indifferent to business matters, such a marplot can get temporary notoriety through assertions of independence of the budget system and, provided there is executive weakness, do great injury to his country."

Although the appropriations for the new fiscal year had already been made and were to go into effect within one week after Dawes' arrival, he prepared a new tentative budget designed to reduce expenditures below the amount of the Congressional appropriations. Such a thing was unheard of in Washington. Once the appropriations had been made, the fate of the taxpayer was sealed.

Dawes slashed right and left. He made Colonel Henry C. Smithers, a tough Army man, coordinator general; called in a dozen more able Army and Navy men; and induced another dozen outstanding businessmen from private life to come into his office at one dollar per year. In this list were two of his brothers, Rufus and Henry M. Dawes. Others were such nationally known names as A. J. Earling, Samuel M. Felton, Colonel John S. Sewell, and former Senator Lawrence Y. Sherman. How much could be accomplished with such a staff under Dawes' guidance may be gathered from a memorandum covering the activities of one day:

"On the first onslaught, the Navy dropped out on a hundred-million-dollar reduction I had put down for them. Admiral Coontz (Chief of Naval Operations) is a tough old buck. I had to accept his statement as far as the present is concerned.

"Agriculture followed by reneging on $25,000,000. Beads of perspiration formed on my forehead and, I regret to say, profane ejaculations characterized my vocabulary. Secretary Mellon, who joined me at the office, joined also in the perspiration, although naturally a cool man. By evening, I had raked up a dependable $305,000,000, notwithstanding the $125,000,000 that dropped out."

In spite of such signal achievements, Dawes never forgot the limits within which his bureau was to function.

"The Budget Bureau," he said at one of the semiannual meetings, "must keep humble. If it ever becomes obsessed with the idea that it has any work except to save money and improve efficiency in routine business, it will cease to be useful. Again I say, we have nothing to do with policy. Much as we love the President, if Congress, in its omnipotence over appropriations, and in accordance with its authority over policy, passed a law that garbage should be put on the White House steps, it would be our regrettable duty, as a bureau, in an impartial, nonpolitical, and nonpartisan way, to advise the Executive and Congress on how the largest amount of garbage could be spread in the most inexpensive and economical manner."

Although the statutory term of office was seven years, Dawes remained faithful to his original resolve to leave at the end of twelve months.

"As I proceed," Dawes said, "I am surer of my position that, as one who must be used to upset the *status quo*, I am not the logical man to continue the operation of the Budget Bureau after it is organized, and after the way is cleared for its operation by the establishment of precedent, custom, and executive attitude and regulations.

"There is a great relief in feeling this way, for I detest this life. Once it is clearly understood by everybody that I am to leave upon the presentation of the first budget, I will have in the minds of all, when I advise machinery and regulations, what Woodrow Wilson called 'the moral advantage of disinterestedness.'"

On June 30, 1922, when his year was up, Dawes had more than made good his promise to save a billion dollars. During his twelve months in office, government expenditures exclusive of debt repayment had been cut down to $3,375,000,000, a saving of one and three quarter billion dollars over the preceding fiscal year. The Federal Budget was not only balanced in that year, but receipts exceeded expenditures by nearly three quarters of a billion dollars, and the public debt had been reduced by slightly over one billion dollars. Even taxes had been lowered. Said Charles Evans Hughes: "Only Dawes, with his experience, energy, and untiring devotion to his task, could have done the job that was done."

Dawes himself noted:

"I am carrying back as souvenirs of this experience the handwritten pasteboard sign on the office door: 'Bureau of the Budget,' and two brooms. I wish I could take back some of the secondhand furniture which we raked up in the Treasury cellars. One cannot successfully preach economy without practicing it. Of the appropriation of $225,000, we spent only $120,313.54 in the year's work. We took our own medicine."

The system Dawes had instituted operated in the Budget

Bureau for eleven years. These years constitute the longest sustained effort at maximum economy in the history of the American government. In 1931, the English Royal Commission on Civil Service unanimously recommended to Parliament the adoption of the American budget system as conceived by Dawes.

But on June 10, 1933, two months after taking office, President Franklin D. Roosevelt abolished the Federal Coordinating Service of the United States, most essential part of the executive control system, without which there could be no adequate supervision of the correlated affairs of the government. Another seven years later, in 1940, Dawes was to say in a public speech:

"Some day, a President, if he is to save the country from bankruptcy and its people from ruin, must make the old fight over again, and this time the battle will be waged against desperate disadvantages. Against him will be arrayed the largest, strongest, and most formidably entrenched army of interested government spenders, wasters, and patronage-dispensing politicians the world has yet known."

If the Roosevelt Administration wanted someone to tell it how to "end slovenly fiscal housekeeping," no one was so well qualified as "Dawes who set up the centralized Federal budgeting system and showed results," Arthur Krock wrote in the New York *Times.* "But," Krock commented ruefully, "the spenders in the executive group" were not interested.

Chapter Fifteen

❀

THE "DAWES COMMITTEE"

Chicago had no monopoly on the crime wave of the early 1920's, but with its mobs fighting gory war for territory in which they would furnish illicitly brewed beer, alcohol for bathtub gin, and liquor for speakeasies, and with racketeers and gunmen moving in on some union labor organizations, Chicago yielded to no American community in her disrespect for law. The corrupt crowd of William Hale Thompson held the city hall, and Len Small's evil-smelling cohorts were in control of the state government at Springfield. Downstate, the Ku Klux Klan was in the ascendency. Labor hoodlumism made building operations in the nation's second largest city as dangerous as a battlefield. Needed home and business construction had to be abandoned or delayed.

In April of 1923 Dawes announced the formation of an organization whose aim it was to counteract these influences. The organization was to be known as the "Minute Men of the Constitution."

In his statement announcing the formation of the organization, Dawes hit out at "the wide disrespect for law, the cowardice of political leaders in evading issues involving good government when they tend to antagonize organized minorities, and the arrogance and lawlessness of certain unworthy leaders of special groups. . . . The organization," he hoped, "could reach our political parties over the minority organizations formed for selfish purposes, and over the ambitions of candidates for office and down into the hearts and consciences of law-abiding citizens.

"The country needs a new Bill of Rights, just as it did when the

211

Declaration of Independence was signed. We need to protect the country from those who are trying to dig under the cornerstones of the Constitution. Our organization is not a political body, but we are going to fight for clean politics. Neither is it antiunion. It is not against the closed union shop, but it maintains that union disputes should be settled in a legal manner."

The first company of the Minute Men was put together in Evanston under the captaincy of a former First Army Division machine-gun captain, who had brought sixty fellow American Legion members to Dawes' residence for the purpose. Most of these sixty took leaves of absence from their businesses, professions, or employment to canvass for members. In six weeks they recruited 6,000 members for Evanston Company No. 1.

"In this effort to support law enforcement I did not turn to any but young men, including with them only a very few gray heads," Dawes wrote. "Youth is a matter of soul and spirit and, therefore, in its essence is not to be measured in years. The reason I did not turn to my business friends was not because they are not patriotic citizens, but because youth always furnishes the energy and translation of idealism into immediate and unquestioning action.

"The older man is cynical and reform-weary. He has participated in so many efforts for good which have failed. He wishes well and votes well and applauds constitutional principles at public dinners. But after many years of experience he needs some demonstration that his work is really going to be effective before he will join, in earnest, this kind of activity, which requires him in the early stages to subordinate golf, dinner engagements, ball games, and business itself to its calls."

In June Dawes himself slammed down the top of his bank desk and began setting up companies throughout the state. There were no dues for membership, no pay for organizers, and every precaution was taken that membership should not yield any monetary profit to anybody. Expenses were negligible. All meeting places were furnished free. Audiences as high as 5,000 heard some of Dawes' speeches; crowds of 3,500 were common. While Evanston, with its enrolled membership of 7,300, was the largest, there were Quincy with 3,500 and Moline with 1,500, down to as low as 100 in some communities. In its heyday the organization reached a membership of 42,786, and had 154 companies in 42 of the 102 counties in Illinois. It had some members in all but eight counties.

Some of Dawes' downstate meetings furnished real fireworks. At Joliet, where the sheriff had been slain by gangsters, Dawes went to address a citizens' meeting. Less than fifty people turned out. The mayor who was to introduce him had left the city. Dawes stood up and said:

"I have been getting audiences of 1,000 to 3,000 people in other towns, and it hasn't been considered a disgrace to introduce me. Your mayor ran away like a yellow dog. I won't insult these men who are here with me by addressing fifty people. This town isn't worth the powder it would take to blow it up."

With that he walked out of the room. A few days later he was invited back to address a meeting of 500 civic leaders. He took General Dumont of France as a guest, and enrolled 400 members in a Joliet company.

Both in Chicago and downstate Dawes was constantly threatened with physical violence. He refused to heed the fears of his friends that he might be slugged. He never was.

The Minute Men's first test came in Cook County in a judicial election and against labor bosses. Two high and respected judges, Denis E. Sullivan, a Democrat, and Jesse E. Holdom, a Republican, were attacked as "injunction judges." Dawes rallied his twenty Cook County companies behind the two judges, asserting the union leaders were guilty of misrepresentation.

"Judges Holdom and Sullivan, under the law, were required to issue these injunctions when a proper bill was presented to them," he said. "They merely followed the law as they found it. An attack upon judges who follow the Constitution and the laws of Illinois should be condemned by all classes of citizens because the security of all is bound up in the enforcement of the law and a social condition which means their protection from illegal acts. A labor injunction restrains men who want to assault and kill from carrying out such practices. It does not prevent a man from striking, nor does it prevent him from going to work. It is an arm of the law intended to protect society in the peaceful carrying on of the affairs of life.

"In the coming judicial election, therefore, we find an attack being made by men assuming to represent minority organizations upon judges who have done their full duty in carrying out the law. Under these circumstances, if Judges Sullivan and Holdom should be defeated, it would be an encouragement to all other judges to disregard the law at the behest of minority organizations rather than to enforce it."

The fight on the judges was made by a group of labor leaders, the ablest of whom, Dawes considered, was James C. Petrillo of the Musicians Union. Twenty companies of Minute Men in Cook County, backing the judges, rang doorbells and manned the polls on election day. The heavy majorities for Sullivan and Holdom in the suburbs, running nine to one in Evanston and almost as much in others, carried the day. The Fifteenth Ward in Evanston, heavily labor, went five to one for Sullivan and Holdom, and Dawes commented: "No better evidence could be had of the bluff and pretense of radical labor leaders when they claim they can influence the good citizens of labor organizations against the safeguards of law and order."

The Minute Men were accused of being anti-Ku Klux Klan. This accusation was true. For the program of the Klan included religious and racial intolerance, and the Klan considered itself to an extent independent of the regular law enforcement agencies.

"The opposition of the Klan," Dawes announced, "only emphasizes the necessity of what we are doing. Why does not the Ku Klux Klan, which professes to be for law enforcement, come out from behind their sheets? The truth of the matter is that they are taking the law into their hands in many sections of the country. Lawlessness is not helped by more lawlessness."

The Minute Men were also accused of being antiunion. That this accusation was false is perhaps best shown by the fact that the Steam and Operating Engineers Local of Chicago unanimously and in a body endorsed the purposes of the Minute Men, and that among the Minute Men themselves could be found a majority of the members of that Union as well as of many other labor unions.

"The question is often asked," Dawes said in a speech at Decatur, "if our organization was formed to fight for the open shop. I reply that the Supreme Court of the United States has held that the right to collective bargaining under which employee and employer may establish the closed shop is a constitutional right. If we advocated the open shop we would be striking at the Constitution just as the lawless labor leader does when he orders an American citizen assaulted in an effort to establish the closed shop. We will always have with us these economic contests, and good citizens will differ on the open and the closed shop. These contests should be waged under the law which protects the inalienable rights of the individual."

But while the Minute Men had no intention of opposing labor, they intended just as little to yield ground to gangsters who had seized control of some of the labor unions. As Dawes put it:

"The labor demagogues did not inspire us with political trepidation. This movement is in the interest of all labor—union and non-union—and all classes of citizens. It is simply a movement for good government, equally important to all. Union labor is, in the great majority, patriotic. In Chicago, it is suffering under a leadership in part composed of gunmen and criminals, who impose a slavery through intimidation upon their membership to which only the autocracy of Lenin and Trotsky can be compared."

The conceded accomplishment of the organization was victory in the bitterly contested Cook County judicial election of 1923. Its opposition undoubtedly caused the withdrawal of William Hale Thompson as a candidate for re-election as mayor in 1923, and it was instrumental in the nomination and election of many law enforcement candidates on a statewide nonpartisan basis in Illinois in 1924. But beyond this result, the organization had brought about a public awakening on the part of the citizens to the necessity of watching state elections, preventing fraud at the polls, and counteracting unfair propaganda.

However, there was trouble brewing elsewhere on the globe. Germany had defaulted on a reparations payment and France and Belgium had sent troops into the Ruhr. The British had taken exception to the French and Belgian action, while the Germans threw up their hands and asserted that they simply could not pay. And so Dawes was called to head a committee of experts which was to solve a hopelessly tangled situation.

With all that has happened since, it is difficult to realize today how important the question of German reparations was to the well-being of Europe and indeed of the whole world back in the year 1923. After the end of World War I, it seemed a settled proposition to all thinking men that Germany should pay for the damage she had wrought in an unprovoked aggression. A Reparations Commission had been set up to formulate the terms of settlement.

The figures appearing in the numerous reports of that commission staggered the imagination: the war debt of Germany was set variously at sixty-seven, eighty-six, and finally thirty-three billion dollars. Then, while German mouth harmonicas, shipped in part payment, flooded France, the German currency collapsed and inflated to a point where German bankers were eager to pay twelve thousand billion marks for one American dollar.

The average man with a cursory interest read at intervals of such apparently futile political starts as those made at Boulogne, San Remo, Hythe, and Brussels; of the Spa Conference, "Paris Decisions," "London Ultimatums," and the actual payment by Germany of one billion gold marks on September 21, 1921. Then followed news of defaults, moratoriums, conferences and counterproposals, and finally the military move which sent the French and Belgian armies marching back into the Ruhr on January 11, 1923.

The United States did not claim reparations from Germany. Whatever sums came out of Germany were to go to France, Great Britain, Italy, and Belgium, with some payments to Japan, Greece, Portugal, Yugoslavia, and Rumania. All America hoped to recover were the relatively small expenses of the American Army of Occupation in Germany, and the ten billion dollars in war and reconstruction loans made to the Allies. But since the French asserted that they could not pay their debts unless the Germans did, even these modest hopes of the United States were to prove illusionary.

Secretary of State Charles E. Hughes, in his address at New Haven, Connecticut, on December 21, 1922, made his historical proposal that the reparations question be referred to a committee of experts who would make an effort to solve it from an economic rather than a political viewpoint. A year later, the Allied powers accepted the Hughes proposal and issued the invitations to General Dawes and Owen D. Young to participate. They were invited as eminent American citizens and not as authorized agents of the American Government. Great Britain chose Sir Josiah Stamp and Sir Robert

M. Kindersley; France, Jean Parmentier and Edgard Allix; Belgium, Baron Maurice Houtart and Monsieur Emile Francqui; Italy, Dr. Alberto Pirelli and Prof. Federico Flora. In extending the invitation, the Reparations Commission of the Allied governments designated Dawes to act as chairman.

The Allied governments were especially anxious that Dawes should accept. As General Purchasing Agent for the A.E.F., United States member of the Military Board for Allied Supply, and in a role which amounted to diplomatic representative of Pershing during World War I, he ranked, so far as Europe was concerned, as one of the American big four—Woodrow Wilson, Pershing, and Herbert Hoover being the other three.

On December 27, 1923, General Dawes, Owen Young, and Rufus Dawes, brother of the General, who had been selected by Dawes and Young as chief of their personal staff of assistants, conferred for two hours with Secretary of State Hughes. Next day they sailed aboard the liner *America,* of the United States Shipping Board, for the session of the "Committee of Experts" in Paris and Berlin.

Dawes and Young were acutely aware of the magnitude and importance of their task. Restoration of the productivity of Germany was a world necessity. The two Americans and their associates faced the necessity of finding means to balance the budget and stabilize the currency of Germany first of all. Their studies aboard ship convinced them of the accuracy of what the French statesman Louis Barthou was to tell them in the opening session at Paris: "It may be said without exaggeration that the peace of the whole world depends upon the settlement of the reparations problem."

Dawes summed up his view of the situation as follows:

"The question of reparations in each country concerned involves both an economic and a political problem, and a proper settlement of it in any one of them or among all of them necessitates a compromise between economics and politics along lines of expediency which recognizes the real essentials of both.

"In negotiating settlements of such a nature, men of official position, endeavoring to avoid offense to public opinion, tend to advocate proposals sacrificing economic principles for temporary political objectives, while economists, on the other hand, in applying economic principles, tend to disregard existing public sentiment which, however prejudiced, ignorant or temporary at first, must eventually determine the fate of the settlement."

Before boarding ship, Dawes had discussed his assignment with Roland Boyden, formerly observer for the United States on the Reparations Commission, and with Dwight Morrow.

"In our talk with Morrow and Boyden a divergence of views manifested itself of which, no doubt, we will see constantly the counterpart during our work abroad," Dawes wrote. "Boyden seemed to think that to give Germany 'the will to work' the limit of reparations should be fixed now—that productivity in Germany depends upon removing the menace of indefinite reparations. Morrow, on the other hand, believes that the stabilization of the currency and the balancing of the budget are the important things now as the first step—that an endeavor to fix reparations now means an impasse with France, which does not propose to estimate the present strength of an impoverished Germany in such a way as to foreclose the case finally. Morrow feels that given a currency system and a reformed budget, Germany will commence to revive as Austria has, notwithstanding that vast and unsettled reparations overhang the country and its people."

All through the trip across the ocean, Dawes and his staff continued to familiarize themselves with their assignment. There were daily conferences aboard ship.

"Ship Captain Rind has been very considerate of us and set aside the children's play room as our place of conference. The significance of this choice was not wholly lost on us. Through some mysterious subconscious mental agreement, probably arising out of a desire to forget the more appropriate actual designation, we are calling the conference room 'the dog house.'

"These daily conferences on the boat, involving as they do the constant repetition of thought on this unfamiliar question—this mental exercise is doing to the mind what physical repetition of exercise does to the body. It is not only adding to our knowledge but is preparing us for this kind of work when we land next Monday. I really attach more importance to the exercise which my mind has had than to the knowledge which it has acquired in the last week."

Dawes quickly formed a deep liking for Owen Young. "I am

delighted with my associate, Owen D. Young. He is all that Harbord has said and more. He has intellectual poise. His ability, after patiently listening to a detailed discussion, to summarize his conclusions in a few sentences is remarkable. The elimination of the nonessentials marks all his processes of thought. Added to that, he inspires not only confidence but friendship and trust."

The capacity of Young's mind to cut through details to the heart of the problem became more and more precious to Dawes as the days went by. For the man who was to head the "Committee of Experts" soon began to lament in his private notes that he found himself "knee-deep in experts."

"Am getting rather 'fed up' on expert opinion as I read long arguments of 'experts' winding up with diametrically opposite conclusions. I realize the value of 'expert' opinion, but I realize also the danger of its unqualified acceptance. Where a man has acquired his 'expertness' merely as a judge and observer of the work of other men whose burdens he himself has never borne—in other words, where he lacks a definite and personal experience in a practical participating way with the work itself—I regard his opinions and advice of negligible value.

"My reading of the economic arguments, pro and con, inspires in me a feeling of apprehension when I see myself designated as an 'expert.' Is it possible that my common sense is suspected? All international economists deal with a subject so vast that it defies comparison with other subjects upon which we are accustomed to call in experts. For this reason, these economists enjoy a general range of possible asininity, wider and more unchallenged than any others. By some of them one must set great store—by others, none. One thing is certain, the European situation needs something besides theoretical discussion.

"Less and less I am impressed with detailed argument. The more I hear, the more clearly I see that if, as a Committee, we are to make progress and really be helpful, we must be something quite different from a debating society. Just now my mind is upon those methods which I must adopt as Chairman to accomplish results.

"Nothing is more important at the inception of important work than humility of opinion. If one does not have it, he can never be sure that he has all the facts, much less the proper sense of their relative importance. I think Young and I are humble and open-minded."

The American group arrived in Paris on January 7. An assembly of former wartime associates had met on the station platform to greet Dawes. But if they expected to see him with his famous black cigar they were disappointed. For Dawes, faithful to a promise he had made to Marshal Foch, had given up cigar smoking, and had instead adopted that famous underslung pipe which a friend had given to him, and which caused the smoke to travel through a wooden channel fifteen inches long. Soon the "upside-down" pipe would become Dawes' hallmark.

Paris was beckoning, but Dawes had work to do. "As this detail is a working one," he wrote, slipping into military lingo, "I am declining all invitations. It certainly seems like old times to be lying awake nights thinking over difficult problems. It is the irony of fate that Paris, the playground of the traveling American, is, and always has been for me, the place of strenuous endeavor night and day and little else."

But he did find time for his close friends. Pershing was in Paris completing his book, *My Experiences in the World War,* and they were to be much together. General Payot was running the railroads in the Ruhr and, as it was important for Dawes to know about the Ruhr, he called in his old wartime coadjutor. He recorded dinners and luncheons with eighty-four-year-old Clemenceau, with Foch, with Sir Robert Horne, who had been Lloyd George's wartime chancellor of the exchequer, and with Charles M. Schwab and other old friends. Foch asked for an upside-down pipe and wrote Dawes that he had adopted it for his smoking.

On January 14, 1924, Dawes made his speech at the opening session of the Committee. It was straightforward and hard-hitting in the best Dawes tradition:

"This is no time to mince words. What, today, at the inception of our work, have we found? In the first place we see an impenetrable and colossal fogbank of economic opinions, based upon premises of fact which have changed so rapidly as to make the bulk of them seem worthless even if they were in agreement. With all due respect to the great ability of those experts who have wandered through this gloomy labyrinth, they could not have failed to come out in the opposite direction. They were confronted with the necessity of finding stable conclusions where no conditions were stable. If in their computations designed to clarify the mind, they dealt with the mark, the next week the mark was something else; if they dealt with the dollar, the pound, the French or Belgian franc, or the Italian lira, there was one value in foreign exchange for each, and another in internal purchasing power; if they dealt in gold there were values in prewar gold and postwar gold to be considered. In general, we failed to find much value in economic arguments based on what ought to be instead of what is.

"While immense libraries of legal arguments, of more or less obsolete statistics, and of economic discussion were being laboriously compiled for five years, the economic foundations of Germany have well-nigh crumbled away.

"How could anyone, expert or nonexpert, suggest anything worthwhile about a German budget if the money collected through taxes and disbursed under the budget would not buy or pay for anything? The first step we should take, it seems to me, is to devise a system to stabilize Germany's currency, so that we can get some water to run through the budget mill. Let us build the mill after we find the stream to turn its wheels.

"We are less concerned for the moment with the present capacity of Germany to pay, than with the present capacity and courage of this Committee to act. Why waste time in formalities and meaningless courtesies and conventionalities?

"The house is afire. We propose to find some water to put it out, without the further use of mathematics involving the fourth dimension."

Next morning, the speech appeared in twenty different languages all over the continent. Troubled Europe heaved a sigh of relief. These plain words were the first ray of hope in many years. Owen Young said no more than the truth when in a speech in New York, nearly eleven months later, he reported:

"The installation speech of General Dawes, which was published in full in the newspapers in all the principal countries of the world, created a change in the public opinion of Europe. His directness, his courage, and his determination dispelled despair and doubt and gave hope and confidence to the masses of the people in Europe and a feeling of pride to the people of America. From that time on the Committee was no longer the 'Experts Committee' but the 'Dawes Committee.' "

Dawes' expectation that he would have to plow his way painfully through expert opinions was agreeably disappointed. "I never met an abler body of men," he wrote after the first meeting of the group. "It would seem impossible for such a group to adjourn without some accomplishment." Yet he was not overoptimistic. "When our work here is over," he said, "we shall get either garbage or garlands. I'll run the risk of the garbage."

Never did an international committee more quickly grapple with its problems. Between its opening on January 14, and its adjournment on April 9, the full committee held fifty-four meetings, the subcommittee on the budget held sixty-three, and the subcommittee on the stabilization of the currency, eighty-one. After a short time, Dawes was able to write into his diary:

"The first draft of the bank plan has been worked out in detail. We are now approaching some of the essential points of possible controversy. What substantial thing can be given Poincaré for whatever tangible he gives up in the Ruhr in order that Germany, under a new plan, can put herself in shape to commence on a general reparation effort? Many feel that if Germany be made strong enough to pay she will be strong enough to refuse to pay.

"But what if she is not made strong enough to pay, does not Europe face disaster, anyway? It is clear that every program is attended by dangerous contingencies. The only course we can take is a plain one—to assume that peace, well guarded, and not war, is the normal state of modern man."

Dawes kept the Committee in almost continuous session. Subcommittees met in the morning, plenary session took up the afternoon. Dr. Hjalmar Schacht, head of the German Reichsbank, was immediately sent for, and at the close of his testimony the committee had reached the opinion that an independent gold bank should be established in Germany.

"Schacht made a remarkable revelation of character during his questioning," Dawes wrote. "He frankly intimated that as long as he was the President of the Reichsbank, he was the bank."

But Dawes thought he got his best picture of German despair and desolation from M. Grassman, representative of labor: "Grassman made a very powerful and moving address. Why must the chief burdens of society fall most heavily upon those to whom it is most indebted?"

Dawes' notes on the work of the Committee are once again scanty, indicating the pressure under which he worked. The Dawes Plan that came out of the conference is history. But for an appraisal of Dawes' own work during the many meetings, we depend on the notes and memoirs of other participants.

"Those who did not know Dawes at the outset of our deliberations," Sir Josiah Stamp wrote, "knew of him, and that he was noted for his prompt action, vigorous and picturesque speech, with a special pipe of his own that stood for his personality almost without a cartoon, and having toward polite society an attitude around which hung an anecdotal cluster, in which the real and apocryphal were equally entertaining and inextricably mixed. We expected much from him and got more than we had expected. He kept himself free from detailed contention, and, therefore, stood as a final court of judgment, to which we had the less need to have recourse because he was always there. He kept the contacts with the outside world during the proceedings, freeing us from embarrassment but creating no feeling of aloofness or indifference.

"He had an eye for essentials and smooth working. And if leadership is encouragement, enheartenment at a critical time, and getting the best out of a team, he was a born leader. Some of us soon learned that underneath the 'Hell and Maria'-ness of a rather mythical violence was a singularly generous nature, punctuating faith in himself with strange essential humilities and an almost extravagant appreciation of the qualities and works of others. These characteristics go a little way toward explaining the uniform success he has had in his career in getting results, whether in France or as Director of the Budget, in the Dawes Committee, as Vice-President, as Ambassador, or in his bank, for he trusted his assistants and rejoiced in any limelight they could get, and it never affected one whit his own individuality."

And Owen Young:

"It was the charm of a unique personality, the sympathy of a

sensitive man with a capacity to understand different and often conflicting points of view, and finally the generosity of spirit which excited the admiration of every member of the Committee. General
Dawes became more than the impartial chairman of that diversified
group. Their several individual backgrounds and national interests
would naturally invite disintegration. The cohesive force which
held them together and brought a unanimous report on every point
considered by the Committee was General Charles G. Dawes."

French Jean Parmentier wrote how Dawes delighted the sessions with such apothegms as:

"Common sense when applied to great affairs is the height of
statesmanship. . . . Economic peace is the best antidote for war.
. . . A man falls in love with ideas simply because he created them,
not because they are worth creating. . . . We must not fear the
consequences of truth—only the failure to tell it completely."

Sir Josiah Stamp had listed ten critical points on each of which
the Committee might have split and gone home without agreement.
That it did not split, Stamp wrote, was due principally to Dawes, its
captain and leader.

On April 9, 1924, the Dawes Plan was completed. It was a
report as lengthy as the Versailles Treaty, but its terms were made
understandable in a summary prepared by Young and included in
the report. So intense was American interest in the agreement that
its 39,927 words were cabled to the United States that day at the rate
of 2,700 words per hour—the biggest single transmission by either
wire or cable up to that time.

Dawes himself wrote the letter of transmittal to the Reparations
Commission. In this document which would go into the archives of
the world he gave all credit to his associates:

"In their vision—in their independence of thought—and, above
all, in their high and sincere purpose which rises above small things
over which the small so often stumble, my colleagues have shown
themselves worthy of this trust. That their work, which I now place
in your hands, may assist you in the discharge of your great responsibilities is their prayer, and the knowledge, hereafter, that it has so
done will be their full reward."

Germany accepted the plan within the week. Secretary of State
Hughes wrote to Dawes: "Permit me to congratulate you upon your

extraordinary achievement. The more the question is considered the more clearly it appears that in this plan may be found the hope of salvation in Europe and that if it were thrown aside the result would be economic chaos. You and your associates have made a contribution of first magnitude to the peace and security of the world." Even President Coolidge, in what must have been for him an extraordinary burst of enthusiasm, cabled: "You and your associates represented not the American government, but the American mind."

The Dawes Committee had held the only completely successful conference on international governmental affairs between the end of World War I and the midway point of the twentieth century.

Whatever happened later in Europe because of the timidity among Allied statesmen and the rise of the maniac Hitler and the even more cunning and evil Stalin, these things are the record of the Dawes Committee: Its plan worked for its entire limit of five years. Germany had a normal parliamentary regime in that half decade— the only time it did between the dethronement of Emperor Wilhelm II and its dismemberment after World War II. For those five years Germany paid the reparation which the Committee had found was in its capacity to pay. For those five years Germany's economy, currency, and credit were re-established, and Europe had the greatest period of tranquillity between the two world wars.

While the public was hailing Dawes and his committee, he and Owen Young were driving in a cab through the streets of Paris. In the words of Young:

"The Committee being hailed in the European press as the saviors of civilization, General Dawes said to me at dinner in Paris, 'Say, Young, if we have saved civilization, don't you think we ought to investigate it and see if it's worth saving?' Realizing the importance of basic research, I accepted the daring challenge.

"Several hours later, how many I will not say, the General turned to me in the taxi that was bringing us home, and without referring to our earlier conversation said, 'Maybe she ain't worth it.' "

In October of 1924, after he had returned to Chicago, Dawes received a cable from Young in Paris: "Plan effective and in operation. Referring to your garbage and garlands, I am thankful you are receiving only garlands." Dawes, then campaigning as the Republican Vice-Presidential nominee, replied: "Sincere congratulations on your great success. Relative your remarks about garlands and garbage. My steady diet in this campaign is a mixture of the two."

As in all diaries, there are gaps and omissions in the diary of General Dawes. There is no mention that for his work as Chairman of the Reparations Committee of Experts he was awarded the Nobel Peace Prize. Nor is there any record of the fact that he never cashed the check which accompanied the Prize, but endorsed it over to the Walter Hines Page School of International Relations for which money was being raised at that time.

Chapter Sixteen

✿

COUNSEL FROM COUSIN CAL

$\mathcal{T}$he Republican national convention which met in Cleveland on June 10, 1924, was the first such party gathering to be broadcast over the radio, the nation's newest industry. Listeners all over the country put on their earphones or gathered closely around their loud-speakers, to hear a college president delivering the longest nomination speech in the annals of American political conventions in behalf of the most taciturn of all Presidents of the United States. Between the hours of five o'clock in the afternoon and ten o'clock at night on June 12, they would hear the convention stampeding twice to nominate two different Vice-Presidential candidates.

For four years the Republican party had chafed under the taunt that its Presidential nominations were made in smoke-filled rooms. Henry Cabot Lodge, whose strange ruling on the volume of the oral aye and nay adjournment vote four years before had set the stage for the smoke-filled room, was again present as a delegate. But for all of the influence he exerted this time, he might as well have stayed at his home in Cambridge.

The majority of the 1,109 delegates, gathered in Cleveland's shiny new convention hall, wanted most of all to do something for Frank O. Lowden, recent Governor of Illinois, who they felt had been euchred out of the 1920 nomination. They would gladly have nominated him for President. But Calvin Coolidge had been in the White House for ten months, and not to name him was unthinkable.

With top place on the ticket foreclosed, the delegates were determined to make amends by nominating Lowden for Vice-President.

Lowden, however, had no hankering for the Vice-Presidency and had emphatically so declared.

Among the men whom Lowden had informed of his decision, there was Mark W. Woods of Lincoln, Nebraska, the same man who had pushed Pershing into the Nebraska Presidential preference primary in 1920. Although Woods had failed then in sending to the White House a former Lincoln man, he was unabashed. If he could not make one former Lincoln man President of the United States, he would at least try to make another one Vice-President. That other man was Charles G. Dawes.

Woods broached his plan to Dawes. Again, he received no encouragement. Dawes felt that his friend Lowden should receive the nomination and, if the ticket won that November, should try for the Presidential nomination four years later. Then Dawes changed the subject to talk about the impending commencement exercises at Marietta College, which he meant to attend and make the occasion for a substantial gift to his old alma mater.

But Woods was not easily discouraged. Even though Dawes had been noncommittal, Woods felt certain that he would accept the nomination if it were presented to him as a *fait accompli*. Woods went on to Cleveland and went to work at once.

A tyro in politics, Woods knew no delegates except those from Nebraska. The only other two people at the convention whom he knew well were two men sitting in the press section: William Jennings Bryan, covering the convention for a newspaper syndicate, and a Texas correspondent who, four years earlier, had shared his enthusiasm for Pershing and now shared his admiration for Dawes.

"You know I share your high regard for Dawes, Mark," Bryan said to him. "If you succeed, your party will have a Vice-Presidential candidate who is abler than its Presidential candidate. I don't believe though that you control your own delegation."

Bryan was right. Of the nineteen delegates from Nebraska, ten were supporting the former Senator and then Circuit Court Judge William S. Kenyon. But among the Kenyon backers was Representative A. W. Jefferis of Omaha, among whose ambitions was that of becoming Senator. Jefferis might be open to any suggestion that would bring him to favorable public notice in Nebraska.

And so Woods buttonholed Jefferis and explained his proposition. He painted in glowing colors the great political and other benefits that would fall to any man heard over the radio in a nominating speech. Hundreds and thousands of miles away, in every part of the country, people would be crowding around radio receivers, attracted by the novelty of listening to a party convention. No man from Nebraska had ever been able to command such a nationwide audience, and if he, Jefferis, were to place the former Nebraskan Dawes in nomination, there would not be a home in the entire state to remain ignorant of it. His would be an historic performance, especially if it should turn out that Dawes was the choice of the convention.

Jefferis was convinced. His switch brought the Cornhusker delegation caucus over to Dawes.

The overwhelming sentiment of the convention, however, was in favor of Lowden. Lowden was given the nomination. Nebraska and New Jersey gave their entire strength to Dawes, and scattered votes from sixteen other states ran him up to an unexpected 149 votes.

While the convention adjourned to await Lowden's reaction, Woods canvassed Lowden's supporters to secure pledges for Dawes if Lowden should decline. And up to June 12, 1924, no man in American history had ever refused a Presidential or Vice-Presidential nomination bestowed upon him by one of the major parties.

After a few hours, the unprecedented had happened. Lowden declined. The convention, led by the big state delegations from New York, Pennsylvania, Illinois, Michigan, and Texas, stampeded as noisily and enthusiastically to Dawes as it had supported Lowden a scant five hours before. Dawes' margin over Herbert Hoover, the next candidate, was nearly three to one—682½ votes to 234½ votes, despite the fact that William M. Butler, chairman of the Republican National Committee, was working for Hoover.

"The Republican candidate for Vice-President," wrote William Jennings Bryan in a syndicated newspaper article, "is a successful businessman, a man of character, patriotism, and civic enthusiasm. In all public positions which he has held, beginning with Comptroller of the Currency, he has acquitted himself creditably. He goes into the campaign a more active factor than the Vice-Presidential candidate usually is. He is a more vigorous personality than the President."

Dawes received news of the convention's action in Marietta.

"My nomination occurred unexpectedly to myself while I was at my old home in Marietta, attending the commencement exercises of the college from which I was graduated," his journal reads. "There is one recollection I shall always treasure. It is of the gathering of thousands of the people of the town the next day to hear me speak briefly from the front porch of the old family home. The church bells were rung in honor of the occasion. Some people may claim the Vice-Presidency doesn't amount to much, but just then it seemed to me the greatest office in the world.

"The old proverb 'A prophet is not without honor save in his own country' embodies a general truth with but rare exceptions. The prophet in this case was one who had spent a more or less mischievous boyhood in the town, and his reflection was that the only explanation of the stirring scene was that those who really knew him then had for the most part departed this life."

Three days later Dawes stood before his house in Evanston, in the rain, and addressed two thousand of his neighbors, both Republicans and Democrats, who had come to call on him in spite of the weather.

"Before such a gathering I could not be partisan," Dawes said. "As human beings, whatever may be our party, we are bound to differ on many subjects, but as good citizens we can unite to demand of those who represent us in political debate that they represent our differences honestly and from the standpoint of truth—not from the standpoint of prejudice and passions. The man who distorts facts, the man who preaches pleasant doctrines to one portion of the people and another pleasant but absolutely inconsistent doctrine to another portion, is a menace to the safety of our fundamental institutions. As good citizens, irrespective of party, we must demand from our political leaders a strict adherence to the truth, including disagreeable truth.

"I have recently returned from Europe where I have seen in prostrated industry and human suffering the effects of demagogic political appeals to the passions and prejudices of the different people, as distinguished from appeals to their reason and common sense. To the very brink of the abyss has Europe been brought by this method of treating serious questions, involving great elemental and

economic principles. To save herself, she has abandoned the demagogue and returned to common sense. As to the demagogue on the
stump in the coming campaign, whatever may be his party, I want
it distinctly understood that I will ask no quarter, and will give
none."

On July 1 Dawes went to Washington to discuss campaign plans
with President Coolidge. The two men who were now ticket mates
had not been especially close to each other before their nomination.
In Dawes' papers there are copies of only a few letters that had
passed between them, among them one from Coolidge dated November 23, 1923, which reads:

"You know I am no hand to write letters unless I have some kind
of business, but it does not seem right for me not to see you and hear
from you once in a while."

The Washington visit was to have a tragic ending. During dinner of July 2, fourteen-year-old Calvin Coolidge, Jr., felt ill and left
the table.

"While I did not realize that there was anything serious about
Calvin's illness, I think the President must have sensed it from the
first," Dawes said. "He seemed to lose all interest in the conversation
and the dinner soon ended. I was to leave that night to continue my
talks with Young and Morrow in New York on the preparations for
putting the Reparations plan into effect. As I passed the door of
Calvin's room I chanced to look in. He seemed to be in great distress.
The President was bending over the bed. I think I have never witnessed such a look of agony and despair as was on the President's
face. From that moment I felt a closeness to Coolidge I had never
felt before, and have never lost. I had gone through the same great
sorrow that he faced."

A blister on the boy's foot, contracted while playing tennis on
the White House lawn the day before, had caused blood poisoning.
Celebrated specialists hurried to the White House for consultation.
Their efforts were of no avail; death came on Monday night, July 7.

Calvin Coolidge had little heart left for the campaign. The
brunt of the stumping was to fall on Dawes.

At this stage, the outcome of the election was far from a foregone conclusion. The Republicans had then no reason to expect the
boon they were to receive from the Democrats, who made a spectacle

of themselves in a slugging, snarling 103-ballot McAdoo-Smith dead-lock in Madison Square Garden. This, too, was the first Democratic national convention ever to be broadcast, and a nation listened in as the oldest of the national parties signed its own 1924 death warrant.

Senator Robert M. LaFollette of Wisconsin had been nominated by the third party. On July 7 the Socialist party formally enlisted under his banner.

There was in the third-party platform a plank which called for congressional veto of judicial decisions. And Eugene Debs, the Socialist leader, had backed LaFollette with the words: "I think it is wise for our party to make no nominations under the circumstances, but at the same time to hold the Socialist party intact, adhere strictly to its principles, and keep the red flag flying." These were the two issues on which Dawes intended to base his campaign.

Both the President and William M. Butler of Massachusetts, chairman of the Republican National Committee, differed from Dawes in their ideas on how the campaign should be run. Early in August President Coolidge sent to Dawes one of the most unusual letters ever written by a Presidential candidate to his Vice-Presidential running mate. It is such an extraordinary document that Dawes put it in his lockbox, where it remained for the rest of his life. It ran:

THE WHITE HOUSE
WASHINGTON

August 2, 1924

My dear General:

Thinking you may have the same difficulty in writing a speech of acceptance that I had four years ago, I am going to venture to try to help you.

The more simple you can keep it, the better you will like it. You have for your guide, of course, the Party's platform, and you might get some suggestions out of my message to the Congress and the speeches that I have made since that time. If you keep as much as you can to an expression of general principles, rather than attempting to go into particular details of legislation, you will save yourself from a great deal of annoying criticism. More people will agree with you if you say we ought to have protection, than if you begin to discuss various schedules. More people will favor opposition to high surtaxes, than the adherence to specific rates.

I know how irksome it is to attempt to restate what others have said, instead of having perfect freedom to branch out in any direction you might wish. But that is the penalty we have to pay for running in pairs. Should you think that I could possibly be of any help, do not fail to run down here any time, or communicate with me in other ways, always keeping in mind that my telegrams and telephones are public property.

It may interest you to know that I was much pleased to learn the other day that I am kin to Manasseh Cutler, through the Rice family, and therefore kin to you. We are both kin to John Quincy Adams.

With kindest regards to you and Mrs. Dawes, I am

> Very truly yours,
> (Signed) CALVIN COOLIDGE

Brig. General Charles G. Dawes
Chicago, Illinois
P.S. Whenever you go anywhere, take Mrs. Dawes along.

Chairman Butler wanted to make economy in government expenditures the dominant issue, and gave instructions to that effect to Dawes in what amounted to a ukase. Dawes disagreed. To him, the paramount issue lay in LaFollette's call for congressional veto of judicial decisions.

"This proposition," Dawes stated, "is to abrogate the threefold division of power—executive, legislative, and judicial—which is the basis of our Constitution, and to make the executive and judicial power subordinate to legislative power. Its effect likewise would be disastrous to the rights of states, to which are reserved such rights of government as are not specifically delegated to the federal government by the Constitution. It would be practically equivalent to a government of pure democracy, which history has proved is most futile and disastrous for the proper protection of the people."

While Coolidge undoubtedly agreed with Butler on the matter of what the issue should be, neither the President nor the National Chairman pressed their points. Dawes sent his acceptance speech, stressing the issue raised by LaFollette, to the President before its delivery, and Coolidge made no suggestions for changes in the speech other than in the LaFollette section where he thought it better to use the phrase "an important issue" rather than "the predominant issue." Dawes delivered the speech on August 19, from the porch of his Evanston home, to a crowd estimated at fifty thousand people which filled the yard, the street, and a park running down to the shore of Lake Michigan.

Once the campaign had opened, Dawes' relations with both Coolidge and Butler were the most cordial. His one acrimonious brush was with Representative Everett Sanders of Indiana, chairman of the Speakers' Bureau of the Republican National Committee. Sanders claimed the right to censor the speeches of Dawes and all other speakers for the national ticket. Dawes went to the offices of the National Committee in Chicago and spoke his mind:

"Everett, I was nominated for this office at Cleveland by all or part of the delegates from thirty-seven of the forty-eight states. I was not a candidate for either President or Vice-President. I assume that the men and women who nominated me knew of my record of independence. I intend to be guided by my own conscience and my own judgment of the issues to be presented and the manner of their presentation. If that is not satisfactory to the National Committee then I will not speak under its auspices. I will conduct my own campaign and pay my own expenses."

Sanders argued that Dawes was planning a course that would wreck the Republican party.

"What about Maine?" Sanders asked. "The Maine Republican Central Committee has forbidden anyone to mention the Ku Klux Klan there. If you make the speech there, that I understand you intend to, regardless of what may happen in Maine we will lose Indiana by 150,000 votes."

Dawes knew full well that Indiana and Maine were the two most completely Klan-dominated states in the north. But the descendent of Manasseh Cutler and future cofounder of the Chicago branch of the National Conference of Christians and Jews would not soft-pedal this issue.

"I intend to speak on the Klan in Maine," he replied. "I may make many mistakes but I think I can make the campaign without discredit to myself or the party. If I go into office I want to go with the respect of the people of this country. The occupancy of a public office, unless decorated with public respect, is a curse to anyone."

The showdown was not long in coming. Dawes opened his campaign at Augusta on August 23. A Ku Klux Klan official, high in the councils of the Republican party, sat on the platform a few seats away from the Vice-Presidential candidate. Dawes opened his speech:

"I first desire to speak relative to the Ku Klux Klan."

Taking as his text Josiah Quincy's statement, "Society is never more certainly in the path of destruction than when it trusts itself to the guidance of secret societies," Dawes continued:

"Government cannot last if that way, the way of the Ku Klux Klan, is the way to enforce the law in this country. Lawlessness cannot be met with lawlessness if civilization is to be maintained."

This speech had precipitated the issue that the more timid members of the Republican party had most feared. There were widespread rumors that Calvin Coolidge would take vigorous exception. But three days after the speech was delivered, the Maine Republican State Central Committee chairman wired to the President and to the National Committee at Chicago that, in his opinion, Dawes' speech had saved the Republican campaign there instead of injuring it. This was what Dawes would have expected. His diary reads:

"When I arrived at Augusta and it was learned I was to mention the dread word 'Ku Klux,' the state committee was in a state of extreme apprehension which it took no pains to conceal. Under its orders no Republican state candidate had been allowed to refer to the subject in his speeches. However, before an audience of six thousand people, I started my speech: 'I first desire to speak relative to the Ku Klux Klan.'

"Knowing there can be no reaction to right except a right reaction, I had no misgivings as to the reception of the speech by the public. It was, I am told, the only argumentative statement on the Ku Klux subject made by a candidate during the campaign."

President Coolidge, whom Dawes saw at Plymouth Notch, Vermont, the day after the speech, remarked that it was "good."

"The President, Mrs. Coolidge, and I took lunch in the little dining room off the sitting room. During the lunch Colonel Coolidge, the President's father, took no part in the conversation. In the sitting room afterwards he said nothing, but after a time he rose and left the room. The President and Mrs. Coolidge were sitting where they could see out of the window, and although I could not do so, I knew what was happening. About thirty newspapermen, waiting outside to tackle me, waylaid the Colonel. The President rose abruptly, and with considerable impatience said: 'I asked him to say nothing.' Mrs. Coolidge replied: 'I don't think you need worry about your father.' When finally I met the newspaper phalanx outdoors, I asked them what they had said to the Colonel. 'We asked him what you and the President were talking about, of course,' they replied. 'What did he say?' I asked. 'My hearing ain't as good as it used to be!' had been the reply of the President's father."

On August 29 Dawes spoke at Lincoln. He received a noisy welcome. Before a crowd of twenty-five thousand people assembled under the hard hot sun of a Nebraska summer, he discussed the farm question, calling it the "most serious economic situation now confronting the United States." From Lincoln, his train was to carry him fifteen thousand miles over the country to deliver 108 speeches to hundreds of thousands in his large audiences, and to millions more who listened on the radio.

Dawes hammered away at radicalism in any guise. He made the most of Debs' red flag statement.

"Here is the alignment and here are the two flags," he told his audiences. "Neither President Coolidge nor his party platform assumes that the Constitution of the United States is an outworn document of old-fashioned ideas to be discarded for the principles of the new socialism. Robert M. LaFollette, leading the army of extreme radicalism, has a platform demanding public ownership and attacking our courts which are the fundamental and constitutional safeguard of American citizenship."

He struck out at "lack of respect for law," "demagogism," "efforts to catch votes under false pretenses," and unsparingly attacked both Republican and Democratic candidates for their timidity and for "condoning in minority groups acts of lawlessness."

He demanded continuing effort at economy in the federal government, "which is now taking only 28 per cent of the total taxes," and called for more economy "in states, cities, and counties which are consuming 72 per cent of the taxes."

Although the campaign was waged mainly on domestic issues, he also urged the entry of the United States into the World Court. The man who had helped Europe solve its reparations problem was no isolationist. He stressed that in foreign policy there must be no impairment of the right of sovereignty of the United States, or of her right to make her own decisions on her own interests; and with that settled, the United States must do its duty in its international affairs.

"In the United States," he had said in his acceptance speech, "in regard to the question of foreign relations, general opinion seems to have settled upon two great fundamental principles; first, that whatever be our form of contact and conference with foreign nations, the independence and sovereignty of the United States, with the right to determine its own course of action, must at all times, and under all circumstances, not only be preserved by it, but recognized by all other nations; and second, that, with its sovereignty always unimpaired, the United States should undertake to meet its international obligations unflinchingly, exhibiting no moral cowardice and welcoming, in the interest of universal peace and progress, that contact with other nations in which alone relevant facts can be fully developed and common-sense methods adopted for solutions of questions of common interest.

"Here we are, the greatest and most powerful nation on the face of the earth, possessing the capacity for world leadership. To rot morally in a policy of national isolation rather than to contest cleanly in those mental battlefields in which questions must be solved for the advancement of civilization, both here and abroad, is that the temper of the American people? I think not."

These were the principles which Dawes repeated over and again in every one of his major speeches. Some of the newspapermen traveling with him urged that he say something new, or insert some new matter, so that their reports could be somewhat more newsworthy. But Dawes declined. In his next platform appearance, he said:

"Some of the gentlemen of the press accompanying me have been urging that I change my speech. I have not. There is one issue in this campaign and one only—on the Atlantic seaboard, out beyond to the Rockies, to the Pacific waters, in the Southland, or in the great middle area of our country. That issue is whether you stand on the rock of common sense with Calvin Coolidge, or upon the sinking sands of socialism with Robert M. LaFollette."

Dawes was no orator in the accepted sense of the term. His voice, which was high-pitched, had none of the timbre of the silver-tongued spellbinder. He spoke too fast for full radio effectiveness. But his strong points were his winning personality and a deep earnestness and sincerity. Western crowds liked his emphatic gestures reminiscent of Theodore Roosevelt. The red-blooded nature of his campaign, his blunt and emphatic language, and his whole-souled forthrightness pleased his audiences.

It has always been a disputed question how much a Vice-Presidential candidate can help a ticket. There is no doubt that Dawes was of immense help to the Republican campaign of 1924. He was strong in the Western farm belt where Coolidge was weakest. And the fact that the world powers had unanimously adopted the Dawes Plan on reparations and that it went into effect in October, less than a month before the election, gave the Republican party a considerable boost. Everett Sanders, the same man who had tried to prevent him from discussing the Ku Klux Klan, would soon announce from Republican campaign headquarters:

"Dawes has been the most successful Vice-Presidential campaigner in American history. He has won hundreds of thousands of independent voters to the Republican banner. There are five words that we hear so often they have become a chant. They are: 'I like that man Dawes!'"

Dawes himself was having the time of his life—with just one single drawback. Wherever he went, his "Melody in A Minor" was being manhandled by bands of every description.

"General Sherman," he wrote, "with justifiable profanity once expressed his detestation of the tune 'Marching Through Georgia,' to which he was compelled to listen whenever he appeared anywhere. I sympathize with his feeling when I listen to this piece of mine over and over. If it had not been fairly good music I should have been subjected to unlimited ridicule. As it is, a toastmaster once introduced me as 'both a businessman and a musician,' adding, 'It is a regret to me, however, that I find businessmen referring to him as a musician and musicians referring to him as a businessman.'"

On November 1 Dawes closed his campaign with a picnic on the farm of his author friend George Ade, at Brook, Indiana. On the following Tuesday the Republican ticket won, carrying thirty-five of the forty-eight states with an electoral vote of 382, and drawing a popular plurality of 7,339,019. This victory was bigger than even the most optimistic Republican had dared hope. The Democrat Davis won 136 votes, all in the solid South. LaFollette carried Wisconsin.

Dawes himself took no credit for the outcome. He wrote:

"Under a government such as ours, and the method provided for selection of the President, the man who occupies that office, in his temperament, attitudes, and characteristics, will generally well represent the inarticulate opinion of the public as to the kind of leadership the country needs at the time.

"When Coolidge was elected, the world desired tranquillity—a reaction of its people from the excesses of war. That was the subconscious issue of the elections of 1924 in the United States, England, and France. Where the victory of the conservative party associated itself in the public mind with a prospect of a tranquil future, the conservatives won, as they did in our country with Coolidge, and in Britain with the Baldwin government. Where, as in France, the attitude of the conservative party—dominated by Poincaré and his extreme nationalistic Ruhr policy—was regarded as conducive to increased controversy, Herriot and the left were victorious.

"What brought Calvin Coolidge to the favorable notice of our people generally was his action in the Boston police strike, which indicates courage in a period when growing lawlessness in the country had aroused public opinion. Coolidge personifies to our people calmness, common sense with purpose, and splendid courage."

Three days after the election in the United States, the so-called "Dawes Election" was held in Germany. It was to choose a new Reichstag for the German Republic. Supporters of the Dawes Plan won 322 seats, twice the strength of the Fascist opposition of the right and the Communist opposition of the left put together. For the next five years, the term of the Dawes Plan, Germany and all Europe would experience a period of unbroken recovery.

One of the few men not willing to speak in glowing terms about "the Dawes Plan" was Dawes himself. A few weeks before, in Philadelphia, he had been introduced for the hundredth time as "the savior of Europe." He had opened his speech with the words:

"Throughout this campaign I have been introduced as the man who, alone and unaided, all by himself, drew up and adopted what is known as the Dawes Plan. I have explained as best I could all along that that plan was the result of concerted effort. It could not have been possible without the full effort and full cooperation of every member. To have it said repeatedly that I did it alone, just between us—makes me sick!"

On March 2, 1925, the Vice-President-Elect with Mrs. Dawes and their adopted children, Dana and Virginia, left Chicago for Washington. Dawes was still on the greener side of sixty years. His hair was a little thinner than formerly but it had hardly a streak of gray. He was in superb physical condition.

The nation wondered how the vigorous Dawes would perform in this strange office to which he had been elected, an office lying somewhere between the executive and legislative branch and where he presided by constitutional dictum over a body which would much rather elect its own presiding officer as the House of Representatives elects its Speaker.

The answer of how he would perform was not to be long delayed.

Chapter Seventeen

✺

VICE-PRESIDENT DAWES

𝒯he morning of March 4, 1925, held the promise of the most pleasant, comfortable, and generally satisfactory inauguration day in many years. Three days of rain had been succeeded by sunshine ideal for the ceremonies and the brief but snappy parade that were scheduled. "Coolidge luck" was still holding, even to the behavior of the elements.

There had been just one mishap and only a perplexed subcommittee of the civic inaugural committee knew about that. Governors of the states, including a feminine one from Wyoming, were, as their predecessors had from time immemorial, to ride imposingly astride horses in the inaugural parade, spaced in the order of the admission of their states into the Union. But the horse age had about come to its end. More governors than ever before had come for the inauguration of the first Yankee President since Franklin Pierce. There were, in fact, more governors than horses. But the committee had scampered around and remedied the unbalance.

For all the curtailments upon which Calvin Coolidge had insisted in the interests of economy and Coolidge simplicity, the ceremonies were to be impressive. The speech, given out well in advance, was in type in every newspaper office in the land, ready for release when the President uttered the first word of it. It was a good Coolidge speech, stressing economy, promising a tax cut, and calling for an "adequate army and navy."

No Vice-Presidential speech was available. Stevenson, Hobart, Fairbanks, Sherman, Marshall, Coolidge, and even Theodore Roosevelt had assumed the Vice-Presidency with no more than a few pleasantries suitable to the occasion. Charles G. Dawes, who had arrived quietly a day or two before, had given no indication that he would do differently. Unknown to him, a chorus from the Hamilton Club had come down from Chicago and was conducting impromptu serenades. He had given a dinner the night before inauguration. Pershing, who was to have been there, was ill in Cuba and only the Dawes kin and Owen D. Young sat down to table.

The ceremonies were to begin as always in the Senate chamber with the swearing in of the new Vice-President. Then, after a third of the membership of the Senate, chosen at the previous election, had taken their oaths, the Vice-President, the legislative and judicial branches of the government, the governors of the states, the Cabinet, and high officers of the Army and Navy would stand outside on the east entrance while the President, in solemnity and simple dignity, would take the oath of office.

The Senate chamber formed a brilliant setting for the first event of the day. The Senators were crowded to one side of the chamber. On the other side were placed members of the House of Representatives. The Supreme Court occupied the front row, all in black. The man in the huge black robe was Chief Justice William Howard Taft, who had himself taken the President's oath on the snowiest, stormiest of all inauguration days and now was to administer it to a successor. Near the front were the governors of the sovereign states.

Across the aisle sat the President of the United States and his Cabinet. Then came the diplomatic representatives of foreign countries, ambassadors in front, ministers just behind. No glory of uniform is comparable to diplomatic dress, and none ever equaled the equipage of Señor Don Juan Riano Gayangos, the Spanish Ambassador and dean of the Corps on that occasion, although British Ambassador Sir Esme Howard, with gold lace, orders, and decorations, approached Gayangos in elegance.

The galleries were packed. Mrs. Coolidge, Mrs. Dawes, and their parties sat in reserved sections. Everyone of eminence in Washington was on hand. Outside, a hundred thousand men and women faced the Roman portico where the President would be sworn in and address them.

Promptly at noon (Senate clock time), Dawes, correctly dressed and looking a little shy, mounted the podium and took the oath from President pro tem Albert B. Cummins. That completed, the new Vice-President picked up a gold-mounted and inscribed gavel made from a portion of a piano stool he had used as a boy and gently tapped the extraordinary session of the Sixty-ninth Congress to order. The gavel had been presented to him that morning by Marietta Post No. 68 of the American Legion.

Dawes began his speech in a low tone.

"What I say upon entering this office should relate to its administration and the conditions under which it is administered," he said. "Unlike the vast majority of deliberative and legislative bodies, the Senate does not elect its Presiding Officer. He is designated for his duty by the Constitution of the United States."

The full portent of that was not lost on the Senators. Here was a man calling attention to the fact that forty-eight states had participated in his election and certainly he would claim the same interest in the rules that they, each elected by a single state, could claim. Before they could recover, Dawes went on:

"In the administration of this office his duty is to be concerned with the methods of effective procedure as distinguished from any legislative policy of the body over which he presides. It is not for the Vice-President to be personally concerned with the interests of political parties or with the policies or projects involved in legislative action, save in that unusual contingency where, under the Constitution, it becomes necessary for him to cast the deciding vote in the case of a tie. Nor should he, in view of that unusual contingency, assume any attitude toward prospective legislation until the contingency occurs. Any other course would inevitably lessen the weight of his influence in those impartial and nonpartisan matters with which it is his duty, under the Constitution of the United States, to be concerned.

"In my conduct I trust I may yield to no Senator in fairness, courtesy, and kindliness and in deference to those unwritten laws which always govern any association of gentlemen, whether official or private. It shall be my purpose not to transgress in any way those limits to my official activity determined by the Constitution of the United States and by proper parliamentary procedure. But the

Vice-President, in part because he is not elected by the members of this body, not by a state, but by the people of the United States, and his constitutional and official relations are to the Senate as a whole, should always express himself on the relation of its methods of transacting public business to the welfare of the nation.

"For him, therefore, officially to call to the attention of the Senate any collective duty such as an improvement in the method under which its business is carried on, so far from being an irrelevant and uncalled-for action on his part, is a supreme duty."

Dawes warmed to his subject. His voice rose. He shook his finger for emphasis. In past years, he went on, the customs had evolved out of a commendable feeling of the members of the Senate of fairness, courtesy, and consideration for each other. But minorities had taken advantage of those rules and turned them against the interests of the country, and incrusted tradition had stayed the Senate's hand in dealing with such headlong individuals and blocs.

"What would be the attitude of the American people and of the individual Senators themselves toward a proposed system of rules if this were the first session of the Senate of the United States instead of the first session of the Senate in the Sixty-ninth Congress?" he asked, and answered himself: "The impact of outraged public opinion, reflected in the attitude of the Senators themselves, would crush the proposal like an eggshell."

Now Dawes turned to Senate Rule Twenty-two:

"That rule," he contended, "which at times enables Senators to consume in oratory those last precious moments of a session needed for momentous decisions, places in the hands of one or a minority of Senators a greater power than the veto power of the President of the United States, which is limited in its effectiveness by an affirmative two-thirds vote."

For nearly twenty minutes he vigorously and pungently attacked the rules conducive to dawdling and deadlock, filibuster, obstruction, and circumlocution, the rules that seemed made to order for minority and bloc interference.

The Senate burned. Members of the House of Representatives, a body so large and unwieldy that it can operate only with some form of cloture, were enjoying the proceedings. Others than the members of the legislative branch listened first with formal attentiveness, then with amazement. In newspaper offices all over the land, new eight-column banner headings were written, and the newspapers went to press without waiting for the Coolidge speech. Vice-President Dawes had stolen the headlines from the President.

The things Dawes had said about the rules had been said many times before in the Senate chamber. One President of the United States, Woodrow Wilson, with wide public support, had brought about a modification providing for checking debate by a two-thirds rule. The Wilson device had been used once or twice. But what evoked the Senate's wrath was that Dawes had never presided over a legislative body and had not even waited for the Senate grudgingly to accept him. Here was a man with a great popular following, using the dais and the backdrop of a spotlighted occasion to appeal not merely to glowering Senators but over their heads to the country. Also, and perhaps more consistently than any other man, he had the success habit—he was accustomed to achieve what he set out to achieve.

When the new Vice-President had finished, there was an icy silence among the Republicans, while Democratic Senators exchanged remarks of biting sarcasm. But if the Senate deplored the speech, the nation applauded. In the words of the Boston *Transcript:* "Dawes has no one but the people with him."

Dawes himself noted in his diary:

"It is one thing to write and deliver an address and another to get the public to think it over. The course I followed to bring my inaugural speech to general public attention succeeeded. It was simple, consisting of a delivery so emphatic and jarring upon the atmosphere of the occasion as to compel the general reading of the speech, because of the indignation it created on the spot, especially among Senators. And yet, when the public read the speech, they found it only plain argument and simple statement, not provocative in nature, and addressed wholly to the reason and not the prejudices or emotions of the reader.

"Ordinarily, of course, the Vice-President's inaugural speech has been a minor incident of the program, carried out in the Senate in the morning session, just preceding the inauguration of the newly elected President on the steps of the Capitol outside. For a new Vice-President, elected by the people—and not by the Senate—to discuss in his inaugural the proper conduct of the body over which he is to preside was not customary, but it is difficult to indict it as out of place.

"My forceful manner of delivery was resented: Bernard Shaw was right when he said: 'No offensive truth is ever properly presented without causing irritation.'"

But fate, as if to pour balm on the wounded feelings of the Senators, decreed that Dawes himself should be caught napping only five days later.

Among all of Coolidge's nominations for his Cabinet, only that of Charles Beecher Warren of Michigan to the office of Attorney General met with resistance. Senator Walsh of Montana charged that Warren had been connected with the "Sugar Trust" and was therefore disqualified to head the Department of Justice which was responsible for the enforcement of the Sherman Antitrust Act.

For days Dawes presided wearily over the Senate sessions in which Warren was attacked and defended, and defended and attacked again. At last, late in the afternoon of March 9, he asked Senators Curtis and Robinson, the majority and minority leaders, if there would be a vote that day. They told him that six more Senators had given notice of their intention to speak and, therefore, it would be impossible to reach a roll call. Dawes went to his suite in the Willard Hotel and was fast asleep when the Senate underwent one of the sudden changes for which it is noted. Five of the Senators who had expected to speak abandoned their plans. One spoke. Then Curtis asked for a roll call.

The roll call proceeded. Nine nominal Republicans aligned with the Democrats and it quickly became evident that a tie vote might result. A frantic call went out for the Vice-President. As Dawes hurried from his hotel room, a forty-to-forty vote defeating the nomination was tabulated. And while Republican Senators tried to delay further proceedings until Dawes' arrival, using the very parliamentary tactics he despised, Senator Overman of North Carolina, the only Democrat who had supported the nomination, changed his vote and definitely killed the nomination just before Dawes reached the Chamber.

The incident at once became Washington's choicest morsel of

conversation. Republican Senators sharply criticized Dawes, Democrats ridiculed him. And the Willard Hotel, where Dawes stayed, had to remove from its F Street entrance a crude sign, placed there by a prankster: "Dawes Slept Here!"

A day or two after the event, Dawes was showing a Chicago friend around the Capitol. The two friends sat down in the chamber of the Supreme Court. An uninteresting case was being argued, and the lawyer arguing it was a bore. Justice Van Devanter was nodding. Justice Holmes was pulling his mustache in an effort to keep awake.

Alert Chief Justice William Howard Taft, who had seen his old friend enter, scribbled a message on a piece of paper and sent it to Dawes. It read: "Come up here. This is a good place to sleep."

Dawes took the lesson to heart. Never again was he to take a chance on the uncertainties of the Senate.

With the special session of the Senate in adjournment, Dawes stayed over in Washington to make a speech at a dinner honoring William Jennings Bryan on his sixty-fifth birthday. After fending off some good-natured jokes about his own "activity and inactivity in the Senate," he paid a tribute to Bryan as "a clean man in every way." About the three occasions on which Bryan had unsuccessfully run for President, and the other three times when, just as unsuccessfully, he had backed Democratic candidates, Dawes had this to say:

"I have been listening to speeches telling of Colonel Bryan's fight for the commoner and against the forces of plutocracy. I knew him before any man in this room did. We were young together in Lincoln. At that time I represented the commoner and he represented plutocracy. He lived in a two-story house and had a one-horse surrey. I lived in a coffee-mill cottage and had neither surrey nor horse. He often would come by our house and take us for a ride.

"Since that time he has, three times directly and three times indirectly, taken the National Democratic Party for a ride."

After the speech, Bryan went over to shake Dawes' hand. It was the last meeting of the two old friends. That night Bryan went to Dayton, Tennessee, to take part in the Scopes evolution trial. There, on July 26, he died.

Caught napping or not, Dawes had every intention to do what he could to reform Senate rules. Immediately after the dinner in honor of Bryan, he left for a tour to carry the issue to the people. In some of the larger cities on his long itinerary, he addressed audiences of between six and twelve thousand persons.

There can be no doubt that individual Senators and groups of Senators have on occasion used the Senate rules to blackjack or blackmail the Senate. But it is doubtful whether a minority could ever have become as tyrannical as Dawes feared. The bloc system, which plagued the Republican stalwarts in the Senate, did not last long beyond the early twenties. It was liquidated, as was indeed most of the Republican membership, in the economic depression which followed.

Later on, the constitutional amendment abolishing the "lame duck" session of Congress was to do more. Individual filibusters flourished best under the mandatory March 4 adjournment date. But when Dawes' term as Vice-President came to an end, the rules against which he had protested and campaigned were still in effect. The audiences who came to listen to him on his flying tour were perhaps more interested in the man than in his message. No popular movement arose to help him in his efforts at reform. With all the sorrows of the world, and all the follies of mankind, it proved too difficult even for Dawes to arouse and sustain interest in the rules under which a parliamentary body operates.

Dawes' otherwise ineffectual trip had one pleasant interruption: he stayed in Boston for the 150th celebration of Patriots' Day, with its lighting of lanterns in the spire of Old North Church and a re-enactment of the ride of Paul Revere and William Dawes in 1775. General John J. Pershing, who had completed his tour of duty as Chief of Staff, was present to put an Army sergeant on a horse to ride the Revere route, while Dawes helped another sergeant on his mount to retrace the route his great-great-grandfather William had ridden the same night. While the two modern horsemen were on their way, now somewhat lengthened by detours around souvenir stores, tourist cabins, gasoline stations, and other works of man, the assembly in Boston revived a bit of poetry which had been written to give Dawes' great-great-grandfather his due. The poet Longfellow had neglected the role of William Dawes because, he said, "the name Revere rhymed better." A less famous poet, Helen F. More, had had no such difficulty. Her poem ran:

What's in a Name

I am a wandering, bitter shade;
Never of me was a hero made;
Poets have never sung my praise;
Nobody crowned my brow with bays;
And if you ask me the fatal cause,
I answer only, "My name was Dawes."

'Tis all very well for the children to hear
Of the midnight ride of Paul Revere;
But why should my name be quite forgot
Who rode as boldly and well, God wot?
Why should I ask? The reason is clear:
My name was Dawes and his Revere.

When the lights from Old North Church flashed out,
Paul Revere was waiting about
But I was already on my way.
The shadows of night fell cold and gray
As I rode with never a break or pause;
But what was the use when my name was Dawes?

History rings with his silvery name:
Closed to me are the portals of fame.
Had he been Dawes and I Revere
No one had heard of him, I fear.
No one has heard of me because
He was Revere and I was Dawes.

Shortly after they met on the speakers' rostrum in Boston, Dawes told Pershing that their old restaurant keeper, Don Cameron, was ill, and that he had seen to it that Cameron's remaining days would be comfortable. Pershing answered with a check. "I want old Don to know I have not forgotten him."

Dawes was back in Washington for the autumn session of Congress.

"The Vice-President's room—come to think of it—is an impressive one," he wrote. "Its chief ornaments are Rembrandt Peale's portrait of Washington—painted in 1795, and said to be his best likeness—and a great chandelier brought up from the White House after some Rooseveltian alterations of that mansion.

"During the session of Congress, whenever the Senate is not sitting, large delegations of visitors are piloted through the Capitol corridors and either pass by or through the Vice-President's office, depending upon whether or not that official is seated at his desk —his door as a rule being kept open for better ventilation. In case he is there, the visitors all stop and peek in—or walk sideways past the door to look in. It was under these circumstances that the late Thomas Marshall called out: 'If you don't come in, throw me a peanut!'

"To those who have heard the guides solemnly describe the historical relics of the Vice-President's office, the following Capitol legends of the office may seem irreverent, but they are at least worth noting.

"The Dolly Madison mirror from the White House, which is not large and hangs about eight feet above the floor, was hung so, it is said, in order that tall Vice-President Fairbanks could use it to tie his cravats. The fine mahogany cabinet which occupies the west side of the room is interesting only to the old-timers among the Senate employees as the alleged depository of the historic bottle of brandy which Andrew Johnson drank just before he made his inaugural address to the Senate as Vice-President, and which after nearly upsetting him quite upset his speech."

There were now in the Vice-President's room some other unusual objects which Dawes did not mention. On a table awaiting his return were piled up stacks and stacks of gavels. There were gavels made of wood taken from Fanueil Hall, from the Washington elm under which George Washington had taken command of the American Army at Cambridge, and from Admiral Peary's North Pole ship, the *Roosevelt*. There were gavels of ivory and of myrtle wood. Ever since his opening speech to the Senate, they had kept pouring in from all corners of the country, many of them accompanied by the suggestion that he use them on the Senate. There were gavels, too, in the form of underslung pipes. And pipes also had come from everywhere: hand-carved gold and silver pipes, gourd pipes, and peace pipes from Indian tribes.

A few minutes before he went up to the Vice-President's chair for his first time, Dawes turned to John C. Crockett, for more than a quarter of a century Reading Clerk and Chief Clerk of the Senate: "Crockett, I am going up against a job I don't know anything about, and I'm going to lean on you. I want you to help me."

"Yes, Mr. President," said Crockett, using Dawes' Senate title. "I'll quietly whisper any detail of procedure to you."

"No, dammit, Crockett, say it out loud. I know and they know I don't know. Let's not pretend!"

Dawes probably put in a greater number of man-hours in the presiding officer's chair than any of his immediate predecessors or successors. A Vice-President can vacate the chair at will by the simple process of beckoning some Senator to assume it. Garner, whose two years as Speaker and eight years as Vice-President formed the longest continuous service of any high parliamentary presiding officer in this country from its founding to the middle of the twentieth century, occupied the chair relatively seldom, and often took a seat on the floor. Dawes was never in the chamber except to preside.

Impatient as he was with time-wasting tactics, and although he found a way to eliminate some of them, Dawes never resorted to any of the short cuts that Garner used to speed up proceedings. But, for a period of fifty years, Dawes shared with Garner the fame of being one of the two Senate presiding officers (Vice-Presidents or Presidents Pro Tempore) who never had a ruling overturned by the Senate.

"If these Senators whom I have called to the chair during my absence have occasionally been overruled, it is probably because they endeavored to rule so as to further a political motive, something which Senators tell me is occasionally expected in the Chair, but which I have never done," he wrote.

It was one of the boldest strokes of initiative ever taken by the presiding officer of a parliamentary body when Dawes, in the short session of Congress ending on March 4, 1927, assumed nonpartisan leadership in the Senate, forcing cloture not only on the McNary-Haugen bill, but also on the McFadden-Pepper bill which revised the National Bank Act and indefinitely extended the charters of the Federal Reserve Banks.

The national-bank section of the Pepper-McFadden bill had been framed in 1924 by Comptroller of the Currency Henry M. Dawes, brother of the Vice-President. It provided for important modifications in the law governing national banks. At that time, state banks could join the Federal Reserve System if they wished, whereas the national banks were compelled to join. The strictures put upon the national banks by antiquated laws were such that many of them were taking out the more liberal state charters, thus removing themselves from a class that was compelled to join the Federal Reserve System to one that could make its choice. The Government was thus losing control over the Federal Reserve System, and the national banking system was being dangerously undermined. The Pepper-McFadden bill had been drafted to meet this danger, and carried with it an indefinite extension of the charter of the Federal Reserve System which otherwise would have expired shortly.

Dawes brought together in his office some of the most conservative and some of the most radical members of the Senate.

"I know perfectly well that an undercover filibuster is under way against both these bills," Dawes addressed the gathering. "I mean by that, debate on other measures is being prolonged solely to keep either of these bills from being reached. If either one of them is reached, there will be an open filibuster. Without cloture, neither the McNary-Haugen bill nor the McFadden-Pepper bill can get a vote. I propose that you men who oppose the McNary-Haugen bill vote for cloture on it; then, if you have got the votes, beat it. But let's have some action instead of this name-calling that is going around."

Dawes forced an agreement that both bills should be voted on. His energetic action produced the unprecedented situation that the bank-bill proponents circulated the cloture proposal for the McNary-Haugen bill, while the McNary-Haugen supporters circulated the cloture proposal for the bank bill. Both bills passed. President Coolidge vetoed the McNary-Haugen bill, but the McFadden-Pepper bill became law. Dawes later felt that this law had at least warded off threatened catastrophe in the strained financial situation shortly after the renewal of the Federal Reserve System law.

As under his watchful eyes the debate proceeded on the floor day after day, Dawes sat in the Vice-President's chair and jotted down contemplative character sketches of the Senators. If they were uncomplimentary, he omitted the name of the Senator:

"I have often noticed in the Senate that ignorance, when it is a natural gift and not the result of mental indolence, is a rather attractive human quality when associated with courage and sincerity. It creates a sense of their own superiority in the minds of others, without creating irritation. It inspires kindly treatment from the world. But we have some individuals who seem to have been cursed at birth with the double heritage of ignorance and grouchiness. Of these only I speak. None of them would have ever arrived in public life had it not been for an extraordinary endowment with nervous energy. This is the one gift which everybody envies them. Such men, although they are adept and successful publicity seekers, have no great influence; their astonishing amount of misdirected energy cannot make up for their lack of common sense. Their frequent diatribes usually evoke no reply, for, as the Spaniards say: 'It's a waste of lather to shave an ass.'"

"I suppose Senator ——, from sheer weariness or, more likely, because to continue longer would endanger the publication of the speech in the morning paper, will soon conclude. Then we can pass the appropriation bill."

"There are certain men who so like to wield the torch that, while they occasionally and usefully burn away underbrush, they are not content until they burn some houses as well. These house-burners are represented in the Senate. At times, with great public benefit and acclaim, they will burn a rotten structure. If they were to be content with this, all would go well with them in public life. But, unfortunately for their highest ambitions, they always, in their career, try to set ablaze too many good structures, and a common-sense public never makes a hero out of one whom they come to consider a pyromaniac."

"When Boulder Dam is built, there should be on it somewhere a tablet to Senator Hiram Johnson, without whose untiring and able leadership it would have failed. I never saw a man more faithful and effective in a hard fight than Johnson has been in this one."

"Senator Joseph T. Robinson is a man of great ability, of high character, of industry, and exceptional qualifications as a leader. He has the courage of a lion. He never deceives, and his decisions are quick but sound. I regard him as a statesman of the highest rank."

"I am inclined to regard James W. Wadsworth of New York as the ablest of the Senators. This high estimate has not been influenced by a close friendship. I have never had any intimate associations in work or interests with him. But viewed from every angle, not only as a Senator but as one qualified for constructive leadership (mental or moral, military or civil, in Congress or out), I regard him as most unusual."

"Borah always brings to my mind the great parliamentary leaders of the past and, when he speaks, it seems a far cry from the tactics which are bringing general discredit upon Senate debates."

And of Reed, the Democrat from Missouri who had commented on Dawes' opening speech with the acid remark, "His melody of voice, grace of gesture, and majesty of presence were only excelled by his modesty!" Dawes wrote:
"I had a pleasant talk with James A. Reed. Everybody regrets that he is voluntarily leaving public life after eighteen years of brilliant service in the Senate. As an orator, he is in a class by himself, a representative of the able and fearless statesmen of the old school. I have many times been the target of his shafts of wit and satire but, after all, that is really something of a distinction."
For before the term of Dawes' office had reached the halfway mark, his wholehearted forthrightness, fairness, and invariable kindliness had won him the ungrudging respect of the Senate, and made him many warm friends.

On March 4, 1927, the session of Congress which completed Dawes' first two years in office came to an end. The Senate was tied up once again in a dreary filibuster, in which a minority was trying to seat Senator-Elect William S. Vare of Pennsylvania, charged with excessive election expenditures. Important legislation, including a deficiency appropriation bill, failed.

One minute before twelve o'clock, Dawes rapped his gavel sharply and said: "It is customary for the Vice-President, at the beginning and ending of a session of Congress, to address the Senate upon an appropriate topic. The comments the Chair has to make on this occasion will be very brief.

"The Chair regards the results of the present legislative session as primarily due to the defective rules of the Senate under which a minority can prevent a majority from its constitutional right of bringing measures to a vote. This is the only great parliamentary body in the world where such a situation exists.

"On this closing day of the second session of the Sixty-ninth Congress, the Chair commends to the Senate the remarks on the Senate rules which he made on the first day of the first session of the Congress.

"The hour of twelve o'clock having arrived, the Senate stands in adjournment, *sine die*."

James Alexander Reed of Missouri, the uncontested master of invective, ridicule, and sarcasm in his generation, smiled a friendly smile, and, from his Senate seat, waved to Dawes.

Dawes had been enjoying his return to Washington. It was like a vacation, for the work pace, by his standards, was leisurely. Vice-President and Mrs. Dawes gave dinners, big and little, at their home on Belmont Street. Dawes had his own plan of dining, which was the despair of the sticklers for protocol. He would conform only when the occasion absolutely required formality. His dinners for President and Mrs. Coolidge met the prescribed form to the letter during the meal, but afterward there was an informality and a variety of entertainment which kept the President up long beyond his accustomed bedtime.

The dinners that Dawes liked most to give brought together

scholars, musicians, explorers, aviators, financial giants, and just old friends. They caused the saying in Washington that "everybody has a good time at the Dawes dinners, but he is just as likely as not to put a fiddler ahead of the Secretary of State in the seating."

There is an entry in his diary telling of another dinner, one at which he had been a guest. It had been in New York, where Vice-President Dawes had gone for a conference on reparation questions with Charles Evans Hughes and Owen Young.

"On Monday noon, General Harbord gave a lunch at India House and, in the evening, I addressed a joint meeting of the New York Post Society of Military Engineers and the American Society of Mechanical Engineers. Major General Ely, Admiral De Steiguer, General Harbord, General Vanderbilt, and others joined in the discussion after my speech. I made a short visit to the Armistice Ball of the British Great War Veterans at the Plaza Hotel, another brilliant affair; and when I was taken to the center of the hotel, the dancing stopped and the "Star Spangled Banner" was played by the band. I mention these things to give a contrasting background of a tragic and pathetic incident, one which brought me for the last time to the side of a boyhood friend, and has been unrolling for me since the memory of long ago.

"In the midst of all these festivities, I received a telegram from my son-in-law in Chicago, saying '—— —— DIED YESTERDAY CHARLES BACIGALUP UNDERTAKER MULBERRY STREET NEW YORK ADVISES BODY IN HIS CARE.' At Miss Eell's private school at Marietta, Ohio, which I attended at the age of twelve years—fifty-one years ago—I first knew him. I remembered him then chiefly as a good-natured boy who was always laughing, and who, with a front seat in school and a book so held that the teacher could not see his face, would twist his countenance into the most absurd grimaces for the benefit of the rest of us on the back seats.

"Our ways soon parted, but we had become good friends, and the occasion of our next meeting was during the week of my graduation from the Cincinnati Law School in 1886. Tom Dawson (afterward Minister to Chile and Colombia) had won the hundred-dollar prize for the best essay, and was spending a portion of it upon a dinner in a private room of the old Denison Hotel at Cincinnati, to assuage the disappointment of his competitors, of whom I was one.

"When we were seated, —— walked in with a napkin over his arm. He was a waiter at the hotel. He was visibly embarrassed. It took me some time to get him at his ease. That was the last time— forty-two years ago—that I talked at length with him. But I have seen him several times since.

"The first time was on the streets of Chicago, at least twenty years ago, when I recognized him as a dilapidated and disconsolate tramp with ragged clothing. But he had recognized me first and turned away. He would not allow me to catch him. If I walked fast after him, he would walk faster; if I started to trot, he would trot. I knew then that pride had not left him, and a man that keeps his pride is never wholly lost. It was not until years afterward that I heard from him. He appealed for help from a New York public hospital, which I gave him, writing him that he could call on me any time. But he did not do so for another space of years. When, several years ago, once more in sickness, he asked aid, I sent it, then continued to send him a monthly check thereafter until his death.

"When on Monday morning I visited the undertaker to arrange the burial, he told me that when —— cashed my checks at his lodging house, he had said that I was his friend, and when he died alone in his room and was taken to the morgue, the lodginghouse keeper told the undertaker to notify me. The last time I saw him was at the City Morgue yesterday morning. Owen Young and I were unrecognized when we went there with the undertaker, and while the search was being made for his body, which was there with eighty others. Owing to some mistake in his name on the commitment papers, the first body shown me was not his. But on the second steel litter which was drawn on rollers from its alcove, there beneath the terrible mask left by long years of poverty and dissipation, I saw the face of my boyhood friend. His wasted body was covered by an old and frayed overcoat. He had died uncared for in any way.

"Besides the morgue attendant, Mr. Young, and myself, there were present three soldiers in uniform, who had been looking for a missing comrade. As I stood uncovered, they took off their caps, and one of them asked: 'Is he your brother?' 'No,' I replied, 'just a friend.'

"But as I walked away, I thought, 'Are we not all brothers?' "

Chapter Eighteen

❁

"I TAKE BACK NOTHING"

"I do not choose to run for President in 1928," President Coolidge said in the South Dakota Black Hills on August 2, 1927, exactly four years after he had assumed the Presidency.

If this carefully and puzzlingly worded statement did not preclude a Coolidge draft, it did open the door for the nomination of another Republican presidential candidate. Four names were almost immediately under discussion: Hughes, Hoover, Lowden, and Dawes.

Charles Evans Hughes took his name out of the debate at once. Dawes, although his stand was not quite as unequivocal, made it clear from the beginning that he had no intention of pressing his candidacy in any way. To his brother Henry, who wanted to know his feelings in the matter, he stated:

"I have had friends who have been President and it killed them. I have no desire to end my life that way. However, no American can admit that he would consider being President other than a great accomplishment. As far as I and the Presidency are concerned, I am like a chip on the tide of the ocean, and I don't know and am not going to try to control where it might drift."

"But there is another point to consider," Henry Dawes urged, "and that is your obligation if you can do things in the office some other man might not be able to do."

"That's all bosh. The man nominated will be either Hoover or Lowden. Essentially I think as they do and there is nothing I can do that they could not do."

But editorials all over the country continued to push his candidacy. The *North American Review* thought the situation called for a revival of the precedent set at the very beginning of the Republic, when Presidents were succeeded by the Vice-Presidents who had served under them—Washington by Adams, and Adams by Jefferson. "There could be no more auspicious solution of the problem created by President Coolidge's self-denying choice than to hark back to that rule of our early days and to select for his successor the man who had served with him as Vice-President and who, in doing so, has vitalized, energized, and magnified that office as was never done before," said a leading editorial in the *Review*. "The first occupant of the office declared it, with peevish ineptitude, to be 'the most insignificant that ever the invention of man contrived or his imagination conceived.' Nobody would ever dream of thus describing it during the tenure of the incumbent. Nor would it be questioned that the roll of Presidents would be enriched by having added to it in 1929 the name of Charles Gates Dawes."

Dawes paid them no heed. On September 10 he went to New York to say farewell to Pershing who was leaving the country to attend the American Legion convention in Paris. Dawes used the occasion to pay public and eloquent tribute to Democrats Woodrow Wilson and former Secretary of War Newton D. Baker.

"President Wilson and Secretary Baker conferred on John Pershing the title of Commander in Chief of the American Expeditionary Force and he was all the title indicated," Dawes said. "Our great war President, Woodrow Wilson, and his able Secretary of War, Newton D. Baker, protected the American Army from political mischiefmakers. Thank heaven, and them, Pershing did not, like the Generals of our Civil War, have political assassins firing at his back while he was facing the enemy. The nation should always be grateful for the courage, conviction, and action of Wilson and Baker."

This was not the kind of talk a candidate for the Republican nomination was expected to make. But the Dawes-for-President movement was mounting nonetheless. In the beginning of December, when Dawes returned to Washington for the session of Congress, he made an effort to stifle the boom with a statement only slightly longer than Coolidge's announcement:

"I am not a candidate for the Presidency. I favor the nomination of Frank O. Lowden, assuming President Coolidge is not a candidate."

It was well understood that Dawes was tied to Lowden by cords of loyalty. But practical politicians also understood that Lowden's candidacy did not have a chance in the changed situation within the Republican Party. They continued to press Dawes. But he turned a deaf ear to all entreaties.

Thus, while Lowden's campaign continued listless, and Calvin Coolidge loomed in the background as an unknown quantity, Hoover scouts redoubled their activity, touring the country in the quest of delegates for their candidate.

Dawes, meantime, absented himself from politics and resumed a favorite extracurricular occupation of his, that of lecturing at the Army War College on the military principles of supply in allied armies. Generals Pershing, Mason Patrick, Edgar Jadwin, and many of Dawes' old associates of World War I attended the lectures, as did many young officers, among them one Captain Dwight D. Eisenhower, later to be President of the United States.

"I like this experience at the War College best when I can get off the platform and down into the bull pen with these military experts," Dawes wrote. "To present to their keen intelligence and immediate comprehension and acceptance certain new principles of warfare, the recognition and establishment of which only dire necessity made possible, brings to me that satisfaction which always comes upon those rare occasions when one can impart relevant information and constructive suggestions to experts."

In June, 1928, delegates to the Republican national convention began to arrive in Kansas City. Speculation was still revolving around a draft of Calvin Coolidge. Lowden had an undetermined number of delegates, but was undoubtedly short of the 250 he had expected. Hoover forces believed that, barring a strong resurgence of the "Draft Coolidge" sentiment, they would have the 545 convention votes then required for nomination.

The "Draft Coolidge" movement collapsed. Lowden withdrew his candidacy. In the one and only ballot of the convention, Hoover received 837 votes. A last-ditch group of 74 voted for Lowden, and

171 more were divided among Curtis, Watson, Norris, Coolidge, Goff, Dawes, and Hughes.

"Hoover triumphed in his fight for the nomination through ability, inherent merit, and persistence in organized effort," Dawes wrote into his diary. "He is a man of courage and character. I have always admired him, having come to know him, his attitudes, and his methods during the first year of the American budget and in France during the post-Armistice period of the war. The attacks on him during the preconvention campaign only strengthened him. The justified association in the public mind of a man's name with real accomplishment in the public service and in the service of humanity is always his best protection against the tongue of slander."

It was on August 7, 1927, five days after Coolidge's famous statement, that Dawes had been the starred orator at the dedication of the Peace Bridge at Buffalo. The event had been memorable. Vice-President Dawes, Secretary of State Frank B. Kellogg, and Governor Alfred E. Smith of New York were the ranking American officials, while the British Empire was represented by the Prince of Wales, future King Edward VIII, Prime Minister Stanley Baldwin, and Premier MacKenzie King, of Canada.

The Vice-President and the Prince sat in the center of the span and exchanged greetings over a ribbon stretched across the bridge. Then Mrs. Dawes cut the ribbon with a pair of gilt scissors, and the two official groups went to a platform on the American side where Dawes delivered the principal address of the occasion before an audience of seventy-five thousand.

The Naval Disarmament Conference at Geneva had just disbanded in failure. The United States and Great Britain, pledged to equality, had been unable to agree upon what in the special necessities of each nation constituted parity. Dawes took advantage of this peace celebration between the two countries with the long Atlantic-to-Pacific boundary to impress upon both of them the need to continue their efforts at eliminating competitive war preparations. Urging that it was unthinkable for the United States and Great Britain to place again upon their people the burden of competitive naval building because of a temporary disagreement among their experts on a matter of interpretation, Dawes laid down the simple proposition:

"If in their respective programs under the principle of equality the United States requires heavy cruisers, which Great Britain does not need, and Great Britain requires light cruisers, which the United States does not need, there is no excuse for inaugurating a competition under which ships will be built which neither of them need."

Dawes' incisive speech produced wide and favorable comment on both sides of the Atlantic. Prime Minister Baldwin was so impressed with it that he asked for, and received, Dawes' signed reading copy as a souvenir. But Dawes had his critics, too.

One group of them felt that his speech was "good common sense, but undiplomatic." Dawes noted in his diary: "Common sense is never undiplomatic."

Other critics felt that the Vice-President, in dealing with royalty, had failed to follow the proper protocol.

"When the Prince and I stepped from our cars," Dawes' diary reads, "I insisted that he precede me on the platform, as that appealed to me as the proper courtesy to show our guests. When he and I went through formal affairs later in the afternoon on the Canadian side, he insisted that I precede him. I mention this merely because some American newspapers criticized at length this proceeding on the American side as indicating that our Government was improperly taking a backseat because I did not step ahead. Washington indulges in much discussion of questions of personal precedence, and to such a degree is offense sometimes taken if the precedents are not followed that the State Department undertakes to give advice in the matter, especially in connection with official dinners and other official occasions! I suppose this saves a lot of petty and undignified quarreling. But I do not think the American people care a 'whoop' about these things."

There was another American attendant at the dedication of Buffalo Bridge who was also soon mentioned in the country's newspapers and those of the world, but not in a tone of criticism. That was Secretary of State Kellogg who, not much later, submitted to the European powers a plan for the renunciation of war which took its name from him, received almost immediate and universal adherence, and was signed by twenty-three nations in September of 1928.

Dawes himself played an important part in securing American ratification for the Kellogg Pact. This Pact, as well as the billion-dollar cruiser-building program for the United States were both on the agenda when the Senate reconvened on January 3, 1929, for the short two-month session left to the Coolidge Administration. Dawes put Vice-President-Elect Curtis into the chair for the first day, and went with Senator Borah to spend most of the day in his own room, laying plans to prevent a filibuster.

"I favor the Kellogg Treaty," Dawes stated, "but I favor the Cruiser bill just as strongly under existing circumstances. It is not proposed to build cruisers to achieve naval superiority, but to attain naval equality under existing treaties. Since the naval experts at Geneva were unable to interpret, in terms of ships, an agreed-upon principle of equality with Great Britain as extending to cruisers, it is now unwise for the United States to stop building cruisers.

"The struggle of the world away from war will be slow and hard, and many steps which, when taken, may seem illogical and backward, will, in due time, be recognized as forward steps. There will be wars in the future, for human nature has not changed. But some may be avoided. About all I can see in this Kellogg treaty is a better chance for peace; but that is a great deal."

President Coolidge was as anxious as Dawes that the Kellogg Pact be ratified. But in spite of all of the steam the Vice-President generated, the vote did not come until January 15, after an impressive address by Senator Borah.

"The final and short speech which Borah made rose to the heights of the historic orations of our forebears in the Senate years ago, when principles of fundamental importance to our nation's life were at stake."

Then, finally, the Senate voted overwhelmingly for ratification. For the result Dawes gave credit to a half-dozen Senators: Borah, Curtis, and the freshman Vandenberg for the Republicans; Robinson, Tom Walsh, and Swanson of Virginia for the Democrats.

The Cruiser bill was also called up, and was to have still rougher sailing. But in the end the clouds dispersed, and the bill was passed.

And finally, the Senate completed action on the bill for the

"Century of Progress" exposition at Chicago. Dawes, who sponsored the exposition, appeared before a Senate committee and was so genial that the committee was disappointed when he told them he wanted no federal appropriation—the Fair would pay for itself.

"*January 24:* Our fortieth wedding anniversary. I brought home to my wife some flowers, which pleased her the more because, I regret to say, I generally forget the anniversary until she reminds me of it. But this time I did not."

Dawes' Vice-Presidential term was now drawing to a close.

"I have found the task of presiding over the Senate, while frequently most interesting and exacting, at times rather irksome," he wrote. "This is natural, for most of my life has been in executive and administrative positions with specific objectives and well-defined authority and responsibilities. In such positions, one becomes accustomed to condensed and clear statements of fact, accompanied by arguments based upon them which appeal to reason and common sense rather than to prejudice or emotion. There are many able Senators of business and legal training whose addresses are a delight. Their public life is devoted to constructive public service exacting in its demand for hard work and, as a rule, useful in proportion to it. Conscientious and considerate, with minds bent upon creating conviction on debatable propositions and projects of immense public importance, they command a respect and influence, when speaking, greatly out of proportion to the size of their senatorial audience. Indeed, the surface indication of a useful speech is often a vacant Senate floor."

And in another mood:

"I consider it no part of my duty to crown candidates for cherry-blossom or sundry other queens and, so far as I have any recollection, at no time since my nomination for or occupancy of this office have I kissed anyone except female relatives."

Nor had Dawes considered it part of his duty to trouble the President with unsolicited advice. Even before assuming office, he had written the following note to Coolidge:

"I am not much of a letter writer, but I will try to say here what I would say to you if I saw you.

"About sitting with the Cabinet:

"I have always thought that unwise, long before it ever entered my head that I would have to pass upon the matter individually. So far as you and I are concerned, such a thing as a misunderstanding is impossible. That never entered my head. But if I should sit in the Cabinet meetings, the precedent would be fixed, and in the future it would sometime prove a very injurious thing to the country, in my judgment.

"The Cabinet, and those who sit with it, should do so always at the discretion and inclination of the President. Our Constitution so intended it.

"And again, the relationship is a confidential one, and the selection of a confidant belongs to him who would be injured by the abuse of confidence—however unintentional. Suppose, in the future, some President, with this precedent fixed, must face the alternative of inviting a loquacious publicity seeker into his private councils, or affronting him in the public eye by denying him what has come to be considered as his right—how embarrassing it would be!

"I have many times expressed these ideas when I had no thought of ever being nominated for the Vice-Presidency, or any other office.

"If ever you want me in some matter where I can really be of assistance to you, you know how greatly I would esteem the privilege of serving you. But it is not necessary for me to report 'Tuesdays and Fridays' in order to be 'prepared for duty.'"

And a diary note read:

"My friendship and high respect for President Coolidge are such that it would be personally a pleasure to sit in his Cabinet, but I will not do so because, in my judgment, it involves a wrong principle.

"The official relations of the President and Vice-President lend themselves to the encouragement of misapprehensions, which are easy to create. I have always sensed the inherent embarrassments involved in the plan of having the Vice-President sit in the Cabinet, as Coolidge did in the Harding administration. After my election, not knowing how Coolidge felt about it, I wrote him stating my views.

"This was done to relieve him—if he shared my views—of any embarrassment, if he desired to carry them out, notwithstanding the fact that he had accepted Harding's invitation. Again I did not want to do him the discourtesy of declining a possible invitation, and I thus avoided any necessity of such a course, however remote."

As the end of his term neared, he wrote:

"The busybodies and mischief-makers, of which Washington has its full quota, flutter around those in public position like birds of ill omen, and have said much about unpleasant relations between Coolidge and myself; but I have paid little, if any, attention to them. And if Coolidge has, I am mistaken."

Like every one else in Washington he enjoyed some of the new Coolidge stories which were springing up almost daily. He wrote of the latest one he had heard:

"I came back to Washington from New York last evening with Frank W. Stearns, the President's close friend and a man universally liked and respected. He is the embodiment of the cautious and considerate gentleman of the old school. He told me of an amusing conversation he had with the President. The latter was standing at his desk one day with a copy of the 'Intimate Papers of Colonel House' in his hand. He looked fixedly at Stearns and said: 'Mr. Stearns, the Constitution of the United States makes no provision for the position of unofficial adviser.' 'Mr. President,' responded Stearns, 'have I ever given you any advice?' 'No,' said the President, 'but I just thought I would tell you.' "

Dawes had had no qualms about doing a good turn to an old friend. Chief Justice Taft, whose Supreme Court was then crowded in quarters in the old Senate Chamber, midway on the long Capitol corridor, had long wanted a home of its own for the Court. At last the bill was passed.

"I received the engrossed bill for the erection of the new building, and signed it as President of the Senate. Less than fifteen minutes later, Chief Justice Taft telephoned, asking whether I had signed the bill. He was anxious to have President Coolidge approve it today. This I arranged within an hour, to his considerable satisfaction. I have always felt grateful to Taft for, in 1886, he marked the papers of our graduating class in Cincinnati Law School, and passed nearly the whole class, including myself. He does not know it, but that was one reason why he got such quick service today. The friendship with the Chief Justice, which I have enjoyed during these last four years, has been one of the pleasant things of my service here. He is beloved by all."

And now the time had come to go to the last big White House reception. Dawes had been to twenty of them under the McKinley Administration, five under Harding, and twenty under Coolidge, and had worked out a plan for enjoying them.

"After marching downstairs and as far as the Blue Room with the official procession, headed by President and Mrs. Coolidge, I do my full duty in greeting those assembled there, even waiting for the judges, diplomats, or generals and admirals (as the nature of the reception determines) to return to the room after they have passed in line to greet the President. Then, generally with Secretary Mellon as a companion, I slip away to the room at the right of the front door where the Secret Service men and my old friend, Ike Hoover, major domo of the White House, generally hold forth. Just beyond its open door, in the main hall, the Marine Band, which plays all evening, is stationed. We have, therefore, three advantages of which the other guests are deprived: we can sit down; we can hear the music; and we can smoke.

"Here we remain until about ten minutes before the official procession, which we must join, starts upstairs again. We can tell when to start back to it by the petering out of the long procession of guests coming from the East Room through the hall to the Blue Room to shake the weary hands of the Chief Executive and his wife. But we have another way of telling. Invariably, Mrs. Dawes gets worried for fear we shall not get back in time, and either comes herself or sends an aide for us."

The President-Elect, Dawes' old friend Hoover, had already arrived in Washington and was staying at the Mayflower Hotel. The new administration was ready to take over. Dawes, and apparently President Coolidge also, were equally ready to lay down their official cares.

"When an administration changes in Washington, it is a tragic time for many. Yet in Washington there is a heartless indifference to ambitious and suffering spirits, for Washington is used to change. When the appointments are finally made, all is outwardly pleasant, for the pride of the disappointed sustains them in the effort to conceal their feelings, and the satisfaction of the successful is restrained to be in 'good form.' Yet, under the placid surface of things, currents of deep feeling are surging.

"The White House offices, where I called this morning, bore mute evidence of the passing of power. The halls ordinarily filled with newspapermen, photographers, candidates for office, Senators, Representatives, and visitors who have come to pay their respects, were almost empty. My old friends there, some of whom came to their places thirty years ago under the McKinley Administration, like Rudolph Forster and Latta, all had time to leave their work for a chat. The President was not seeing different men every fifteen minutes. He, too, had plenty of time. The crowd was up at the Mayflower Hotel, where the President-Elect is staying, and there is the chief center of news and interest.

"But I could not help but think that, of the two men, the President is the more fortunate. He has finished his work, a great and successful one, and leaves with public acclaim, while the President-Elect must take up great and difficult burdens."

In his last days in the Vice-Presidency he wrote his appraisal of that office:

"It is largely what the man in it makes it—which applies to all public offices. The fact that the Vice-President in the Senate Chamber cannot enter into debate is considered a disadvantage, yet for that reason he is removed from the temptation to indulge in the pitiable quest of that double objective so characteristic of many Senate speeches—the placating of general public opinion and an opposing local constituency at the same time. For his prestige as a presiding officer, it is to his advantage that he neither votes nor speaks in the Senate Chamber. Outside the Senate Chamber his position as Vice-President gives him a hearing by the general public as wide as that accorded any Senator, other things being equal. If he lacks initiative, courage, or ideas, he of course will be submerged; but that is true also of a Senator or any other parliamentary member. Whatever many have said to the contrary, as any one discovers who has occupied the office, the people hold it in great respect."

He spoke out against some of the flummery of the office, one of them motorcycle escorts. He thought these screeching convoys were "usually to feed the vanity of local politicians and they endanger life and limb.

"After several narrow escapes due to the high speed, which the escorts generally insist on increasing when street travel and traffic is heavy, I proceeded on the theory that the motorcycles were escorting me, and not I the motorcycles, and compelled my chauffeur to slow down to a reasonable speed. To the ordinary citizen on the street, these escorts are not only dangerous but extremely annoying."

As if to render Dawes' departure still less painful, the Senate, in February, became involved in a double-barreled filibuster, one against the naval appropriation bill, the other against a bill to increase the number of federal judges. Senator Cole Blease of South Carolina blandly informed the Senate that, unless his state got another judge, no one would. While Blease talked on every other subject but that of judges, Dawes went to his office off the Senate chamber. Novitiate Senator Arthur Vandenberg of Michigan left the floor and came to Dawes' office.

"Do you know Martial?" the Vice-President asked.

"I have read him," Vandenberg replied.

The Vice-President, a teetotaler, crossed over to the case where Andrew Johnson had kept the ill-starred bottle of brandy. The case was now filled with rare books. He pulled out a volume of Martial and read:

"My action is not one for assault or wounding or poisoning; it concerns my three she-goats. I complain that they are lost by my neighbor's theft; this is the fact which the judge prescribes to be proved to him. You, with a mighty voice and every gesture you know, make the Court ring with Cannae, and the Mithridatic war, and insensate Punic perjuries, and Sullas, and Mariuses, and Muciuses. And now, Postumus, mention my three she-goats!"

Dawes reread the last six words from the Latin.

"Jam, dic, Postume, de tribus capellis!

"Did you ever," Dawes went on, "listen in an American courtroom to anything like the lines that Martial wrote?"

"I did!"

"Well, you'll hear it in the Senate, too. What I've read is eighteen centuries old, and it is still urgent."

The situation in the Senate had reached a deadlock. "The most determined obstructionists are fawned upon, cajoled, flattered, anything to get their acquiescence so that the Senate may do its constitutional duty." Among the subjects discussed in the delaying tactics was a local District of Columbia bill, providing the site for a new food market. "Now the Senate fritters away its time over a place to sell spinach," Dawes wrote.

"*February, 27, 1929:*   I am spending the evening alternately in my office and in the Chair of the Senate while that body, tangled in the web of its rules, flounders hopelessly. The Senate is a paradise on earth for the congenital troublemaker.

"*Midnight:*   Have been in the Chair, listening to the filibustering speeches droned out by the obstructionists. A humiliating spectacle is presented by this powerful body, helpless of relief from an absurd situation except by the sheer wearing out of the physical strength of those determined that the majority of the Senate should be denied its rights. It is a travesty on common sense, and an outrage upon American institutions.

"Am now going to sleep on the sofa in my office beneath Peale's portrait of George Washington, who was an exponent of direct action; a sleep which will be subject to interruption but affording relief from the sight of grown men acting like spoiled children."

"*1:35 A.M., February 28:*   My fitful slumber has been disturbed during the last hour and a half by quorum calls announced each time by two rings of the bell in my office. Curiosity about what was going on led me to arise at the last bell and re-enter the chamber of the 'greatest deliberative body on earth.'

"The Senators were resting uneasily but, thank heaven, quietly, in their seats, having sent the Sergeant at Arms to arrest Senators who have not answered the roll call. When these recalcitrants are brought in, they will listen to a continuance of driveling and irrelevant talk.

"Will go back to the Senate lobby and listen to the probable profanity of the arrested Senators as they are brought in. This is to me one of the few pleasant incidents of such proceedings.

"*Later: 2:30 A.M.:*   When I reached the Senate, the Senators were standing in the middle of the Chamber, gathered around the chief filibusterer, who was laying down the conditions upon which the business of the Senate could proceed tomorrow.

"All demands for the allotment of time tomorrow on the pending bill were finally granted by 'unanimous consent,' and the Senate recessed at 2:45 A.M. until 11 A.M. today.

"*Later: February 28, 1929:*   One hundred and eighty-four bills and four resolutions were passed by the Senate. The session began at 11 A.M. and ended at 7:30 P.M.

"Almost all were passed after 4 P.M., when the calendar was taken up, and within a period of three and a half hours. A very deliberative body, indeed!"

Altogether it had been a busy session. The Seventieth Congress, in the last two years of the Coolidge administration, passed 1,037 public laws, the largest output in the first 163 years of the nation's history and being approached only by the 921 public laws of the Eighty-first Congress.

While the Senate would not change its rules, eighty-eight of the ninety-six Senators on March 3, 1929, gathered in the historic chamber in an unprecedented action to sing the praises of their fighting presiding officer. Democratic Leader Joseph T. Robinson, his voice choking with emotion, presented the Senate's gift, a silver tray.

"During the four years that you have served as Vice-President, no instance is recalled in which your decision has been reversed on appeal by vote of the Senate," Robinson said. "In this respect the record is without parallel. Remembering that, on numerous occasions during these four years, this Chamber has been the scene of fierce debates, participated in by skilled parliamentarians, it is surprising that you, being without judicial experience, have avoided successful challenge for error in decision.

"It must be pleasing to you in this hour to be assured, by one with some degree of responsibility, and by the Senators opposed to the political organization with which you have been affiliated, that only unlimited confidence in your impartiality has made such a triumph, such a record, possible.

"No mere intelligence, however great, if influenced by partisan or personal favoritism, could produce such conclusive evidence of the respect and good will of both the Democrats and the Republicans with whom you have worked during the last four years.

"Fairness and promptness have marked your conduct. Firmness and justice have characterized your decisions. This declaration is believed to be the conviction of every Senator.

"To the tribute respecting the high standard of your official conduct, another should be added, a tribute which cannot fail to inspire in your own breast sentiments of pride and gratification. You enjoy the friendship, the affectionate esteem, of all with whom you have been associated here: members, officials, and employees of the Senate.

"Clarity of thought, generosity of disposition, and decisiveness are, indeed, a fortunate combination of traits which have endeared you to us all."

And Borah of Idaho said:

"Over the Senate of this Congress and the preceding Congress has presided one of the most distinguished of living Americans, a man high in the confidence and esteem of his countrymen long before he became presiding officer of this body. Of his career and his distinction generally, there is no occasion perhaps, at this time, to speak. But of him as a presiding officer there is occasion to speak. His uniform courtesy, a stranger to favoritism or partisanship, his keen interest in the great problems before us, his acknowledged and exceptional ability—these are the things which have won the respect of and endeared him to every member of the Senate. It may well be understood what an inspiration is found in the standing and high character of such a presiding officer. We take leave of him in deep affection and with a sense of gratitude which will go with us through the rest of our lives."

Moist-eyed, Dawes wrote some lines on a piece of paper which he handed to old John Crockett, the Reading Clerk:

"Senators, I had intended to reply personally, but I find I cannot trust myself to do it.

"My dear friends, you have done a very generous and kindly act. You have done me a great honor. I thank you from the bottom of my heart."

At noon on Inauguration Day, Dawes made his final statement to the Senate, graceful but unyielding:

"I have tried to be worthy as best I could and, in the occupancy of this Chair, I have never consciously deviated from the duty which inseparably attaches to it, that of impartiality in partisan, personal, and sectional differences.

"At the time of parting between friends, there is no place for acrimony, and I assure you there is none in my heart. But I could not be true to myself and to my conception of the duties of this position if, as I leave it for the last time when, if ever, disinterestedness should characterize my convictions, I did not speak again of the collective error of this great and powerful branch of government.

"Alone among all the great deliberative bodies of the world, the Senate of the United States, under its rules, has parted with the power to allot its time to the consideration of the subjects before it in accord with their relative importance. This defect of procedure is fundamental. I take back nothing."

Chapter Nineteen

❁

HIS EXCELLENCY THE AMBASSADOR

Dawes looked forward to his return to Chicago "where I have ties of business." But especially would he "enjoy the quiet things of life: books that do not speak until taken in hand and addressed; the peace of a well-ordered house; the recollections of an active career; and the pondering over the lessons which experience alone can teach."

There was just one thing he had to do before going home. He would go to the Dominican Republic as soon as his term as Vice-President expired and carry out his promise to President Vasquez to put the financial affairs of that country in order.

In February Dawes had just finished his skillful job of piloting the Kellogg Peace Pact and the billion-dollar cruiser-building bill through the Senate when he had a visit with President-Elect Hoover. The President-Elect talked of his anxiety over the growing bitterness between the United States and Great Britain, and of his fervent desire to get an Anglo-American agreement on the smaller categories of war vessels—there was already the battleship treaty. He wanted a man as Ambassador to Great Britain who would have to embody an unusual combination of experience, skill in dealing with a variety of people, and personal charm. And the man Hoover thought fitted the description was Dawes.

The man whose Buffalo speech had convinced a large body of opinion in both English-speaking nations that another effort at agreement should be attempted presented compelling reasons why some one else should be chosen. He thought that Henry L. Stimson, whom

274

Hoover had chosen to be his Secretary of State, might have some one in mind. Stimson was Governor General of the Philippines and would not be able to return and assume his new duties until late in March. Dawes, however, agreed to accept if Hoover continued to feel he should after Stimson's return, and after the outcome of the election between Baldwin's Conservatives and MacDonald's Labor party had become known.

With a commission of his own selection, Dawes sailed for the West Indies in March, and after four weeks had established a system of executive control of expenditures of the Dominican government similar to the budget system he had set up in the United States. As he prepared to board ship for home at the end of April, 1929, a cable from President Hoover informed him of his designation as Ambassador to the Court of St. James.

What he had wanted most was to get back to Chicago and assist his brother Rufus in getting the preparations for the Chicago World's Fair under way. But Hoover, who twice before had wanted to draft Dawes and twice had failed, now knew how to appeal to him.

"When one reaches my age in life and but a few more years are available for the allotment of its remaining activities; and when, as in my case, one has very definitely decided what those activities would be, he does not relish the idea of being wrenched away from them and diverted into something new," Dawes wrote. "Of all the activities I would have chosen for myself, diplomacy would have been the last. Hoover *got* me the only way he could have *got* me. He believed the world was in for an armament race, and he knew that every such previous race had ended in devastating war. He believed I could be useful in connection with international reduction-of-armament matters and the new diplomatic status which we all hope has been created by the Kellogg treaty.

"He mentioned the difficulty he was having of inducing men of large affairs and unusual administrative and executive qualifications to accept appointment to the Cabinet. He said that three had recently declined to be considered, in view of the treatment accorded nominations by the Senate, treatment which amounts to a trial before the public on *ex-parte* evidence and upon any charge an enemy chooses to make. Criticism would in no way deter me from trying my wings in difficult public service. I have reached an age where I am no longer unduly elated by public praise or depressed at all by public criticism. It can be a question of only a few months until it is determined whether the assignment given to me is to be a success or a failure."

And so Dawes put his personal affairs in shape for an absence of indeterminate length, and reported in Washington. He arrived on May 15.

President Hoover put Dawes up at the White House—partly as a gesture of friendship, and partly to facilitate Dawes' work. A work-room had been set up immediately adjoining Dawes' bedroom.

Dawes and Henry L. Stimson, the new Secretary of State who had just returned from his post as Governor General of the Philippines, began at once to work out the details of Dawes' assignment. Both men saw eye-to-eye in their enthusiasm for a limitation-of-arms program which Stimson later was to call "the last concrete achievement of the postwar movement to turn swords into plowshares." Indeed, a general reduction of armaments enjoyed at that time the almost solid support of both Democratic and Republican Parties. It also had the backing of General Pershing and, among younger officers, of Major General Douglas MacArthur, son of Dawes' old friend Lieutenant General Arthur MacArthur. In addition, the new administration, which had gone into office on a strong majority, was still in its "honeymoon," the most favorable time in the life of any administration to secure concerted action. Herbert Hoover, one-time head of relief in Europe, knew better than most Americans the harrowing distress that follows in the wake of war, and was anxious to make determined peace efforts while in the White House. Beyond the ocean, Ramsay MacDonald's Labor party had just won the British election and was more eager than the Conservative party had been to improve relations with the United States. Great Britain was among all nations most heavily indebted to the United States, and American public opinion felt that a limitation of British naval construction would produce savings which might go to reduce the British debt. Finally, a general disarmament conference was planned for the year 1932. An Anglo-American agreement was essential to set the stage for that general conference. "If the United States and Great Britain can agree upon what constitutes parity of fighting strength," Dawes wrote in his diary, "the result will be a naval reduction by the three great powers (the United States, Great Britain, and Japan) and probably France and Italy. If we cannot reach such an understanding, the cause of naval disarmament is lost for the present."

Against this background, Dawes and Stimson worked out the three main topics that the Ambassador's talks with Ramsay MacDonald would cover. First of all, the two countries would have to reach an accord on the naval strength each of them required for its security. Next, they would have to study the question whether a reduction in their naval construction programs then under way could be agreed upon without endangering security needs. And finally, the two countries would have to get together on the thorny question of just what constituted equality between their two navies, particularly in the cruiser category.

Dawes' assignment was one of peace or war, of life or death. It was of the kind to which he could devote his whole-hearted attention, and all of his considerable energy. And again, time was of the essence.

Dawes' arrival in London was planned to coincide as nearly as possible with the accession to power of the MacDonald government. Less than a week after his arrival, Dawes was scheduled to speak before the Society of Pilgrims—and it was this address which would set the pattern of his negotiations with MacDonald.

Dawes had written his Pilgrims' speech in Chicago. "This address I took with me to Washington to submit to President Hoover and Secretary Stimson, as tending toward 'limiting debate' upon the matter, since the discussion then would naturally be as to modifications in the address, rather than in generalities," he wrote. Dawes remembered only too well the hopeless maze of conflicting "expert" opinions in which the settlement of the reparations question had been all but lost. This time, he intended to make it abundantly clear that, while the professional naval men would be heard and their findings be given weight, the central problem itself would be settled by responsible statesmen and not by the technicians. The experts would in the main be expected to work out specific problems assigned to them by statesmen.

He found that Hoover and Stimson agreed with him that this was a point of such paramount importance that they spent all of three days on the formulation of the pertinent passage, consulting a number of American officials and even British Ambassador Sir Esme Howard. After seventy-two hours, the crucial paragraph emerged in a version that no expert could misunderstand:

"At the beginning of the work, the contribution of the naval experts to the problem should be a definition of abstract equality. It is certainly possible for naval experts to arrive at a definition of fighting strength of ships. Thus, for instance, one might find a yardstick with which to determine the military value of individual ships. These ships might differ in displacement, size of guns, age, speed, and other characteristics; yet such an agreed, properly weighed value might be given to each of these differing characteristics as to make it possible to compare, for example, the cruiser fleets or combined fleets of two navies, and establish a parity between them."

With his Pilgrims' speech settled, Dawes found that he had still time enough for a whirlwind trip to Chicago where brother Rufus was having difficulties in raising the monies necessary for the projected Chicago Fair. The enthusiasm for the idea which Rufus Dawes had encountered in 1928 had, by May, 1929, turned to indifference.

Charles Dawes, scheduled to sail for England on June 7, appeared in Chicago on May 24 and announced publicly that he assumed full responsibility for financing the Fair, and expected to raise ten million dollars from Chicago sources before he sailed.

"In making this decision," Dawes wrote, "I was wholly actuated by a sense of loyalty to my brother and indignation at the position in which he had been left in a great civic enterprise, through no fault of his own. My first step was to call to my office peremptorily, and without explanation, certain civic leaders whose friendly attitude I regarded as essential to unify the different elements behind the Fair. These were mostly friends whose unselfish, constructive, exacting, and remunerative work for Chicago in the past had placed every loyal citizen in their debt; men with whom I had cooperated for years and whom, at times, I had followed as a worker under them.

"But I met them now as enemies. To me their indifference in this civic enterprise was inexcusable, and I addressed them somewhat as I once did a wartime congressional committee. But I knew my men. Behind my harsh language was a call to duty for their city in a crisis, a call from a friend; and to that kind of summons no one of them, during a lifetime, had ever failed to respond. After the three hours we remained together, the World's Fair, changed by our agreement to 'The Century of Progress,' had a united civic sponsorship behind it. I shall never forget their kindness and loyal offer of help in time of need."

With the "Century of Progress" exposition started on its way, and the ten million dollars' worth of bonds entirely underwritten, Ambassador and Mrs. Dawes, their adopted children Dana and Virginia, and his nephew Henry, who was to be his secretary, sailed for England as scheduled.

"I have never been a diplomat," Dawes said on his arrival in London. "I have many faults. But somehow I am sure you will put up with them, as have my own people."

Two days later, His Excellency Ambassador Charles Gates Dawes and Mrs. Dawes were riding to Windsor Castle in an open landau sent to Windsor railroad station to meet them and with British outriders in blue and white livery. They were to be received by King George who, because of illness, had not received a foreign diplomat for a whole year. When they left the Castle nearly two hours later, after a short private conference between the statesmen and a long foursome conversation in which Queen Mary had joined, they parted friends.

That night, Dawes was on his way to Scotland to see Prime Minister J. Ramsay MacDonald. "I had been asked by the President to show MacDonald my Pilgrims' speech," Dawes wrote. "My purpose, of course, was not only to submit it to him for comment, but to secure his acquiescence in the program of our government which it contained, and his agreement to relegate the present discussion of the question of the freedom of the seas and other controversial questions, pending the settlement of naval reduction as the probable first step to be taken."

The Sunday conference between the Prime Minister and the Ambassador at Logie House, Dunphail, Morayshire, was friendly and frank. MacDonald approved of Dawes' plans in full, and sat down to write out in longhand a statement to the press:

"We have had a conversation regarding the present position of naval disarmament as between the United States and Great Britain. It has been informal and general and most satisfactory. His Excellency proposes to refer to the subject at his Pilgrims' dinner on Tuesday night, and I shall do the same almost at the same time at Lossiemouth, and that is intended to be the beginning of negotiations. We both wish to make it clear that the other naval powers are expected to cooperate in these negotiations, upon the successful outcome of which the peace of the whole world must depend."

Their official business settled, the two men went riding over the moor to Glen Ferness by way of Lochindorb. By the time they approached the ruins of Lochindorb Castle, once the stronghold of the Wolf of Badenoch, greatest of Highlands bandits, MacDonald was smoking the upside-down pipe with which Dawes had presented him. With a Scotsman's pride, the British Prime Minister assured his guest that some Chicago gangsters might perhaps accumulate greater wealth, but none of them would ever achieve greater or more lasting fame than the Wolf of the Highlands.

When Dawes returned to London he had every reason to feel satisfied with the results of his first few days in Great Britain.

"I was much impressed with MacDonald," Dawes wrote. "His constructive purpose in this navy matter is unquestioned. His ability to deal with it and the clearness of his mind upon the subject were fully demonstrated. He was agreeable, confidential, and frank throughout all our interview, and I left with a high respect for him."

But although much had been accomplished, there was yet more to be done before the delivery of the Pilgrims' speech. If naval disarmament around the world was to be achieved as a step in the eradication of the seeds of a second world war, the cooperation of Japan, the third great naval power, was essential.

Dawes, whose common-sense procedure on Buffalo Bridge had incensed a part of the American press, had been carefully briefed by State Department officials in Washington on the diplomatic protocol a new Ambassador was expected to follow. Among his first duties was that of calling on the ambassadors of other nations in the chronological order of their appointment. Any violation of this order, he had been warned, would be considered an insult by the country whose ambassador had been slighted. Yet the Japanese ambassador,

Tsuneo Matsudaira, was the most recently appointed among the ambassadors on whom Dawes had to call. If diplomatic protocol were followed, Dawes would not be able to see his old friend of Washington days until some time after the Pilgrims' Speech.

Putting first things first, Dawes, who arrived in London early in the morning, went from the station directly to the Japanese Embassy and joined Matsudaira for breakfast. Thus the Japanese government was given prior notice of the content of Dawes' speech, eliminating all cause for suspicion on their part. The rest of the world never learned of the visit, and the diplomatic sky remained unclouded.

"A matter of the first importance at the present time," Dawes addressed his audience at London's Pilgrims Club, "is that the friends of world peace move unitedly toward that objective with a clear understanding among themselves that any effort which is not a united effort is likely to be ineffective and tending toward disintegration.

"An early agreement on naval reduction would seem to be the next step to be taken toward world peace. As to any other controverted questions between any nations or between Great Britain and the United States, their future peaceful settlement will not be endangered by the cessation of an enormously expensive naval competition in progress during their discussion."

A series of long and difficult negotiations followed the Pilgrims' speech and MacDonald's almost simultaneous speech at Lossie-mouth. The attention of the chancelleries and of the peoples of the world was on London where the two English-speaking nations were making a concerted effort to assure durable peace. "One of my most frequent callers on business has been Matsudaira," Dawes recorded, "and I have called at his embassy at least as many times. Each tries to save the other the trip necessary to get together."

But Dawes' activities were a healthy mixture of business with the highest pleasures known to him, the pleasures of the mind.

"Half the time MacDonald and I spend together, we talk of things other than international relations," Dawes wrote. "His knowledge of history and literature is exact and comprehensive. It is a delight to be with him. He talks of the problems which he has on hand—and few men have more difficult ones—and in his views, so

far, he has never descended from the high levels of sincere friendship. I have faith that he will stand all tests without loss of public
respect, irrespective of what happens to him politically."

Slowly, signs of progress began to appear. On July 29 Dawes,
Hugh Gibson, American Minister Ray Atherton, MacDonald, and
First Lord of the Admiralty Alexander held an important conference.
"When we left, the only remaining question involving naval parity
between our two nations which was unsettled related to the cruiser
class, and that was much simplified. . . . We agree to equate by
1936."

Two days later Dawes had his first talk with one of the great
figures of the century, Winston Churchill:

"I had never met him before," Dawes wrote. "We talked over
his coming trip to America, and he outlined what was in his mind
to say. He said, frankly, he did not favor a naval-limitation agreement. There was an interesting but general talk.

"He is a man whose relentless ambition may carry him to the
top. That might be a relatively short time in this country where
parties are breaking down and the electorate is restless. Churchill
makes a point of telling one from the United States that he is half-
American and has a great affection for the United States. I put
my own value on that statement, and it is a high one. But, as much
as any Englishman I have ever met or in fancy created, he typifies
John Bull to me, and he has my admiration for that."

Although Churchill at that time did not command an influence
that would have given his opposition to Dawes' efforts any serious
weight, the negotiations lagged and dragged. The experts, it seemed,
were resolved that no agreement should be reached before they had
had their day in court.

". . . I am more depressed than I have been since we began
our conversations," Prime Minister MacDonald wrote to Dawes
on August 22. "You will remember that we started on the yardstick
which was the proposal for Geneva. You were to give me a formula,
and we both agreed that it should be examined by subordinate experts. That has all gone. In your speech to the Pilgrims, you said
so truly that the statesmen should handle this matter and, as there
was the desire for an agreement and as a naval conflict between the
countries was unthinkable, the technicians should not thwart the

statesmen. That has gone, and we are back in exactly the same atmosphere, and facing exactly the same presentation of the problem, as we were at Geneva. We are drifting away from the only road that offers a solution of a problem which does not consist of reality at all, but of words and appearances. Experts and lawyers make nearly all the reefs on the seas of life upon which men and states founder."

And Dawes himself thought he saw "the beginning of an effort to fit a yardstick to the settlement instead of a settlement to a yardstick."

Three more weeks, dozens of conferences in London and in Washington, and endless cabling between the two capitals had to be gone through before Dawes, on September 13, could record:

"Differences of naval technical opinion have now been so reduced that, quantitatively, they concern less than 25,000 tons out of an aggregate tonnage of both nations of about 2,400,000 tons. The only point upon which the naval experts are apart is whether three of the American cruisers are to be 10,000 tons each with eight-inch guns, or there is to be substituted for these three cruisers four smaller cruisers, say of 7,500 tons, with six-inch guns. Thus has a mountain shrunk to a mouse."

Now that it was nearly over, Dawes could pay a left-handed compliment to the experts: "I confess to satisfaction with the way in which we have used the naval technicians, for never, in my judgment, could there have been a naval conference in which the consultations with them have been more continuous and thorough on both sides. . . . At no time did we let them get the middle of the stage, where their continuous bonfires would have presented to the audience the appearance of a general conflagration."

With the agreement sealed, MacDonald sailed for the United States on September 27—the first British Prime Minister to visit this country. Before leaving, he had had time for only a short note to Dawes:

"When I have a little more leisure, I really must put on paper an expression of some of the obligations we all owe to you for what you have done since you set foot on our shores. I feel that, if this were to end one's service to the world, it would have been worth while."

Dawes sailed for the United States shortly after the British Prime Minister, to spend a few months at home.

Almost a year and a half earlier, on July 10, 1928, Dawes had noted in his journal:

"The situation in the country points to a coming business change. The credits of the country which, under natural laws, eventually grow beyond a proper proportion to the cash in which they are redeemable, give evidence of reaching that stage before many months. Will it, when reached, make nervous the depositing class, as used to happen in the days prior to the establishment of the Federal Reserve System with its large credit-creating potentiality? Will the American people, as they sometimes do during the closing of a period of prosperity, while it still persists, suddenly turn over in bed—that is, wake up some morning with their outlook changed from an optimistic to a pessimistic view of the future, as they did in 1893? Such an action might mean political revolution, now as then. As the Bible has it: 'Jeshurun waxed fat, and kicked!' Since prosperity often begets folly and sometimes panic, these changes have their source in the instincts more than in the intelligence of the people. Their date cannot be predicted with any certainty.

"Yet there are signs at present of the conditions which, in the past, have accompanied such changes in their first stages."

And on January 22, 1929:

"It is a difficult thing successfully to encourage, at the same time, tight money conditions on the stock market and easy money conditions for legitimate business. The Federal Reserve Board is finding that out. Money flows to any safe point of highest interest rates—nothing can stop that. Until general deflation sets in, credit conditions will grow worse, no matter what the Federal Reserve Board does. Expanded credits, when they are general, can never be liquidated in an orderly manner. They collapse. History proves that."

In February of 1929 Dawes had begun to believe a business crash almost inevitable.

He spent the morning of February 18 before the session of the Senate with Arthur Leonard, a business associate of Chicago, later to be President of the "Dawes Bank," "going over some important personal matters. In these days of a strained credit situation in the country, the wise businessman is making preparations for a possible credit contraction of serious proportions. This will come at any time when there occurs any lack of general confidence, and perhaps before.

"Men may talk of the new business conditions which make the old danger signs obsolete, but there is one unchanging element in the situation and that is human nature. All human nature is subject to the law of reaction. When men have moved in a mass in one direction for a long time, under the influence of optimism, they always move in the opposite direction when pessimistic."

And now in the month of October, 1929, as Dawes returned from the United Kingdom, the stock market collapsed in the panic he had predicted. There may have been some at that time who thought the panic no more than a passing crisis. But Dawes, early in November of 1929, noted in his diary:

"This panic, in my judgment, is the beginning of a major depression in general business. It is easy to be philosophical in a panic when one is out of debt. There is widespread agony and despair among the venturesome in life, but it is the plodder's day of triumph. After having passed through the panics of 1893, 1907, and 1914 (the latter two as a businessman), I am in a position in this one to sense the suffering of one class and the melancholy satisfaction of the other. The latter feeling is natural but not creditable. I notice that some who have escaped disaster in this upheaval through mere accident, pickled in the vinegar of their own pretended righteousness, are the most severe in their criticisms of the unfortunate.

"For several years, I have been expecting it and getting my house in order to meet it. It should have occurred two years ago and, for at least that length of time, I have been warning my friends to get out of the stock market.

"It was in the panic of 1893, when I was twenty-eight years old, that I learned the greatest financial lesson of my life, which was that ninety-day notes become due. Before that time, I had regarded them as renewable forever. At the time when that panic broke, I owed in the neighborhood of $200,000. I passed through it without failure, but my agonies of anxiety and worry, and my strenuous endeavors of that period, terrible as their memory is, have proved themselves the safeguard of my business life. They taught me the dangers of debt. I have borrowed since that time, but never recklessly, and never without a plan for repayment worked out at the time I contracted the debt. Out of my experience, I have given advice to a number of young men during the last two years, as to what was ahead of them. I can recall none of them who took my advice. So probably it would have been with me before 1893. I doubtless would have listened to but not acted upon conservative advice. Experience alone teaches the ambitious young.

"To me it seems that the signs of the coming of the present catastrophe were more pronounced than those of any other through which the United States has passed. History shows that there is no such thing as an orderly deflation of generally overexpanded credit. Human nature remains the same. The law of human action and reaction is immutable. Federal Reserve banks, low production costs, low inventories, and all the other things which the optimist has regarded as 'making a change in conditions as compared with the past' have not changed human nature. The longer the spree, the deeper the following depression and the longer the sobering-up time."

But depression or no depression, Dawes had work to do. Within two weeks after his arrival in Chicago, he sold $6,125,000 worth of the bonds of the Century of Progress Exposition that had been guaranteed by leading Chicago citizens. Then he went on to Washington to begin his preparations for the Five Power Naval Conference in January, 1930, to which Great Britain had invited the United States, Japan, France, and Italy.

The American Delegation to the Conference was to consist of Secretary of State Stimson as chairman, and the delegates Senators Joseph T. Robinson and David A. Reed, Ambassador Dawes and Dwight Morrow. Secretary of the Navy Adams was added, and Hugh Gibson was also appointed at the insistence of Dawes. Admiral W. V. Pratt and Rear Admiral Hilary P. Jones went as advisers.

Dawes' role in the conference would be far different from the man-to-man diplomacy he had been able to carry on with Prime Minister MacDonald. Then he had been the highest ranking American dealing with the highest ranking Britisher. Now, Secretary of State Stimson would be the top intermediary between the United

States Government and the governments of the four other nations. Dawes' changed status became evident at once.

"Matsudaira called and fully reported on the Japanese naval proposition. I told him I would not enter into a discussion of it with him, that our Naval Conference delegation had been appointed and that, although I was a member of it, I did not propose to change the *status quo* here in London by personal negotiations at this time, unless specifically directed by my Government or by the chairman of our delegation. I told him that I would, of course, transmit any information he desired to our Government."

Nonetheless, Dawes had been charged in Washington to deliver a talk which, just as his Pilgrims' speech had done earlier, would set out the American aims in the forthcoming negotiations. The speech, which was delivered in November before the Institute of Journalists, was in fact a supplement of the Pilgrims' speech. After expressing his confidence that the five Naval Powers would meet in the spirit of the Kellogg Peace Pact, Dawes summed up the purpose of the Five Power Conference:

"The specific objective of this present negotiation is the abolition of the general competitive building of fighting ships, and their reduction in number, so far as is consistent with the national security and domestic necessities of the respective naval powers."

But privately and in conversation with Ramsay MacDonald, Dawes was apprehensive. The Conference, he feared, would turn into a "four-language talkfest with days wasted on jabber and translation of jabber." And in his diary he added:

"I do hope that, by some departure from the conventional, the Conference can properly create a public sense of its earnestness and its determination to indulge in constructive work rather than declamation."

There was another danger threatening the success of the conference. At the Reparations Conference, where Dawes' word had been law, distracting social activities had been forbidden. Now again, Dawes proposed that "the work of the conference can best be done if there is no debauch of 'gorgeous social affairs.'" The British Government, however, host to delegations from four other nations, had announced that there would be four public functions.

"The four public functions arranged for the delegates are just four too many, in my judgment. I have engaged in too many inter-allied conferences during the war not to understand the folly of the present society program and its possibilities. At the least, we have probably added weeks to the length of the Conference. First impressions are of vital importance in their effect upon the delegates themselves. If they are led to believe that time and expedition are not of value, they will act accordingly."

While Dawes, in the nature of his assignment, did at no time during the Five Power Conference act as the American spokesman, he neglected nothing which might smooth the progress of the Conference.

"Dwight Morrow and I are spending much time with some of the delegates, realizing they can do much to make or mar the success of the Conference. The part of wisdom at a 'unanimous consent' party is to look after wallflowers who, feeling neglected, may prove to be poison ivy in disguise." And, in particular, he carried on many private talks with French Premier Aristide Briand, who became his close friend. For it was from France, and from Italy, that Dawes expected most of the trouble of the conference would come. Lloyd George agreed. "Briand is constructive but, in this conference, his feet are tied; the knot is very, very tight," he told Dawes.

The conference was slow in making progress. In March the United States and Great Britain had equated their tonnage at 1,200,000. A month later an agreement had been reached between the United States, Great Britain, and Japan. France and Italy were still standing apart. While France, Dawes was convinced, wanted to join in an agreement, Fascist Italy was beginning to feel her strength, and refused to settle for anything less than parity with France.

"I am far from regarding a five-power pact, even under the present circumstances, as unattainable," Dawes wrote on March 22. "Even if most of the nations have given up hope of anything but a three-power pact, I am glad to say that is not the case with our nation."

To complicate matters, Secretary of State Stimson, in spite of the success he had achieved so far, was under constant fire from home, being accused of "poor management," "timidity," and "lack of leadership." This criticism from the back seat reached such proportions that on March 28 President Hoover felt it necessary to issue a statement expressing his firm support of the work of the delegation in London. The conference, Hoover felt, was making much better progress than the public realized. At the end of its first month, it had been near failure—but since then, it had survived the fall of the French government, an adverse vote in the British Parliament against MacDonald's government, and an election in Japan in which the Minseito Peace party had emerged triumphant. It had resulted in an agreement among three of the five participants. And hope had not yet been abandoned that the other two participants would be brought into line.

How the situation and Stimson's role looked on the ground emerges clearly from an entry in Dawes' diary. "Stimson is a safe leader, not afraid to take individual responsibility where necessary, without hesitation, and yet wise enough to explain all he does to his delegation. As a result, he has a united delegation behind him. As a body, they are strong men, and only capable leadership would satisfy them. Their attitude toward him during all these difficult negotiations, composed as they are, is of itself a tribute to his unusual qualifications for the place. He is carrying a heavy load, but never shows the white feather or a slackening of effort because of discouraging circumstances."

France, meanwhile, had been attempting to convince England and the United States that she would have to have either a large navy or a security pact. But the United States declined flatly to become party to any security pact. The only obligation America was willing to shoulder in case of naval threats to French security was "to examine the situation as it may affect the interests of herself and her nationals." No security pact or even consultative pact came out of the conference. When the drafting committee set to work in April to prepare the final form of the treaty, they were writing a five-power treaty insofar as the postponement of replacement of capital ships until after 1936 was concerned—and a three-power treaty which limited tonnage of cruisers, destroyers, and submarines. Three nations were to scrap a total of nine ships: Great Britain five, the United States three, and Japan one.

If this was not a complete success, it was far from being a complete failure. Agreement had been reached among the three largest naval powers. As for the rest, Ramsay MacDonald announced in a speech: "The French, Italians, and ourselves will pursue the search for a complete naval agreement." It was not until April of 1930 that all hope for agreement with Italy had to be abandoned when Benito Mussolini launched an Italian naval rearmament program of imposing dimensions.

To Dawes, the British Prime Minister wrote:

"But for you, the success which has been attained could not have been reached. Further than that, I am happy beyond words that the relations between the United States and ourselves have been so wonderfully changed. That alone, I think, is an achievement which means much for the future good of the world and, in that, your part has been as big as mine."

As the various delegations returned home to seek ratification of the treaty, Ambassador Dawes prepared to relax in the fulfillment of his regular duties when he received a cable from Acting Secretary of State Joseph P. Cotton:

"You will proceed to Washington as soon as possible for consultation. What we want you back for is to help in defending the Treaty in the Senate, and we regard this matter as important."

In June the fate of the treaty still hung in the balance before the Senate. Stimson, alluding to a British newspaper editorial praising Dawes as "the one man in the United States who understands the value and use of the calculated indiscretion," wrote to Dawes:

"The treaty represents the most advanced step yet taken in naval reduction, and, at the same time, secures parity for the United States, which could be attained only by fifteen years of a naval race at the cost of two billions of dollars, during all of which time we would have naval inferiority and starvation of other useful government activities. It protects us both in the Atlantic and the Pacific.

"We must, of course, be patient with people who exclaim over a knot in the kitchen door instead of showing appreciation of a great architectural accomplishment.

"For myself, I should welcome a *Dawes' indiscretion* from you. Tear off your dress suit and say 'Hell and Maria.' The situation is almost ludicrous, and yet there is danger of people losing their perspective."

In a special session of the United States Senate, however, the treaty was ratified on July 21, 1930, with the support of all but nine votes. From the day when Buffalo Bridge was dedicated to the day of that ratification, no man had worked as long and unflaggingly for this result as Dawes.

Chapter Twenty

❁

THE TORNADO AND THE DOVE

𝐼t was on Friday, the thirteenth of December, that his Excellency the Ambassador of the United States of America, Charles Gates Dawes, gave his first formal dinner at Prince's Gate. Among the guests were Her Royal Highness Princess Beatrice; Prime Minister Ramsay MacDonald, and Miss Ishbel MacDonald; His Excellency the Japanese Ambassador, and Madame Matsudaira; His Excellency the French Ambassador, and Miss De Fleuriau; His Excellency the Spanish Ambassador, Marques Merry del Val, and the Marquesa; Lord and Lady Astor; Sir John and Lady Hanbury-Williams; and many others. The gathering included a number of famous artists and authors—but the renowned comedian Leon Errol, whom Dawes thought "the funniest man on the stage," who had been a guest at the Embassy for a whole week, did not sit down to table.

The dinner began in an atmosphere of exquisite correctness. But as it proceeded, things began to go wrong. They were small things at first, and the guests ignored them.

One of the waiters, to all outward appearances an excellently trained servant, began to fill the water glasses with lemonade. His deft hands removed plates before the diners had finished the course. As he passed a tray with the fish course around the table with one hand, he removed the silver for the fish course with the other. He took a plate with crackers from the table—and the crackers slipped and buried the food on one of the plates.

The guests, with the tact and nobility of thoroughbreds, gracefully overlooked the series of *faux pas*. But now this same waiter reappeared with a tray, stumbled, and nearly emptied it into the lap of one of the ladies.

A spoon dropped from his hand and fell under the table. He quietly took a candle, got down on his hands and knees, and began to crawl about in search of the lost spoon.

"It seems this waiter has found his way to the sherry," one of the ladies remarked.

"Sorry, ma'am," replied the waiter, sitting up on his haunches, "there is none in the house, but I shall be glad to go out and get some for you."

There is no telling what Leon Errol would have done next if Lady Astor, at this point, had not seen through the prank Dawes and Errol were playing on the assembly. Now they confessed, and Errol was introduced and sat down at the table with the others for the last course. And after the dinner he entertained them so delightfully with his letter-mailing trick and with stories that Prime Minister MacDonald broke an appointment in order to remain, and he and the other guests stayed on until long after midnight.

Charles Dawes' hospitality quickly became as famous in London as it had been in Washington. Although he served no liquor at Embassy functions, since he did not intend to flout abroad the prohibition laws that were in force at home, the Embassy attracted countless American visitors. On each of the three occasions when he celebrated the Fourth of July in London, he served food and refreshments to more than twenty-five hundred Americans.

Like all American Ambassadors to Great Britain, he had to dig into his own pocket for most of his expenses. In the two and a half years he was at Prince's Gate, he served food, from reception sandwiches to dinners, to visitors from home at the rate of more than five thousand a year.

"Caro," a journal entry read, "tells me that, at lunch or dinner in the last month, we have entertained at the Embassy about two hundred and fifty Americans. On assuming this office, I determined that, if I could help it, our visitors from home would never experience a 'cold' Embassy such as I once encountered in 1897, during my first trip to Europe. Caro is entitled to the credit for the way we take care of people. She is a born executive and, with her perfect tact and kindly heart, she keeps the Embassy, with its large staff of servants and a continual capacity load of transients and house guests, a place of comfort and happiness."

American statesmen, businessmen and professional men, artists, writers, actors, and simple tourists made it a point to call on Dawes.

"I have to cross the ocean to see my favorite statesman," wrote Will Rogers. "But I'll tell you that, when you come over here to London and see Charley Dawes performing, it is worth the trip. He makes you mighty proud of your country. You ought to hear him tell about his experience with ferocious mothers. I doubt if a charging elephant or a rhinoceros is as determined or hard to check as a socially ambitious mother."

There is no doubt that social climbers were among Dawes' greatest trials in London. The only person who can introduce an American woman at the British Court is the American Ambassador. Then, and probably still today, one who has curtsied before a King or Queen has achieved a mark of distinction in some circles of American society. And so, dowager after dowager besieged the Ambassador to assist her and her daughters in securing the much desired day in court. Dawes had little patience with such ambitions.

"At dinner, a wealthy American woman kept referring to Lord this and Lady that," he wrote in his diary. "I tried as tactfully as I could to bring the talk back to things in our own country, but she would roam back to her lords and ladies. Finally, I said to her: 'You were born in a little town in Wisconsin. Your husband was born in a little town in Ohio. America has given you all you have. Your interest ought to be there. Let's bring the conversation back to American topics.'"

And in an address before the Masters and Fellows of Trinity College, Dawes remarked:

"We have recently had in London a body of American travelers representing a cross-section of the American people, representing the heart and body and soul of the American people; a body of travelers not self-invited, with their minds unoccupied by thoughts of society reporters or fashionable dressmakers.

"They brought no social introductions. The credentials each carried were but the photograph of a son and a few withered flowers from a garden at home to lay on a grave in France."

The reference was to a group of 156 Gold Star mothers for

whom he himself had held a reception in his Embassy. His diary records:

"Lord Jellicoe and Field Marshal Plumer were there, and I introduced them to many mothers whose sons had fallen by the side of their British comrades. The 27th Division served under Plumer. Afterward, we all accompanied the mothers as they laid wreaths at the grave of the Unknown Soldier in Westminster Abbey and at the Cenotaph. It was an affecting and solemn occasion. I was very proud of the simple and unaffected way in which these fine and natural American women conducted themselves, and I could not but think how majestic was their naturalness as contrasted with some of their countrywomen who besiege me with requests to be presented at Court.

"While I was standing near Lord Plumer, someone told us that one of the mothers present had lost two sons in the 27th Division. I told him I would find her and present her to him. His answer was a request to go with me 'to be presented to her.' "

Dawes, who admired Winston Churchill for being typically British—was American, and did not feel that he owed an apology for it to anyone. He did the hitherto unheard-of thing of giving a dinner at the Embassy to the entire staff, including the Marine Guard, secretaries, stenographers, and clerks. And one Independence Day, he presided and made a brief opening address at a dinner where Dr. John Grier Hibben of Princeton University and Lord Reading were the principal speakers. To Dawes Dr. Hibben's speech seemed in poor taste, an abject apology to the British people for the behavior of the Americans. Dr. Hibben explained to the English how and why the Americans were so wrong in international policy. In effect, Dawes thought, Hibben forgave the British all their reparation debts if only in return they would forgive America all her sins. As Dr. Hibben sat down, Dawes rose to make a second speech, an extemporaneous one such as one might hear from any bandstand in any park in any town in America on the Fourth of July. It was a speech straight from the shoulder. The British cheered as lustily as the Americans.

There is an entry in Dawes' diary on another of his numerous speeches in the British Isles:

"My emphatic method of extempore speech before the Travel

Association of Great Britain and Ireland this week was disparaged by one or two English newspaper critics who are accustomed to more repose in public expression." But it was this very speech which brought him a letter from the Right Reverend The Lord Bishop of London, Arthur Foley Winnington-Ingram, P.C., K.C.V.O., D.D.:

"Dear General: I felt sure that I would like you but, after your speech today, I feel that you are 'a man and a brother.' Now could you and Mrs. Dawes step down quite informally and lunch here on Tuesday, the twenty-third, and meet my five brother bishops who help me with my little 4,500,000? They are all jolly fellows, and you would like them, and your wife would enjoy seeing this old place where the bishops have lived for thirteen hundred years."

The British soon began to bestow attention and honors upon "this distinguished American who has attracted such widespread attention in these Islands," and who was reported to have said he would not wear knee-length silken britches at king's levees or royal courts:

"Attended a dinner of the Royal Geographical Society and, afterward, a formal meeting of it when, in behalf of the American Geographic Society, I presented the Cullen medal to John Huburt Mill for his notable contribution to science. Later in the evening, Caro and I attended a musical given by Lady Corey at her home in Belgrave Square, at which Fritz Kreisler was the artist. During the program, to the surprise of some of my diplomatic colleagues who were present, he played my composition and also played it the next night with an encore at his guest concert at Queen's Hall."

The 500-year-old British Society of Barristers and Judges, the "Middle Benchers," thawed sufficiently to elect him to membership. Dawes accepted, took his place at the foot of the table as all novitiate members did, entered into the assignment of "ringing the bell" with gusto, and was voted a "capital fellow."

And the Earl of Crawford, Chancellor of the University of Manchester, conferred the LLD degree on Dawes with the words:

"Strangely in his chariot is the tornado harnessed alongside the dove. And I trust I overstep no limits set by diplomatic reticence if I add that, under the tempestuous exterior and unconventional address, brimming over with picturesque expletives, none of which, however, he claims to have invented himself, he conceals the kindest of hearts and the most loving of dispositions."

But although Dawes discharged his many social obligations as Ambassador with skill and grace, his heart was not in this kind of activity. His opinion about "gorgeous social affairs" was still the same. Nor was he the only one in a public position to feel that way. Once at a dinner where he was seated next to the Prince of Wales, the future King asked him:

"Do you like this sort of thing?"

"No!" Dawes replied emphatically.

"Neither do I."

"The difference between us," Dawes said, "is that I, some day, will go home to Chicago and do just as I please. You will have to do this the balance of your life."

"Any public assignment," Dawes wrote into his diary, "except a difficult one is unattractive. Aside from the naval work which has now occupied ten months, and in which there was a specific objective, there has been little of importance in this position and, under normal circumstances, the life of an ambassador here seems largely a round of social events, public speaking on noncontroversial subjects, and idle enjoyments."

Obviously, a man like Dawes could not be idle for long. After a short "vacation" trip to Chicago during which Dawes completed the financial arrangements for the "Century of Progress" fair, Dawes returned to London and there made plans for an archaeological excursion to Southern France, to the Altamira Cave, and to other Spanish sites of central interest in the study of prehistoric man.

Archaeology had long been one of Dawes' strongest extracurricular interests. He had financed an expedition of the Smithsonian Institution, to further its studies of the early history of exploration in America and to assist it in a search for a Mayan codex which would allow the decipherment of Mayan writing. His companion on the trip to France and Spain was to be Dr. George Grant MacCurdy, director of the American School for Prehistoric Research

"There is not much doing at the Chancery, and I am putting, without trouble, two hours a day into archaeological study," Dawes wrote. "I am going to give all the time I can to Dr. MacCurdy's treatises, as I want to be more nearly letter perfect when I make the trip with him. I had a long talk with Sir Auckland Geddes, chairman of the Rio Tinto Company, Ltd., about the archaeology of the Niebla area and the Rio Tinto mine which we shall visit."

At Les Eyzies, which MacCurdy called the center of Paleolithic cavedom, and at Cap-Blanc, Combarelles, Font-de-Gaume, Cro-Magnon, Laugerie-Basse, and other famous abodes of prehistoric man, Dawes for two weeks was to forget the plight of the present. On part of the trip Dawes was accompanied by the Infante Don Alfonso and the Infanta Beatriz.

"I stumbled and crawled along the deep limestone passages of Combarelles and Font-de-Gaume, and saw in their inner depths, in Combarelles, 250 meters from the entrance, the pictures executed by Paleolithic man 25,000 or more years ago, under conditions of great personal discomfort. It seems to me he must have sought these more remote and difficult sections of the caves to indulge his artistic instincts, not so much because he was seeking a shrine for the pictures themselves, as some archaeologists say, but a protected place, so that if his enemies did find him unawares, they could attack him in only one direction, and then only after he had been put on his guard again."

Thé day on which this note was written, after ten hours underground in torrid heat, was August 27, 1930, Dawes' sixty-fifth birthday.

On his return to London, Dawes found the situation of modern man not much more comfortable. "Between India, unemployment, Palestine, the safeguarding question, and an insecure tenure, necessitating the continual adjustment of a constantly shifting and indefinite alliance with the Liberal party under Lloyd George, the Prime Minister is 'Old Man Trouble's own child' just now.

"MacDonald is disturbed by the French military program involving large appropriations and fortifications and aeroplanes and a large naval construction, planned to commence soon, although the latter is not yet in the appropriation stage.

"He has been unable to get Briand to agree to American and British participation in the discussion between Italy and France as to the naval settlement, which they could not reach at the Naval

Conference. MacDonald maintains that this discussion should be considered as an extension of the negotiations of the London Naval Conference, and should be under similar methods and preparatory to the deliberations of the Disarmament Conference of the League of Nations.

"They do not agree to this or, rather, France does not agree. He regards this as discouraging, and fears that France is going ahead with a naval program which will force Great Britain to follow.

"MacDonald, in discussing the situation in India, told me that Great Britain would at any cost maintain law and order and British prestige, which alone assures peace in India."

The woes of Great Britain were to occupy many words in Dawes' reports to Washington. The future of that country as a world power, he thought, lay largely in India, "divided by castes, religion, tradition, and conditions thousands of years old." The Indian situation, he wrote to Stimson, he believed "was more serious than at any time since Queen Victoria was crowned Empress at the Durbar in 1877." In the Imperial conference in October, 1930, he detected further enkindlement of the flames of nationalism and the shaking loose of the cement which held the British Empire together.

"Perhaps most of England agrees with the views of Lord Rothmere that 'the Indianization of central authority in India means the ruin of the British Empire.'" Winston Churchill came to luncheon with Dawes to tell him that even a discussion of the Indianization of central authority in India was "immensely dangerous."

On October 26 the time had finally come when the treaty that had come out of the London naval conference was to be officially deposited in London. Although France and Italy had signed some parts of it, they were still at loggerheads concerning its main points.

"The attitude and appearance of De Fleuriau and Bordonaro, the French and Italian Ambassadors, appealed to their own and our sense of humor," said Dawes' written account of the ceremony. "The scene was like a schoolroom, the good little boys sitting at their desks doing their sums dutifully under the eyes of an approving teacher, and the two little bad boys sitting all alone. We all laughed about it with De Fleuriau and Bordonaro, who appreciated the ludicrous appearance of their isolation."

The French-Italian situation, however, boded ill for the disarmament conference that had been scheduled to take place in 1932. None of the countries involved were doing the spadework that the United States, Great Britain, and Japan had done to prepare for the naval conference of 1930. As early as spring of 1931, American Secretary of State Stimson believed the conference foredoomed to failure. President Hoover, however, felt there was yet time to save it.

Leading European statesmen, among them the German Foreign Minister Curtius, had let it be known that in their opinion Charles Dawes would be the best possible President or Vice-President for the 1932 disarmament conference. But in January, 1931, Dawes went to see MacDonald, to convey to him the reasons why the United States would not sponsor the selection of an American for that office. In Stimson's view, Dawes informed MacDonald, the most complex problems of the conference directly concerned Europe alone, "and, while the United States is sympathetic toward the effort for a settlement, it cannot properly assume a responsibility for its outcome, whether a success or a failure."

MacDonald was no more hopeful than Stimson.

"I found the Prime Minister frankly pessimistic," Dawes noted. "He sees no progress in the French and Italian naval situation. Nor does he look happily at the attitude of France and Germany toward the Disarmament Conference. He fears that Germany may end up simply using it for the purpose of making a declaration against the Versailles Treaty. He made no demur to Stimson's reasoning."

For a short moment, the situation improved. France and Italy had reached an agreement "in principle," but the agreement was not to develop any further. The German-Austrian customs union was to make any talk of disarmament in France impossible. Briand resigned, and Dawes noted in his diary:

"Briand's resignation as Minister of Foreign Affairs menaces the success of the disarmament conference and of other European efforts for peaceful adjustments for the time."

Dawes, at his London listening post, heard the rumbling of unrest all over Europe, and faithfully reported it to Washington.

"To keep our State Department informed about the progress of the constantly changing naval negotiations between Great Britain, France, and Italy requires the American Ambassador to perform functions similar to those of an informed newspaper correspondent conveying confidential news, not for publication but for use in the determination of policy by those charged with responsibility for it."

With an obdurate and fanatical Hitler daily gathering strength in Germany; France disturbed by the implications of the German and Austrian customs union; Italy and France deadlocked in their naval negotiations; the first faint thunder from the war clouds in Manchuria; and the pillars of Empire weakening for Great Britain in India, Palestine, and on the Suez, Ambassador Dawes, in the late spring of 1931 wrote to his brother Rufus in Chicago:

"I fear the time is arriving described in Isaiah 33:7: 'The ambassadors of peace shall weep bitterly.'"

Chapter Twenty-One

❁

"THIS WEEK IT'S ENGLAND"

"Diplomacy," Dawes wrote during his term as Ambassador at the Court of St. James, "is not hard on the brain, but it is hell on the feet." And indeed, the distances the Ambassador had to cover on foot, in trains, or aboard ship were enormous. On May 22, 1931, he was on another ocean voyage to report to Washington.

On his second day at sea, aboard the SS *Bremen*, he wrote in his diary:

"Governor Franklin D. Roosevelt of New York sent a note by his son, Elliott, inviting me to dinner last night in his stateroom. No others were present. Roosevelt's service in Washington was under President Wilson as Assistant Secretary of the Navy. As I seldom visited Washington in those days, I had never met him, to my recollection, though he said we had met at Bordeaux, France, during the war.

"It was a regular Rooseveltian occasion, both delightful and strenuous. I do not know when I have enjoyed an evening more, and we were both surprised, being still fresh and in the full height of conversational activity, to find we had consumed four and a half hours when we separated or, rather, when I left his room. With common experience in civil service, common experience during the war, common friends and acquaintances by the score, we forgot all political difference which, after all, is never a real barrier; and, naturally, we forgot to look at the clock."

While Dawes felt that President Hoover ought to be re-elected, he held out little hope that this would happen. At the occasion of

302

the 1930 elections Dawes had noted: "Hard times and prohibition went hand in hand to beat the Republicans. There is no occasion to philosophize. Events are in the saddle. Prohibition cuts squarely across party lines. As the result of the election, two new leaders stand out: Governor Franklin D. Roosevelt of New York, a wet Democrat; and Dwight Morrow of New Jersey, a wet Republican." By now, Dawes was convinced that Franklin D. Roosevelt would be the next President of the United States.

"In this world-wide and serious business depression, the majority of the people in most of the countries thus affected seem in opposition to their governmental administrations. The reasoning of the average man everywhere is simple. He wants a change of things, so why not start out by changing administrations? In times of adversity, he will regard any action, good or bad, wise or unwise, on the part of an existing administration as wrong. In other words, his attitude is determined by his feelings rather than his reason.

"Existing administrations, however, while probably doomed to early defeat, may have a chance to come back into public favor later if they act courageously, but not if they fail to act. If they act wisely, posterity, which ignores popularity in forming its judgments, will applaud them. Posterity will even condone an unwise act if it is sincere and courageous, but for indecision and inaction in time of crisis it has only condemnation.

"I hear much criticism of President Hoover for his unquestionably useful effort to mitigate the situation. It is to his credit that he is being criticized for doing too much instead of too little."

Next day, Dawes had another long conversation with the future President Roosevelt. In a session "lasting until midnight," they talked of the League of Nations, Winston Churchill, diaries, and, above all, economy in government. Dawes had gone to the boat from the House of Parliament where he had heard Churchill speak on the Budget, and had written in his diary:

"Churchill interests me more and more as an orator. He is not the equal of Arthur Balfour and does not have the deep, spiritual qualities of Ramsay MacDonald, but he is a great orator, and he draws blood from the opposition when he speaks. Churchill spoke of his 'present loneliness,' an obvious allusion to the fact that the Conservatives seem to be making an outcast of him at this time.

Churchill has great vigor and courage, and it seems to me the Conservatives might well be using his talents."

Governor Roosevelt in the boat conversations had been prolific in his praise of the Federal Budget System established by Dawes. He asked for, and received, a sizable file of material which Dawes had furnished to the British Royal Commission on Civil Service, and which contained some of his views on governmental economy. In returning the material later, Roosevelt attached a handwritten note:

State of New York
EXECUTIVE CHAMBER
ALBANY

Franklin D. Roosevelt
Governor
Dear General:

Are you going to have any copies of this made? If so, I should much like to have one, to make the heads of my departments read it. The budget system as such, in Albany, is pretty good, but there is no comprehension of the idea that the whole amount of an appropriation does not have to be spent.

Faithfully,
FRANKLIN D. ROOSEVELT

Roosevelt in his 1932 campaign was merely to expand the views expressed in his two ocean talks with Dawes. Dawes subsequently changed his early good opinion of Roosevelt when Roosevelt changed his views on economy in governmental administration.

The gloom of the depression ravaging the United States fell across the ocean to meet Dawes on his way home. The passengers aboard seemed "soaked with pessimism, and the press reports indicate clearly that business in the United States is growing worse. With unerring but not premeditated accuracy, I select the worst possible time to go home and raise money for the exposition. However, as I came out all right in the panic month of 1929, I will not prejudge the possibilities." Before the ship reached the American shore, Dawes received radiograms from both Hoover and Morrow to call on them immediately on his return. The word "crisis" would be the leitmotiv of their conversations, as it would indeed be of Dawes' remaining years in the public service.

"Had two long and interesting visits with Secretary Mellon. One thing I note in this terrible business depression, undoubtedly the worst in this country since 1873, is that even the richest men are worried. All have been met by very large and unexpected demands for money to salvage their speculating friends and to assist in meeting past commitments of their enterprises. Mellon is one of the richest men in the United States; but, just as I found with every other business leader in New York, his face was 'sicklied o'er with the pale cast of thought.'"

Home in Chicago, Dawes found "a bankrupt city government already in default on city obligations, and so far unable to get remedial legislation from the legislature which would enable it to help itself. It cannot even raise money to pay the city employees. The banks are unwilling to take any more of the city's obligations until, through the enactment of new legislation, they have a chance to be paid back." Nonetheless, Dawes sold over a million dollars of Century of Progress exposition bonds "sufficient to carry building to the latter part of 1932."

But now the storm in all its fury was breaking in Europe. En route to Springfield, Illinois, where Hoover was to speak, the President and the Ambassador discussed the situation. The Bank of Austria was about to fail. If that happened, the Reichsbank in Germany would be compelled to declare a moratorium.

"This would precipitate a world financial crisis, affecting our own country materially, as the New York banks alone were reported to have $500,000,000 of German acceptances," Dawes wrote in the record of his train conferences with Hoover. "The New York bankers had been telephoning Hoover before he left Washington, requesting governmental assistance in the European difficulty.

"Hoover was considering what he could do to relieve this situation. His present thought was to suggest a reparations moratorium all around, for one or two years, funding the payment due to the United States for that time. France, in that case, would have to forego receiving reparations, at present amounting to more than she is paying the United States. Hoover could not propose such a plan without being assured by leaders of the opposition that Congress would ratify it in December. European finance is tottering, but this moratorium might help tide things over.

"Meanwhile, the Bank of Austria's gold reserve, like that of the Reichsbank, is becoming dangerously low, and the recalling of short-time loans by America, and our favorable balance of trade, continue to draw the life blood from European finance. In our own country, banks are closing every day, and money is being hoarded in safe-deposit boxes."

On June 21 Hoover announced the foreign-debt moratorium. It was a move in the self-interest of the United States. Dawes said in a supporting statement:

"In these days of commercial and financial international dependence, no great nation is immune from the effect of credit collapse of any other great nation. That always involves a possible world-wide credit collapse. That is why the world now rallies to the cause of German credit relief."

But in spite of all efforts, the German financial situation grew rapidly worse. The country declared a bank moratorium and a gold embargo. Other central European countries were about to follow suit.

"This morning, William R. Castle, Under Secretary of State, telephoned me that the President desired me to return to London as soon as possible and be there while the German loan negotiations between the representatives of the three nations concerned were taking place. He stated that the President said, in view of my reparations and financial experience, he thought the earlier I got back to London, the better, that the situation was very serious because of conditions imposed by France, and he feared the negotiations would be prolonged for several weeks."

Dawes prepared to return to London, to remain as long as needed. He had, he said, "remained in public service so long that I have no longer any private employment." The Central Trust Company of Illinois which he had founded had by now been merged with the National Bank of the Republic, to become the Central Republic Bank and Trust Company, a $350,000,000 institution. While it was still generally known as the "Dawes Bank," Dawes had retained little more than a sentimental interest in it. But the institution stood on solid feet, and Dawes left for England without any fear for its fate.

"Among the lessons this generation is being taught is the interdependence of the European nations upon each other, and the fact that no nation can permanently prosper economically upon the calamities of others," Dawes wrote. "It is also evident that public opinion here and elsewhere is changing its attitude somewhat on the whole question of reparations and debt payments. If they can really be settled on a basis satisfactory to all concerned, so that they no longer can be used by nationalistic politicians as a basis for creating ill feelings among neighboring people, the prospects of continuing peace and more effective disarmament will be greatly improved. The present world-wide economic crisis has rescued these questions everywhere, here and in Europe, from a matter of public discussion to a matter of public feeling. In this is some hope, for when the public feels, it acts."

Stimson, in London as another crisis came, favored a $500,000,-000 loan to Germany from the Bank of England, the Bank of France, and banks in the United States. Hoover, Dawes, Morrow, and Mills, huddled in the White House, were unanimously against this, because "the amount proposed would be entirely insufficient to restore normal German credit, whatever be the form the loan would take, even if American bankers would participate, which they won't."

Hoover proposed instead a stabilization and assurance of the existing volume of short-term credit to Germany, which amounted to $1,400,000,000. This would have to be agreed to by foreign bankers. The maintenance of this large volume of credit to Germany, Hoover felt, plus the $400,000,000 relief from reparations payments which he had brought about a month before, would do more to assure stability of the German credit structure than the loan.

With the German situation thus for the moment saved, Dawes embarked for England. Before he was halfway across the ocean, the report came that the Bank of England was in distress. The Old Lady of Threadneedle Street, up to her neck in commitments, was losing gold at a disturbing rate. Sensational press reports charged France with abetting these gold withdrawals.

"It is evident that another week-end crisis is on," Dawes wrote. "Last week it was Germany; this week it's England."

On August 2 the bolstering of the Old Lady began. The Federal

Reserve Bank of New York, and other Federal Reserve Banks, agreed to purchase from the Bank of England up to $125,000,000 of prime commercial bills. The Bank of France committed itself to take an equal amount.

"Everybody informed," Dawes wrote, "knows that England's credit situation is in a crisis, demanding the same kind of help which England, in the past, extended to those in similar circumstances. But it was difficult for England, which has always extended credit in the past, to ask for it now.

"The arrangement is referred to this morning in the English press as a tripartite arrangement between the United States, England, and France, of which England will be the first beneficiary. It is of mutual interest to all concerned, of course, and, while England is primarily benefited, the United States and France act because of benefits to themselves. But the form of the press statement is an indication of how England repels the thought of assistance."

On August 16 Dawes recorded:

"Through the fifty-million-pound loan to the Bank of England by the Federal Reserve Banks and the Bank of France, the pound has been stabilized for the present, but confidence in British economy and financial stability has been shaken. Great Britain now seems to face inflation and currency depreciation or the adoption of a partial moratorium such as that already existing in Germany."

But on August 30 a credit of $400,000,000 to the United Kingdom was arranged, with the United States and France to peg the pound sterling at par. MacDonald called Stanley Baldwin and Neville Chamberlain, Conservatives, and Liberal party leaders such as Sir Herbert Samuel and Sir Samuel Hoare, into consultation on emergency legislation to meet the crisis. MacDonald's own Labor party refused him its support, only Chancellor of the Exchequer Philip Snowden and Secretary of State for Dominions J. H. Thomas going along with him. Arthur Henderson led the Cabinet and the majority of the party in opposition. Meeting with King George at Buckingham Palace, MacDonald, Baldwin, and Samuel agreed to form a national government. Labor displaced MacDonald and made Henderson its parliamentary leader.

Lights burned late in the American Chancery every night in September, and Ambassador Dawes received and cabled tens of thousands of words about the imminence of a general election in the United Kingdom, the silver predicament, the straits on gold with Great Britain close to going off the gold standard, the ugly Chinese-Japanese situation, and other troublesome conditions around the world.

"These are momentous times. In this general election in Britain, democracy is undergoing a supreme and decisive test on this side of the ocean. What will be the outcome? In Germany today, there is a governmental crisis. In Manchuria, Japan and China are on the brink of war. In all the countries of the world, economic crisis. Fear and continuing uncertainty—of these alone we are certain.

"In the breaking up of old conditions, many old controversies may be settled. That at least seems probable. If the Nationalists come into power in Germany, for instance, reparations will be wiped out. Germany will then settle that question for herself, and the world will accept it, for it cannot secure reparations by going to war for them."

During his stay in England Dwight Morrow had often visited him and on every visit home Dawes had had long talks with Morrow. They also carried on a steady correspondence. Morrow died on October 6. Dawes wrote in his diary:

"My dear and faithful friend, Dwight W. Morrow, died suddenly yesterday at his home in Englewood, New Jersey. I loved him as a brother and mourn his loss. Among all the leading men of our country, of whom I have known some intimately in my public and private life during the last forty years, I regard Dwight Morrow as the ablest.

"He died full of accomplishment but, even so, only at the threshold of a great career of public usefulness. The words on General Gordon's tomb in St. Paul's apply to Dwight as well: 'At all times and everywhere, he gave his strength to the weak, his substance to the poor, his sympathy to the suffering, and his heart to God.'"

No sooner had one problem been settled than Dawes' diplomatic skill was needed to deal with trouble elsewhere on the globe. In the night of September 18, 1931, a Japanese army at Mukden, engaged in night maneuvers, used an alleged explosion on a railway to seize the capitals of three Manchurian provinces and other key points, leaving to the Chinese troops no choice but to withdraw from the region. Within two months Japanese troops had occupied every important city in southern Manchuria with the sole exception of Chinchow.

On November 9, 1931, Dawes attended the annual Lord Mayor's dinner. MacDonald, whose nationalist ticket had won a landslide victory in October, was the principal speaker. During the Prime Minister's speech, a messenger brought the American Ambassador a message. Secretary of State Stimson wished to speak by telephone on an important matter. The United States Government, Stimson told Dawes, wanted him to go to Paris and represent it during the meeting of the Council of the League of Nations on November 16, "to consider and act upon the Manchurian situation in a continuation of the effort to avert the threatened war between China and Japan."

Dawes' first move was to get in touch with Matsudaira, the Japanese Ambassador to Great Britain. Next he went to see Sir John Simon, who had succeeded Lord Reading as Foreign Minister. Then Dawes, Matsudaira, and Sir John huddled. It was evident that Matsudaira was a sorely perplexed diplomat. The Japanese military forces which on September 18 began the movement acted without the approval of the Japanese Premier and the Foreign Minister. It was, in fact, almost a mutinous act, at least an act of defiance by the militarists in their long contest with the Japanese moderates. Matsudaira frankly told Dawes that he would be representing, not the Japanese Empire, but the moderates as against the militarists. He did not know which faction would finally be triumphant.

These London conferences, and his talks with M. Briand, the President of the League of Nations Council at the Quai D'Orsay, convinced Dawes that it was doubtful whether either the Japanese Government in Tokyo or the Chinese Government in Nanking could control the movement of their troops in the field:

"During much of the time, it seemed as if we were dealing with two separate governments in Japan, and no government at all in China, representing real power of decision."

The League took jurisdiction, because both Japan and China were members, and both the Council and the Assembly of the League were in session in Geneva at the time of the aggression; and, also, China appealed to the League. The Council, by a vote of thirteen to one, Japan dissenting, demanded that the Japanese evacuate the occupied territory by November 16, and called upon China to guarantee the safety of the Japanese in the evacuated territory. Japan did not comply.

Dawes was then a man of recognized broad competence, and a seasoned diplomat of high standing throughout the world. Consequently, the American government left it very largely to his discretion to make whatever contribution this country could toward settling the issues and preventing war between China and Japan.

Whether he attended or did not attend the meetings of the Council of the League was at his option. This question came up at the first parley between Briand and Dawes. The American Ambassador informed Briand that he regarded the United States as following League leadership in the negotiations. But he said: "A parallel cooperation by the United States, reserving its independence of action and decision, would be more effective in securing peace than if, by attendance at the meetings to the curiosity of the world press and justified apprehension of my Government, I became involved in the discussion of methods of an organization of which the United States is not even a member."

"If, however," he added, "in the future, I come to believe the greatest influence of the United States for the common objective of peace can be exercised by my attendance at the meeting of the Council, I will not hesitate to attend."

Dawes remained at his station in the Ritz Hotel in Paris day and night for four weeks, accepted no outside invitations, held many conferences with other negotiators, was in frequent telephone talks with President Hoover and Secretary Stimson; and so unremitting was the task that he wrote: "I was virtually a prisoner in my office. My cables alone ran well over one hundred thousand words in four weeks."

His relations with the Chinese and the Japanese representatives on the Council of the League of Nations were unique:

"Upon receiving messages from their governments which, if presented to the League, would create an impasse and tend to bring about a failure of the negotiations, both Sze and Matsudaira would first bring the situation to my attention. During those days also, Sir Eric Drummond, Secretary General of the League and thus representative of the Council, would call for a preliminary discussion of the different situations and the course it seemed wise to take from the standpoint of the Council. Sir John Simon and I also would exchange calls. This made it possible for me, on several occasions, to exercise an influence in preventing stalemates which might have occurred if the representatives of Japan and China had first gone directly to the Council, where the nature of the difficulty was sure to have become public before it was settled. It was evident during these negotiations that, whenever a matter was given to the League Council for confidential discussion at a closed meeting, it became public property in the press the next day."

Out of the sessions of the Council of the League, and not least out of Dawes' own efforts behind the scene, there came a unanimous report of the Council, one to which both China and Japan agreed, arranging for the dispatch of an impartial commission of inquiry to Manchuria. In a statement written by Dawes, the United States, not a member of the League, gave her approval and support to the action, and to the appointment of the Lytton Commission. As Dawes left Paris in the company of Sir Robert Cecil, he was hopeful "that this resolution has at least brought about the prevention of a general war between Japan and China at this time, making possible a comparatively peaceful stabilization of the Manchurian situation, and insuring further peaceful discussion of the unsettled and fundamental issue involved."

But on the very day on which Dawes and Cecil disembarked from the channel boat, the Minseito Cabinet of Premier Shidehara fell, and the "war" Seiukai Cabinet came into power. On January 2, Chinchow, the last Chinese bastion in Manchuria, fell to the Japanese.

In London another tough assignment was waiting for Dawes. On December 21, 1931, Stimson called him by telephone to say that the President and the Secretary of State desired him to be chairman of the United States delegation to the Disarmament Conference in Geneva in February.

"I told him I did not feel competent to engage in the technical negotiations which, to such an extent, this convention would involve. My suggestion was that Hugh Gibson would be better qualified. The discussion indicated, however, that he and the President were fully resolved in the matter.

"Upon inquiry whether my appointment was satisfactory to Senator Claude Swanson, who will be a member of the delegation, he replied that it was. I told him that, under the circumstances, I would accept. This is certainly a difficult assignment. If I had not had some experience in international negotiations and did not know what I was taking on, I would feel highly honored. As it is, the appointment leaves me cold. However, I will do the best I can."

Dawes embarked immediately for the United States to discuss his prospective duties as delegation chairman, and presided over the first meeting of the delegation at the State Department. But by now, President Hoover had trouble on another front. In an effort to prop up the nation's sagging economy, he had proposed the establishment of the Reconstruction Finance Corporation to make loans to distressed banks, railroads, and business.

The proposal met with strong opposition in Congress. A foe of the legislation was John N. Garner who, as Speaker of the House of Representatives, held the highest office of any Democrat in the nation. Such an institution, he shouted, might serve legitimate business at first, but, "when that need is past, it will linger on as a pipe line to the United States Treasury for chiselers and drone businesses, which will not be entitled to the use of the people's funds which partisan favor will give them."

Garner admitted, however, that the need for emergency help was great. He agreed to support the legislation if he were assured that it would be abolished when the need no longer existed, and that the men appointed to administer it would be "Republicans like Charley Dawes and Democrats like Jesse Jones." He was given the assurance.

Dawes, by now a keen and experienced judge of international affairs no less than of financial troubles, felt that he would be able to do more good by undertaking an urgent task at home rather than a hopeless task abroad. Late in January he resigned his position as Ambassador and chairman of the Geneva delegation, and a few days later assumed his duties as president of the Reconstruction Finance Corporation.

From 10 Downing Street, London, MacDonald wrote to Dawes:

"I grieve much that the announcement which appears in today's paper means that you are going to leave us. We have had a very good time together, which I think has been completely undisturbed by disagreements or misunderstandings. How happy the world would be if every country's relations with the others had been conducted in the spirit in which you and we have managed as regards our own. When you wander back here to be lazy, or for any other purposes, do remember that, as long as I am above ground, there will be somebody who will expect to see you and who will greet you with gladness."

So acute was the country's economic plight that Dawes and Jesse H. Jones began work before the Senate had confirmed their nominations as directors of the Reconstruction Finance Corporation. Oddly, the borrowed room where they worked had been Dawes' office thirty-five years before when he, a thirty-two-year-old Comptroller of the Currency, had his first nationwide experience in rescuing tottering banks. It was banks again that were to receive first attention now.

The directors heard that they could have their choice between first deciding the claims of the largest bank empire in the nation, or those of the railroad system with the greatest mileage. The decision was to put plasma in the bank's blood stream before giving oats to the iron horse. On the first day of operation, a $15,000,000 loan went to the Giannini Bank of America. While the RFC Directors were debating the loan to the Giannini bank, Orris P. and Mantis J. Van Sweringen, controlling a three-billion-dollar transcontinental group of railroad lines aggregating 28,631 miles, stood in the bustling corridor of the drafty old building, waiting their turn.

There is less personal documentation of Dawes' activities in the first of Washington's alphabetical agencies than of any other period of his adult life up to that time. At the end of his term as Ambassador to the Court of St. James, he abandoned his habit of keeping a diary and notes, never again to resume it. The pace he now set at the RFC was too grueling. In their efforts to rescue the nation's economy, he and his fellow RFC directors would be working many months on sixteen-hour days for seven days a week.

At the end of his first month at the RFC, it had expanded from the original two floors to occupy the entire building, formerly the Department of Commerce. Something like one thousand loans had been studied and processed. To 858 banks and trust companies had gone loans of $158,000,000, nearly $61,000,000 to railroads, and about $10,000,000 to mortgage-loan companies and building and loan associations. These sums were to be dwarfed by the pouring out of billions in both Europe and at home in later years, but in 1932 they were impressive.

While two decades later the wisdom of Garner's epigrammatic statement that "you can lick a depression easier than you can liquidate a government agency" was in a fair way of being proved, but the RFC for at least the first dozen years of its life was to be one of the best administered, the least partisan, and the most helpful to the nation of all modern-day government agencies.

In June, after four months at the Reconstruction Finance Corporation, Dawes resigned and returned to Chicago. For the balance of his years, he would be in private life.

Chapter Twenty-Two

❀

"LOOK, JOHN—IT'S ALL PAID!"

On June 17, 1932, Charles Gates Dawes walked into a meeting of the directors of the Central Republic Bank and Trust Company of Chicago and demanded that he be elected chairman of its Board. The bank was in trouble as, in varying degree, was every other bank in the United States. But in Dawes' judgment, it was solvent.

Dawes' own holdings in the Central Republic amounted to fifty-two shares, with a par value of $5,200, but a market value on that day of only $2,444. The Central Republic had come out of a merger of the Central Trust Company of Illinois, which Dawes had founded but with which he had had no active connection since his election to the Vice-Presidency of the United States, with the National Bank of the Republic. His faith in the soundness of the institution, still referred to popularly as the "Dawes Bank," was such that the firm Dawes Brothers, Inc., of which he was the largest stockholder, had invested several hundred thousand dollars in shares of the bank.

Banks in and around Chicago had been taking a terrible beating. On the day Dawes resigned from the Reconstruction Finance Corporation, twenty-five suburban banks had closed their doors. On June 22, bank runs began in Chicago's Loop. On June 23, the Carroll chain of seven banks failed to open. On June 24, eight more of the smaller banks in the Loop remained closed. At the end of the most tempestuous week of bank runs and closings any great city in the land had ever seen, the Central Republic and four other big banks in Chicago had alone managed to stay open.

But the confidence of the public was badly shaken. On June 25, a Saturday, long lines formed in front of the tellers' windows in the five big downtown banks, and crowds collected in LaSalle, Clark, Dearborn, and Monroe streets. The hundreds of thousands of Chicago's unemployed, dependent entirely on their dwindling bank accounts, could not take a chance on losing their deposits or having them frozen behind closed tellers' windows. And on this Saturday, rumors had spread through the city that even the big five were no longer solvent.

Shortly before noon that day, President Melvin A. Traylor of the biggest of all Chicago banks, the seventy-year-old First National, climbed up the marble pedestal supporting a pillar in the savings department of his bank to address the depositors present. He told them that, with all that was happening in Cook County banks, they could not be blamed for doubting, but he wished to assure them that the First National Bank was as solvent as ever.

That night Charles G. Dawes made a decision and went to bed for the first night's sound sleep since he had returned to Chicago. On Sunday, he would summon the other Chicago banks and announce that, on Monday morning, the Central Republic Bank would not open its doors. To the Sunday morning meeting, Dawes called financial executives of his bank, and the heads of the other big Chicago banks. They knew the story of the past week as well as he did. In six days, loop banks had paid out more than $100,000,000 in currency over the counter. Additional millions disappeared to other cities through the clearinghouse.

After the meeting with Dawes, Traylor called his own bank associates to meet in the First National Bank. He then went to the hotel room of Jesse H. Jones, a director of the Reconstruction Finance Corporation. Jones, a delegate from Texas to the Democratic national convention, and a leader in the movement to nominate John Nance Garner for President, had arrived for the convention which was to meet the following Tuesday. Later, Jones recorded:

"Mr. Traylor came to my hotel room and asked me to go with him to a meeting of bankers. He did not tell me the purpose of the meeting or where it was being held, but his mien indicated that it was serious and important. We got to the bank about noon. Probably thirty or forty of the leading bankers, bank directors, and men prominent in the business and financial life of Chicago sat around, and an atmosphere of graveness pervaded the room.

"General Dawes was the coolest man present, and he dominated the meeting just as I had seen him dominate many other important gatherings. He was concise and convincing. In a voice which was a blend of force and gentleness, he explained how he had weighed all elements of the situation and now wished to inform the other banks in Chicago, and me as a Government official, that he did not intend to open his bank the following morning. He had no doubt that the bank was solvent, but it was perfectly evident what would happen. The bank's cash would continue to disappear through the clearing-house and by over-the-counter withdrawal by frightened depositors, until the bank eventually would have to close anyway. Such a situation would throw the brunt of the trouble on friendly, trusting depositors, who would have to wait for their money until the bank was liquidated.

"He made it clear that he wanted no assistance, but wished to fulfill an obligation he felt he owed to the other banks so that, knowing his decision, they could use such means as they saw fit to meet their own requirements. It must have been apparent to all of those present, as it certainly was to me, that a continuation of the bank runs and clearinghouse withdrawals would force all banks in the Chicago area to close."

The scene was reminiscent of one held twenty-seven years before in the same room, when the John R. Walsh banks closed, and Dawes had deadlocked the meeting until there was agreement on the equal treatment of all classes of depositors. Dawes would not have hesitated to close a bank under similar circumstances when he was Comptroller of the Currency and held that power; now he did not hesitate to close his own bank.

Traylor, speaking for other Chicago bankers, said they would have great trouble in remaining open; indeed, closing of the Central Republic might start a sweep of big-bank closings that would rock the country. Dawes, who as a director of the RFC had participated in authorizing loans to more than four thousand banks, believed that eventually all banks would have to be closed and curative bank laws enacted. Jones afterwards believed that it would have perhaps been better for all the banks if they had closed at that time and remained closed until the enactment of a bank-guarantee law. Indeed, the banks were closed nine months later, at the beginning of the Roosevelt administration. Then the Vandenberg deposit-insurance amendment to the Glass banking bill was passed over Roosevelt's strenuous objections.

Traylor requested Jones to call President Hoover and recommend government assistance in keeping the Central Republic open. Jones said he did not have sufficient information to make a recommendation, but he would make a quick study. He could not, he pointed out, examine a large bank in a few hours, but he, too, had participated in the authorization of four thousand loans to banks in four months, and his eye was practiced. Then he took off his coat, sat down at a desk, and began to examine bank records. An hour or so later, he telephoned President Hoover.

"I have made a horseback appraisal," he said, "which is, I think, about as accurate, for general purposes, as a detailed analysis of the bank's assets supported by credit information. I think it is too dangerous to the country to allow the Central Republic to close for, if it closes, all Chicago banks will eventually have to and, perhaps, all the banks of the country. I am willing to take the responsibility for making the loan. There cannot be any great loss in the liquidation of the bank, if it comes to that. There is security here, in my estimation, for a loan of $90,000,000."

President Hoover said he would consult the Secretary of the Treasury and some others of his advisers. Not much later he called back and told Jones to "make as good a trade as you can for participation of other banks in the loan, but *save that bank*."

The meeting which had begun at noon Sunday did not adjourn until after four o'clock Monday morning. During the afternoon on Sunday, Wilson McCarthy, another Democratic member of the RFC Board of Directors, arrived in Chicago for the Democratic convention and, with RFC examiners, fingered through the bank's collateral.

New York bankers, joining in the telephoning, insisted that the Central Republic borrow the $90,000,000 for which, Jones had said, there was sufficient collateral. The closing of the Dawes Bank, the New Yorkers urged, might start a wave which within a few days or a few weeks of that calamitous summer, would sweep over the whole commercial-bank structure, first of the Midwest, then of the nation. New York, they assured, would participate in the loan to the extent of $10,000,000.

Dawes insisted that the New York commitment be put in writing. As it was Sunday, it was impossible to get the signatures.

Dawes still strongly insisted he believed his decision to close had been the right one. Because he had been but recently a director of the RFC, he did not want to be a borrower from it. He was certain, he said, that in a liquidation the bank would pay off 100 cents on the dollar, perhaps even without a stockholders' assessment.

At two o'clock Monday morning, with the New York banks inaccessible in time for Monday morning opening, and the Chicago banks insisting that $3,000,000 was about as much of the loan as they could take, it still appeared that the bank would have to close. Then Jones announced that he and McCarthy, as RFC directors, would authorize a loan up to $90,000,000 if the Chicago banks would participate to the extent of $5,000,000. But all terms of the law would have to be met, Jones insisted. The Chicago RFC agency manager and examiners and the Chicago loan advisory board would have to certify that the security for the loan, in their opinion, was sufficient to assure its repayment.

Shortly after 4 A.M. Monday the last details had been arranged. On Monday and Tuesday, the RFC put $40,000,000 into the bank's vault. As collateral for the loan, the RFC took practically all of the assets of the bank.

"As it looked to me then, the country could not afford the shock of the closing of this big bank," Jones said later. "Under the same information and circumstances, I would do the same thing again. From the Government's standpoint, it was a sound loan. There were, however, many sound reasons, both from a local and a national economic standpoint, why the Central Republic and all other banks in the United States might better have been closed in June, 1932, as they were finally, anyway, in March, 1933. Probably twenty million depositors suffered a greater loss in their deposits than they would have suffered had their banks not remained open too long."

This was the one occasion on which Dawes changed an important decision at the behest of others. He had done it on the judgment of the President of the United States, two members of the RFC Board of Directors, and the unanimous opinion of Chicago bankers that it was the best course.

Five weeks later, he submitted a plan for the organization of a new bank to take over the Central Republic Bank and liquidate it. The new bank was called the City National Bank and Trust Company, with a capital of $5,000,000. Dawes was its active Chairman of the Board.

Decline in the value of the Central Republic's collateral in the next few months made it necessary to make a stockholders' assessment. The RFC filed suit in 1936. Without waiting for a decision, Dawes paid his assessment of $5,200. On May 1, 1937, Federal Judge Wilkinson ruled that the stockholders were liable to assessments, but imposed the conditions that executions could not be levied for six months. Yet two days after the decree, Dawes Brothers, Inc., and other members of the Dawes family liable to an assessment paid $1,027,000 to the bank receiver.

Despite the fact that Dawes had assumed the burden of the bank's trouble when his personal holdings were small and he had not been an officer or director of the bank for seven years, the loan was the subject of attacks throughout the 1932 Presidential campaign. President Hoover replied to the attack in a campaign speech in St. Louis in November.

"The central human figure of that bank was a man who had served his country for forty years in high capacities, who in recent years had been absent from the country in a position of first importance to the American people," Hoover said. "You know the use our political opponents have made of this incident. They ignore the fact that General Dawes resigned from the Reconstruction Finance Corporation three weeks before, on his first news that attacks were being made on the bank with which his name had long been associated. He resigned to save that bank without call on the Reconstruction Finance Corporation, of which he has been a director. He knew and appreciated the use that would be made of such calumny in this campaign. He sought to avoid it.

"And you should know that, when that Sunday meeting started, General Dawes stated that he could not bring himself to ask for assistance from the corporation of which he had so lately been a director, but it was upon the insistence of the two Democratic members of the Reconstruction Board sitting in the Federal Reserve meeting in Chicago, and upon the insistence of the leading Democratic banker of Chicago, who was then mentioned as a candidate for the Presidency of the United States, and upon the insistence in New York City of the leading Democratic banker and a leading Democratic manufacturer also mentioned for the Presidency, upon the insistence of the other members of the Reconstruction Finance Corporation, that this was no case of the personal feelings of General Dawes or the effect upon my administration; that it was solely a case of national necessity, and those men then and there jointly offered to take the full responsibility for the action.

"These men acted not because they were Democrats or Republicans, but because they were loyal citizens of the United States. The situation demanded broad vision and comprehensive understanding of the problem, instant decision, bold and courageous action. Only by this was a major disaster averted. And I may tell you that not only were these loans adequately secured but, in the ordinary course of business, they are being paid off."

On January 3, 1933, Dawes wrote to John Pershing: "The last year has been a difficult one, but things have come out very well. I am enclosing for you the first statement of the City National Bank and Trust Company. We are both growing older but, with us as with Mrs. Wiggs of the Cabbage Patch, our vicissitudes have not made us sour."

There is reliable eye-witness evidence that this last statement was literally true. For on that morning, or some other morning much like it, two religious sisters in their black and white habits were ushered into his office. The two good sisters, one of whom was of medium height and ample build while the other was tall and excessively slender, came from a Catholic institution whose aim it was to care for the bodies and cure the souls of wayward girls. They came because Dawes had helped them before and because they needed more help.

The General gave them a reception they had little expected. He jumped up from his chair, strode around his large desk to meet them, and greeted them by giving each of them a resounding kiss on the cheek.

They answered with smiles of delight. Their smiles deepened while Dawes wrote the check.

The sisters were merely a drop in an endless stream of unusual visitors who came to the bank and were invariably admitted to Dawes' office. In this stream, there was also a silent, poorly dressed man who put in an appearance at regular intervals. He would find his way into Dawes' office and then stand around without ever uttering a syllable. "Good morning, there!" Dawes would call out. No answer. "What brings you here today?" No answer. "Lovely day, isn't it?" No answer. And then, Dawes would hand the man five or ten dollars, and he would leave, without ever having broken his silence. Only his eyes had spoken. But once outside of Dawes' office, the man would find his tongue and tell those who wanted to know that General Dawes had supported him for many years, but, apparently, the General did not like the sound of the words "Thank you!" —and so he and the visitor had agreed that the visitor would not open his lips. And that, he added, was indeed a hard assignment—oh, yes, he now was really earning his money.

It is not known how many such people the General kept on what might be called his "payroll." He himself refused to tell, and since he kept very few records on matters of this sort, his papers do not tell either. But those who were close to him during those years and had occasion to observe the callers coming to his office, estimate that the number was between two hundred and two hundred and fifty.

From the panicky days of 1893, when a financial crisis had stopped all earnings of the Dawes Block Company in Lincoln, Nebraska, to the day when he had redeemed the last of that company's bonds, Dawes had carried in his pocket a slip of paper showing the progress he was making in repaying the bondholders to whom, in addition, he was regularly paying interest out of his own pocket. When all was paid off, he had shown the slip to Captain John Pershing as a memento of their hard times together in Lincoln.

Now again, Dawes was carrying a slip of paper showing the progress that was being made on the repayment of the RFC loan to his bank. In 1938, while he and General Pershing were together in Tucson, he showed it to Pershing: "John," he said, "you and I will live to see this one paid in full."

One day in the early forties, as Dawes sat by Pershing's bedside in Walter Reed Hospital in Washington, a thought struck him and he reached for the soiled and worn bit of paper in his pocket.

"Look John," he said. "Here it is—it's all paid."

The RFC loan, running with interest and liquidation expenses to over one hundred million dollars, had been paid in full.

✿

Chapter Twenty-Three

LOOKING BACK

*T*he last years of Charles Gates Dawes' life were in many ways his happiest and most rewarding. His health had always been and still was excellent—he didn't "remember when I have had a serious illness." Mrs. Dawes' health had also remained good. In the sixty-two years of their married life they had rarely been apart—the longest period was during his World War I service.

"I am naturally inclined to be indolent, and have always been, except when I was on a red-hot stove. Lately, there has been nothing to keep me from indulging my indolence," he would say. The "indolence" of the man who, for nearly two generations, had led a life of activity and public service few men could match, would have kept a younger man fully occupied.

Each morning at the same time he rode the fourteen miles along the beautiful lake front from his home to his bank and went to the big carved desk in his office. He would be ready to preside over the board of directors, and available for any consultation. He liked his "crowd." In his business, he had told the committee which had offered him the presidency of the Knickerbocker Bank, he would always have his "crowd." This "crowd" of his septuagenarian and octogenarian days were loyal friends and keen bankers like Philip R. Clarke and Arthur Leonard. The banking institution he had founded in 1932 at the age of sixty-seven and over which he still presided at eighty-five had become one of the largest and strongest in the nation.

In addition to the success of his bank, the outcome of the Century of Progress Exposition of which his brother, Rufus C., was president had given him great pleasure. As Vice-President he had piloted a resolution through Congress to permit the government to invite other nations to participate. It was to be a subsidyless exposition and the legislation provided that not only could there be no federal assistance but the President of the United States could not invite other nations until $5,000,000 had been raised by private subscription. Dawes also saw to it that no assistance could be accepted from any state or municipal taxing agency. It not only paid subscribers back with 6 per cent interest, but after paying demolition costs and restoring the grounds, there was surplus of $160,000 for distribution to charity.

Chicago, his city which never lost its fascination for him, considered him its best-known and most beloved citizen, and, at the occasional luncheons and dinners he attended, the audience jumped to its feet and cheered when he was introduced.

Visitors still came from all over the world to visit the Evanston home or drop in on him at the bank. Some came asking things, others just to shake his hand. Many of them came unannounced.

One day in the year 1950, when Dawes was nearing his eighty-fifth birthday, there piled into his office a group of farmers, merchants, and mechanics in their shirt sleeves. They were the board of directors of a small bank in a small Illinois town who at a meeting had suddenly decided to pay a visit to the most eminent citizen of the state. And so they had jumped into their cars without losing time to get their ties on, and had driven off for Chicago and the Dawes Bank.

Against his habit, Dawes did not rise to greet them.

"My legs are not as good as they used to be," he said with a smile. "But I can still read a bank statement without glasses. I don't want you to think from this that I am unduly interested in money. In my very young days, I had a burning ardor for it, but since then I have been interested in it only intermittently. One of the Rothschilds once said he made his fortune because he discovered there are times when one should not try to make money."

When Dawes said that he was little interested in money, he was speaking the literal truth. Although he was to leave his family in more than comfortable circumstances, his fortune did not bear comparison with those, for instance, of most of the other ninety-nine men who had appeared on Senator LaFollette's famous list. His business acumen had allowed him to achieve financial security comparatively early in his life, and he had been able to give to others who were in need. He had wanted little more.

Yet there is no doubt that he could have increased his fortune a hundredfold if he had wanted to. Once on a trip he pointed to a little settlement and said: "Ten or twenty years from now this place will be one of the most important cities in this state." Those who were with him, including his chauffeur, pricked their ears up and bought themselves a few acres of ground in the community, each according to his means. A decade later, they found themselves in comfortable circumstances because of this transaction. But Dawes himself had not been interested enough to do likewise. He probably took some pleasure in the fact that his prediction had come true and had worked out well for some men he knew. But that was all.

No wonder, however, that the shirt-sleeve board of directors now pressed him for a prediction of the future. He laughed, and replied:

"Oh, no! I am not going to do that. I have never been able to break myself of the habit of making soundings along that line, but they are to satisfy myself and I do not any longer divulge the results."

That day an out-of-town friend was with him in his office, and as they talked between callers, Dawes, in his best anecdotal or philosophical manner, would offer a running commentary on the happenings in his office. Thus, when a young member of a Chicago business firm had left, Dawes commented:

"There are men in his firm with far more impressive titles whose work is far less valuable. This youngster is the sort of fellow who does not need a title. When I was at the White House one day, General John B. Gordon, the great Confederate leader and a close friend of President McKinley, came in to see the President. General Gordon told a story I have never forgotten. At the beginning of the war a young man came to him and said he wanted to get his uniform quickly so that he could drill his men. 'Young man,' said Gordon, 'if you are not a captain in your shirt sleeves, I can't make you one with a uniform.'"

Near the end of the day, also unannounced, came Owen D. Young, who was just passing through Chicago. As the all-day visitor reflected back over the day's stream of callers, some successful and some obviously unsuccessful men, he thought of what Young had once written:

"No man of real quality ever lost General Dawes' affection or respect merely because he failed to succeed. No man ever gained it merely because he held high title or high position. With him, it is always the character of the men. From commanding generals to privates in the ranks, from the most ordinary and inconspicuous individuals to presidents, kings, and princes, he gathers his friends. His sense of reality is never impaired by position, and his dramatic sense is never destroyed by convention."

"Is this a typical day of callers?" the visitor asked.

General Dawes answered: "Well, I do not get lonely. But I have stayed out of the limelight very well." And with a chuckle he picked up a letter which he had received and personally answered. It was addressed: "To the estate of the late Charles G. Dawes."

Dawes was an omnivorous reader, and not of books alone. He went daily through all the Chicago daily newspapers, one New York newspaper, two daily financial newspapers, a few periodicals, and the weekly London *Times* still came to him.

"I once read this newspaper very carefully," he said, pointing to the New York *Times*, "but now I seldom look at anything except the obituary page."

"Why the obituary page?"

"To see how many people live to be ninety," he replied. "You'd be surprised how many make it."

In the afternoon, when the business of the bank had been completed, Dawes would return to his Evanston home, and to his library.

There was little music now in his life. His hearing was failing slowly, and he no longer played his flute or the piano. "I do not get the overtones. Not long ago I tried to play 'Tea for Two,' which I used to play a lot, but I won't try it again. I miss these overtones, too, in music which is being played in front of me or which comes by radio or television."

And so, his books which by now had grown into a library of well over ten thousand volumes, came to mean more and more to him. While other people in his social bracket had indulged in such sundry fads as sailing yachts or blooded horses, Dawes all his life had been collecting books. In addition to his regular library, he had brought together a number of special collections on subjects of particular interest to him, including a fine collection of Civil War materials which he later turned over to the Newberry Library in Chicago for public use. And while the countless exquisite *objets d'art* which he had gathered in his home from the four corners of the globe gave to his library somewhat the air of a museum, his books, whether rare or not, were not museum pieces but well-fingered tomes. Throughout the years, his diaries abounded with notes such as:

"I am reveling in my library again as I used to before exchanging evenings devoted to the acquisition of knowledge for those at Washington, so often devoted to large dinners.

"I am reading the one-time-famous work 'History of Civilization in England' by Thomas Henry Buckle. How cheap and contemptible a book like this makes the alleged historical works being sold by tens of thousands today simply because they detail immoralities. It, and books like it, stand out from the mass of 'best sellers' today like some of the old cathedrals of Europe surrounded by the slums of modern cities.

"On my trip to New York I read a current biography, written by one of the new school of historians, who endeavor to make 'best sellers' by emphasizing at length the scandalous episodes in the lives of ancient leaders, merely using their real accomplishments as background."

Or:

"As I write, I have by my side Appian's *Roman History*, Thucydides, Dio Cassius, Julius Caesar (*Gallic Wars* and *Civil Wars*), Strabo, Plutarch, and Suetonius."

Or again:

"How much there is in the life of the reader who spreads before himself the records of history!

"How alike are men; how old is the race; and how through long ages of struggle it is slowly lifting itself into a higher average of happiness—this is the study of middle age. The study of the young is the method of self-advancement. The successful young man is almost more or less of an egotist. But as he grows old, if he has somewhat of wisdom, how little he grows in his own eyes, and how great in comparison that vast current of humanity pouring down through the ages, its source lost in a dim past, its outlet beyond our sight or ken."

He had always been deeply interested in history. It constituted much of his reading after he returned to Chicago. Now he set about rereading all the history he had read before his war service.

"One never knows, who reads with an open mind, to what conclusions history will lead him. They will differ somewhat according to his age in life, and his life's experience up to that time. This I know: that my present conclusions will be sounder than any I could have formed before my war experience. . . . War, more or less, is a postgraduate course in human experience.

"In an emergency, a great leader never thinks or acts as would the ordinary man. This is one reason why historians so often fail entirely to comprehend the motives and acts of a leader in an emergency. As a rule, the historian's life is one of observation, investigation, and literary production. His is not the 'battling' life. He has not experienced that of which he writes. His literary reactions, however brilliant, are based on the only interpretation of human nature possible to him."

Dawes told visitors he used his deafest ear to listen to people who proposed he write his memoirs, contribute magazine articles, and give newspaper interviews.

"I have controlled that situation now except for recurring August twenty-sevenths. People come in here on my birthday and want statements from me on national and international problems. There was never a time one could discuss the world in just a few minutes. National and international problems today are more complex than in the days when I was trying to help solve them.

"At other times I have been asked to give advice to the new generation. Young men have no desire to receive advice from old men. I have no advice to the young, but Owen D. Young made a suggestion to old men which seems to me to have great merit. He said:

'More harm is done by old men who cling to their influence than by young men who anticipate it.' "

In his day he had been in the heat of many a battle. It may be that the differences between him and his opponents had not been as great as they had seemed.

"John Garner once told me that when he came to Washington he thought Republicans were corrupt, but Culberson, the Texas Senator, told him somewhat facetiously: 'No, John, they are as honest as we are. The difference is that we think the people can be trusted to run the government and they do not.' —I never thought the Republican party was the only party fit to run the government, I merely believed that usually the country's best interests were served by the Republican party.

"Both parties have the same basic political economic philosophy; if they had not, the shock of the change from one party to another would be too sharp for the country to endure. Our national elections are not a contest between systems, but between parties, and there can be profoundly important issues and differences between parties."

Yet how much had the political scene changed since he came back to Chicago nineteen years before!

The work he had done as Director of the Budget, which he considered next to his war service his most important achievement, had been undone by President Franklin D. Roosevelt when he abolished the federal coordinating service.

"This unfortunate action, taken at the inception of the most gigantic peacetime governmental spending operation in history, was one of the chief causes of the present condition of chaos in the business system of our government," Dawes said in a speech. "This action fulfilled the prediction I made in 1921 as the first Director of the Bureau of the Budget in my report to the President, which was transmitted to him by Congress: 'If in the future there should at any time come into office an executive indifferent to the operation of the government as a business machine, there would, under the immutable laws of human nature, immediately spring up an effort on the part of the independent departments and establishments at first to curtail and restrict the activities of the coordinating agencies and then to wipe them out of existence.'"

His peace efforts, too, had been undone—they had not been able to stem the tide of Fascist and then Communist expansion by force of arms. The United States had become involved in another World

War, vaster and more hideous than any war in history. Two of his closest friends in the peace negotiations—Ramsay MacDonald and Aristide Briand—had not lived to witness the new conflagration. But Pershing saw it all.

In October, 1937, General and Mrs. Dawes had gone with General Pershing to dedicate the war memorial at Chateau-Thierry, and to visit the old battlefields, including, Dawes recorded, "a place where with three companions I had once stood, serving quietly and unwittingly as a target for three pieces of heavy German artillery."

That year, too, West Point Military Academy had accepted his gift of the Pershing sword to be presented to the Captain of Cadets at each annual graduation ceremony.

In February of 1938 the two old friends had again been together at Tucson. Pershing became seriously ill. He was never to recover fully his health. In 1948, almost sixty years after the beginning of their close friendship, General Pershing died. Dawes had gone to Washington for the funeral, the last trip he ever took to the national capital.

"My old friends who were coeval with me have been dropping off one by one and for years I have been the florist's best customer."

He had corresponded with Pershing, both of them writing in longhand, from the time the General went to Walter Reed Hospital for his long last stay there. He continued to correspond with Cortelyou until the death of this old friend in 1940. In his last letter, Cortelyou had written that although he was supposed to be retired, "I find myself projected into situations where I have been kept busier than for years," and Dawes had replied: "You are wise; for one who has led the life of intense activities you have, idleness is unendurable and fatal. As the demands of business lessen upon me, I, like you, extend my associations along interesting lines, including prehistoric research."

"I have my own way of recognizing old age," Dawes said. "You are old when you believe people when they tell you how much younger you look than you actually are. Connie Mack came in here the other day and had lunch with me. He is still young enough to manage a major league baseball team, but he knows he is 87 and looks it."

One of the old friends who was still alive was the Japanese

diplomat Matsudaira. Dawes had heard from him shortly after V-J Day. Hugh Gibson, in Tokyo at the end of the war, wrote to Dawes that Matsudaira's home had been destroyed by fire, and he had found Dawes' old friend living in reduced circumstances in a little house in the suburbs. "Madame Matsudaira offered me a cup of tea and apologized because she could offer me nothing to eat, for she had nothing in the house." A peace advocate, Matsudaira was broken-hearted at the war folly of his country. "I recall those pleasant days we worked so closely together for the peace," Matsudaira wrote to Dawes. "I have been elected as the First President of the House of Councillors, which corresponds to your United States Senate."

Matsudaira, too, died in 1949, but not before General Douglas MacArthur had paid him this tribute: "By his wisdom and patriotism he gave the Japanese people in time of greatest need resolute leadership in the building of a new Japan."

The death of his brother, Rufus, was the first break in the Dawes family of four brothers and two sisters. General Dawes had always taken great pride in the close relationship of the four brothers. These four remarkable men differed widely in temperament and personality. Their abilities, too, were widely divergent but complementary. All their lives they formed a tightly knit unit, held together by affection and family pride.

Sometimes friends asked Dawes to give his appraisal of the fifteen Presidents he had known. He would not rate them, but ascribed to four of them outstanding qualities: Cleveland—courage; McKinley—quiet effectiveness; Wilson—intellect; and William Howard Taft—"regardless of how his administration is ranked, he had perhaps the best understanding of the constitutional functions of his office of any of the Chief Executives. His public life was a triumph of principle and usefulness." Rutherford B. Hayes, the first President Dawes ever knew, once made a statement which Dawes thought the truest and most notable remark on politics he had ever heard: "He who serves his country best, serves his party best."

Of all Presidents he knew he believed McKinley gave more thought to the task at hand and less thought to his place in history than any other. He believed that Franklin D. Roosevelt gave more thought to how generations yet unborn would regard him than did all other Presidents he had known combined.

"The reputations of public men depend upon their contemporary environment. But I don't want to go into these things now. I put them in my journal. I discussed people as I saw them contemporaneously. My ideas, whatever they were, can be found not only in these notes I have made for nearly half a century, but in the speeches I made or articles I wrote. The writing was all mine. I never had a ghost writer. I would have been ashamed to palm off the product of another man's mind as a creation of my own."

"I consider the job I did in the war the biggest of my life. Next to that I would put my service as Budget Director. Both were jobs where you could get things done," Dawes would say. And if he were asked for the prescription on how to get things done, he would tell an anecdote: "When Napoleon sent his brother to Italy to command an army, he said to him: 'Hold no councils of War!'"

Around the world, and especially among the European debtor nations, Dawes would be best remembered as the author of the Dawes Plan. And in America he lived on in the memory of men as Ambassador and Vice-President—and as the man who had enriched the language by a picturesque expletive: Hell 'n' Maria! This legend followed him through his entire life, and lingers on.

"I have always been interested in how the public will pick up a single phrase out of a long speech and enlarge it beyond proportion," he said. "I heard Bryan give his celebrated speech on the silver question, but his expression about the 'Cross of Gold' hardly received attention at the time. When Theodore Roosevelt used the phrase about the Big Stick that became his tag, he used it merely as an old proverb to illustrate a point.

"I was testifying before a Congressional committee and was attempting to impress upon them that we had been trying to win a war in Europe and without any thought of a 10 or 20 per cent discount in the money cost. The Army had improved my faculty of expression. But the 'Hell and Maria' phrase which leaped into the headlines was not something I learned in the Army. The public got an idea that I interlarded my conversation with explosive expletives, the mildest and probably only printable one being 'Hell and Maria.' Now I don't think I am a profane man. I know that most of the time I am a mild 'by golly' sort of a man and not at all a 'Hell and Maria' fellow."

This is not to say that Dawes had never been criticized for anything but his supposed profanity. In fact, he had been criticized aplenty for any number of reasons. But this never troubled him.

"I never saw a man suffer long from an unjust attack," he once said. "I never feared attacks when I was in public life. I learned early in my office holding how an unjust attack can be turned to advantage."

No, Dawes' biggest trouble in life had not come from his critics. He himself had been his own greatest troublemaker. But it had been worth the candle:

"Most of my trouble has come from attempted kindness. But most of my happiness has come from the same endeavor."

One late afternoon General Dawes was sitting before a cheerful log fire in his library, talking to a visitor, a friend from Washington.

The day had been a typically "idle" day in the Dawes tradition. He had spent the morning and the early afternoon at the bank, presiding over the meeting of the board of directors, dictating and signing letters, receiving visitors, and signing a good part of one thousand Christmas letters that were to go to customers of the bank. After leaving his office at four o'clock, he had done some work on his two current fund-raising campaigns—one of them for a boys' club sponsored by Herbert Hoover, the other for Marietta College. This was the kind of indolence Dawes enjoyed most.

"I have had eighteen unhurried and unharried years since I came back here as a private citizen," he said. "Mrs. Dawes and I have both been blessed with good health and I have caught up on a lot of things I kept putting off because of other preoccupations. There is still a lot of reading I want to do and I expect I will put in the bulk of my remaining time in this room."

The visitor's eyes turned to the bookcases lining the walls of the library. Over there was the collection of Manasseh Cutler's papers running to some ten thousand pages, and next to it the largest collection in existence of records of the Old Northwest Territory. There were the rare books of the Dawes library which, together with the entire building, would some day go to Northwestern University. In the corner stood a cane that George Washington, during his Presidency, had given to one Colonel Thomas Dawes, the smoke-filled-room-Dawes of John Adams' diary; there was silverware that had belonged to William, the rider of 1775, and his wife Mehitabel. A framed certificate on the wall, dated May 27, 1887, proclaimed that Charles Gates Dawes had authority to practice law in Ohio. About the room were bronze busts of Pershing, Foch, Joffre, Payot, Lloyd George, Clemenceau, Tardieu, Harbord, and Dawes; a breech-loading Spanish cannon Pershing had sent from the Philippines; pieces of Mayan pottery, presented by President Chiari of Panama; a Damascene cigarette case from Albert J. Beveridge; a silver cigar box from the 17th Engineers, and a tobacco pouch from Marshal Foch.

As the visitor looked about he thought of what Booth Tarkington had said of Dawes: "A student of history, he laughs at tradition; a philosopher by inclination, he turns to material things; a musician by nature, he becomes a leading financier."

He could have gone on to say: successful in all things, he was forever concerned about the downtrodden and the failures; he was familiar with panic, crisis, and catastrophe as few men were, but in his own words "incapable of remaining a pessimist overnight," a man who never lost his easy laughter and his faith in mankind.

Dawes in his library that night talked of his country's future. There were some things that troubled him.

"A nation is like an individual," he said, "subject to the same laws and offered by the Creator the same inducements to sobriety and industry."

"It would do the country some good," the visitor suggested, "to hear some of the things you said to me tonight."

"I have said quite enough in my time," Dawes replied. "If I did break my vow never again to give my views publicly on events past or present, it would be in the shape of a five-word prayer for all of us:

"God give us common sense!"

In the evening of April 23, 1951, Dawes once again sat reading in his library. As a chairman of a civic committee, he had this day completed arrangements for the reception of General Douglas Mac-Arthur, just removed from his Far Eastern Command. The reception was to take place on the twenty-sixth.

When the hour came for him to retire for the night, Caro Dawes entered the library. He raised his eyes and looked at the woman whom, in a tribute not meant for publication, he had called "my faithful helpmate for so many years." He smiled to her, sank back into his chair, and closed his eyes.

Death had tiptoed in where a strong man had trod.

INDEX

338

Bull Moose movement, 150, 161–163
Bunau-Varilla, Phillipe, 112
Burnham, S. H., 21, 24, 27, 113
Burrows, J. C., 68, 90
Busse, Fred, 106, 109, 138
Butler, William M., 229, 233

Cabinet, President's, Dawes' views on, 265
Calhoun, W. J., 67
Cameron, Don, 25–26, 249
Campaigns, political. *See* Presidential campaign
Cannon, Joseph G., 143
Canton, Ohio, in first McKinley campaign, 59
Castle, William R., 306
Cecil, Sir Robert, 312
Central Republic Bank and Trust Company, 306, 316–322, 324
Central Trust Company of Illinois. *See* Dawes Bank
Century of Progress Exposition at Chicago, 264, 275, 278–279, 286, 305, 325–326
Chamberlain, Neville, 308
Charities, 36, 41–42, 114, 155–161, 322–323
Chicago Grand Opera Company, 145–146
Chicago World's Fair, *1893*, 33–34; *1933*, 264, 275, 278–279, 286, 305, 325–326
China, relations with, 81, 84, 89
Chinese Exclusion Act, 11
Churchill, Winston, 282, 299, 303–304
Cincinnati *Commercial*, 3
Cincinnati *Commercial Gazette*, 12
Cincinnati Law School, 12–14
City National Bank and Trust Co., 321–322, 325
Civil War, Rufus R. Dawes in, 5–9
Clarke, Philip R., 325
Clarkson, James, 40–41, 48
Clemenceau, Georges, 174–176, 220
Cleveland, Grover, 30, 58, 105, 333
Cleveland *Leader*, 64
Coffroth, Bruce, 22
Collins, Lottie, 28
Columbian Exposition, Chicago, *1893*, 33–34
Comptroller of Currency, Dawes as, 65–93
Conkling, Roscoe, 10
Cooke, Jay, 9–10
Coolidge, Calvin, 202, 225, 258; in campaign of *1924*, 227–228, 231–239; as President, 241, 252, 263, 264–266
Coontz, Admiral Robert E., 208

Cortelyou, George B., 121, 132, 136–137, 149–150, 332; in McKinley administration, 72, 78, 94
Cotton, Joseph P., 290
Cowans, Sir John, 175, 177–178
Cox, Jacob D., 13, 14, 22, 27, 67
Crane, Murray, 51
Cravath, Paul D., 177
Crockett, John C., 251, 272
Cross of Gold speech of William Jennings Bryan, 54
Cuba, relations with, 67, 74–75, 81
Culberson, Charles A., 331
Cullom, Shelby M., 41, 45–46, 68, 102, 106–107, 149
Currency question. *See* Free-silver issue; Monetary standards
Currency reform, 111, 132, 141–143
Curtis, Charles, 69–70, 202, 246, 263
Cutler, Manasseh, 4–5, 14
Cutler, William P., 9
Czolgosz, Leon, assassin of President McKinley, 101–102

Daugherty, Harry M., 203
Dawes, Beman (brother), 12, 92
Dawes, Bessie (sister), 12
Dawes, Carolyn (daughter), 24, 145
Dawes, Charles Gates, ancestry of, 3–5, 8; school years, 10–15; Lincoln years, 17–37; first McKinley campaign, 38–63; as Comptroller of Currency, 64–105; Senatorial campaign of, 93, 106–110; in World War I, 165–191; "Hell 'n' Maria" speech, 193–198; as Budget Director, 202–109; on Experts Committee for Reparations plan, 216–226; in campaign of *1924*, 228–239; as Vice-President, 241–256, 261–274; as Ambassador to Great Britain, 274–313; as president RFC, 313–315; in Chicago bank crisis, *1932*, 316–322, 324
Dawes, Mrs. Charles Gates (Caro Blymyer), 16, 23–24
Dawes, Dana (adopted son), 240
Dawes, Henry (grandfather), 5
Dawes, Mrs. Henry (grandmother), 14
Dawes, Henry (nephew), 279
Dawes, Henry Laurens, 11
Dawes, Henry M. (brother), 12, 92, 157, 208, 252, 258
Dawes, Mary (sister), 12
Dawes, Mary Gates (mother), 8–9, 158, 184